Con Houlihan was born, as he puts it himself, 'in the hill-country above Castle Island, on the sixth of December 1925, in a blizzard.' After working as a teacher, he became a journalist, writing a column three times a week for the *Evening Press*. He now writes for a variety of publications, including the *Sunday World* and *Magill* magazine.

First published in 2003 by Liberties Press
51 Stephens Road Inchicore Dublin 8 Ireland
Tel: Editorial: (01) 402 0805
Sales and Marketing: (01) 453 4363
E-mail: libertiespress@eircom.net

Trade enquiries to CMD Distribution
55A Spruce Avenue Stillorgan Industrial Park
Blackrock County Dublin
Tel: (01) 294 2560
Fax: (01) 294 2564

Copyright Con Houlihan, 2003

ISBN 0-9545335-0-X

2 4 6 8 10 9 7 5 3 1

A CIP record for this title is available from the British Library

Cover design by Liberties Press
Photographs by Peter Houlihan
Printed in Ireland by Colour Books
Unit 105 Baldoyle Industrial Estate Dublin 13

More Than a Game
Selected Sporting Essays

Con Houlihan

CONTENTS

Introduction

'His Was the Word We Grew Up With'

I wish I had my own Con Houlihan story. It seems to be an Irish birthright which I have missed out on. Everybody has a Con story, an encounter, a sighting or an exchange of words which they will recite, delightedly playing the part of Con by using the trademark accent and hand gesture. Somehow I've missed out.

In respect of Con I can claim influence, admiration, envy and the same dietician but little by way of shared adventure. I can relate that I have sat for entire evenings in countries more foreign than you would imagine just listening to people telling Con Houlihan stories. I have spent many happy hours with people who can produce Con quotes the way certain undergraduates can regurgitate Monty Python sketches. I have sat in on many attempts to break down international barriers as Irish people attempt to explain Con and the Meaning of Con to mystified foreigners. I have no story of my own, though.

By the time I got into journalism, the Press Group, of which Con was the principal adornment, was in decline and our paths seldom if ever crossed. I saw him one day when I was a straggly freelance who had been dispatched to cover what action if any there was in an encounter between St Patrick's Athletic and some other team of misfortunates during that time when Pat's were playing at the dog track in Harold's Cross. It was the first time I was ever in a press box. And I was alone.

On the other side of the tracks, so to speak, I could see Con Houlihan moving at glacial pace (but keeping up with play) and mingling gently with the crowd. I sat alone in the glassed-in press box with the distinct feeling that I was making a fool of myself but that to follow Con around would be even more foolish.

I can't remember any detail of the game, just that Brian Kerr complained to the paper afterwards that I had described one of his players as trying a shot from outside the large square. Brian felt I was oppressing a minority religion with my GAA ways.

Truth is, I wasn't paying attention. It was fascinating to watch Con Houlihan move through the crowd. He absorbed words and good wishes from everyone without ever losing that slightly sad aura of isolation he always carries.

I think that sense of aloneness about him, even when in company, is what has made him such a great observer not just of the simple choreography of sport but of life. Those observations of the broader picture are what has made him the great sportswriter he is. When you read Con, you read part of the man, you get what he has distilled from life. And what a unique man. As unknowable ultimately as a great, dark mountain.

Con never liked press boxes and it has always been rare to find him in one. He didn't much like aeroplanes either, I suspect. Our surnames beginning with the same letter, we were often placed beside each other in those spacious economy seats at the back of the plane on Irish soccer trips. Neither of us had much sympathy for Roy Keane and his complaints about legroom. We were pressed so close together that in some American states we flew over we are legally married.

We covered the 1994 World Cup together. That is, we were both at the same matches. Otherwise Con was out exploring and absorbing while the rest of us were hanging around in hotel lobbies complaining that our lives weren't more interesting.

My main memory of Con is second-hand and speaks of Con's demeanour in the face of near-disaster. The Press Group was by then already in the claw of the parsimony and dreadful management which disfigured a great institution and killed three newspapers. Ireland's games were divided between New York/New Jersey and Florida for that World Cup, and for reasons of acclimatisation the team were billeted in Florida for the duration and hopped up and down to the megalopolis for games.

The management of the Press Group, a fine collection of know-nothing cheapskates in shiny suits, had determined that they would save a few bob and miss out on a few stories by not permitting their journalists to fly on the team plane but instead forcing them to lag along behind on a series of cut-price flights on little puddle-hopper airplanes.

On one such trip, the little prop plane ran into a rather large storm. The pilot advised the small group of passengers not to panic, that he was finding a path between storm fronts which would get everyone to Orlando with the minimum of fuss and tummy upset. Then a few minutes later the plane hit a trough of something and began losing altitude. That's a fancy way for saying that it began falling out of the sky. Like a stone. There was panic. The plane kept falling and falling. The ground kept getting nearer and nearer.

And then Con starting singing. I'm told it was 'The Rose of Tralee' but am open to correction. Morale began to rise again. People began to whisper to each other. Not long later, the plane pulled out of its dive. Everyone ordered a stiff drink and said that they would remember two things from the day they almost died: almost dying, and Con singing.

I'm not claiming that he saved the crew and passengers. I'm just suggesting that Con's singing was the perfect metaphor for his career. In all the years of the slow death of the *Evening Press*, in all the time that it was losing altitude, Con was there, implacable and note-perfect on the back page. When the propellors stopped and all that could be heard was the whistling of the air rushing past, Con was there.

His was the word we grew up with. His was the word we waited for before we formed an opinion. His were the eyes we saw things through, and from him we borrowed ears to listen. He was the last of the big guys, the last of a great generation of newspaper writers who could beckon an entire city over and bid them sit down while they told a story.

Con Houlihan seldom told you anything which you didn't know already. Sportswriters don't generally do that. It's a rare day when the radio, the television and now Teletext and the Internet don't beat papers to the punch. But Con told it better than anyone else, with more love and humour and perspective. Like they used to say about the great Jimmy Cannon, he wrote to end all writing. Still does.

Tom Humphries
August 2003

9

'FOR ABOUT AN HOUR AND A HALF IT SEEMED AS IF NOTHING ELSE BUT FOOTBALL MATTERED IN THIS MORTAL WORLD'

THE LOT OF A SPORTS AFICIONADO

There is, after all, a time machine, even if it owes nothing to technology, modern or otherwise. And about four o'clock last Sunday it ferried me back over a great many years.

I was in Flanagans, that landmark in Harold's Cross, having a few not-so-quiet drinks with three alarmingly articulate friends – and there it happened.

The warriors who had battled for Cork City against St Patrick's Athletic came in – and suddenly I was back to the days when I played rugby for Castle Island.

My young self was there amongst them, mulling over a game that had just ended, having fantasies about what might have been. City, you see, had just been beaten by a late late goal that had come like a streak of lightning out of a clear blue sky.

It's all very well talking about positive thinking – but there are times when I feel that the concept should be sent back to the cosy pages of the *Reader's Digest*.

That, I suppose, is rather unfair; there is great need for positive thinking but you can overdo it. And when you have just been rather unluckily defeated – whether in soccer or rugby or hurling or love or whatever – you would be astonishingly mature if you didn't indulge in what might have been.

Mature people, astonishingly so or otherwise, do not play games; sport is the last refuge of the immature. And the faces of those young men in Flanagans told their own tale.

It may sound ludicrous and indeed unbelievable to

people in the real world outside – but defeat even in a little match can make you feel that the sun will never rise again.

I am well aware that Frank Haffey sang in the bath after England had beaten Scotland 10–3 – and, in case you didn't know, he was the Scottish goalkeeper.

Frank used to say: 'I make a living out of football but I don't let it get me down.' Later he repented – and the awfulness of the day in Wembley smote him. And he banished himself to the Antipodes; no doubt he would have gone further if there had been further to go.

Let us return to Flanagan's last Sunday evening; that meeting of Patrick's and City had not been a little game – far from it. The points were precious to both: Patrick's are hungering and thirsting for the championship; City are hovering worriedly above the relegation zone.

The championship pennant hasn't come to Inchicore since those golden days when Shay Gibbons was the Patrick's spearhead; the good people of the environ would dearly love to see it flying over Richmond Park.

And relegation . . . there's the rub. For those immediately involved, it is like a death in the family.

And there is more to it than the fusion of guilt and humiliation. There is the cut in wages. There is the disincentive of playing before smaller crowds. And, paradoxical though it may seem, there is the tougher opposition.

Proverbially it is tough at the top; a strange fact of football life is that it is tougher at the bottom. Down there you meet the ambitious youngsters hungering to ascend and the veterans grimly determined to cling to their profession. I do not expect that Cork City will go down – but a slide can prove agonisingly hard to correct.

I watched last Sunday's game in excellent company. By chance I met John McNamara, a man as devoted to Cork City as that famous cat was to Dick Whittington. And he told me a revealing fact about soccer in the United States.

It is played mostly in the schools attended by the poor – because their parents cannot afford the gear necessary for the gridiron game.

John should know: he used to referee schools football in New England. And his knowledge of the game would flummox Jimmy Hill, not to mention Jimmy Greaves and Ian St John.

On Sunday he made a curious little bit of history – you will find it hard to believe. After about twenty-five minutes' play he dipped into a deep pocket and produced a hip flask. I couldn't have been more astonished if he'd produced a Colt 45 or even a Colt 38.

The hip flask, as every dog and cat in the streets and in the fields and in the woods well knows, belongs in the better seats in the stands at rugby internationals. And it is mainly worn by those who wouldn't know a prop from a post. John, however, has an excuse: his pewter flask was given to him about ten years ago by his brother Jim.

On Sunday morning he filled it for the first time – in, I think, the Punchbowl. And of course on Sunday afternoon he emptied it for the first time – not altogether on his own, it must be admitted.

We were joined in Flanagan's by two other aficionados: Christy Looney is vice-chairman of Cork City; Jimmy Edwards used to be a post-office sorter – for good measure, he is devoted to St Patrick's.

With us there was an American girl who had just witnessed her first soccer game; now she was hearing her first post-match analysis. And for about an hour and a half it seemed as if nothing else but football mattered in this mortal world.

Then John and Christy departed for the Deep South – and Jimmy prepared for a stint as Master of Ceremonies and resident singer in Clarke's of Wexford Street.

It was a good day: I greatly respect people who go into the arena and seek glory while risking humiliation.

The First of the Four-in-a-Row

Kerry Play Dublin in the All-Ireland Football Final, 1978

If a man who fishes for salmon with a stake net had seen his cordage dance as often as Paddy Cullen did in this astonishing All-Ireland final, he would have been very happy with his day's work. But there is an immensity of difference between bending to take out a salmon and stooping to pick up a ball that has got past you – and for long years to come Paddy will now and then rack his brains and try to find out what happened him yesterday.

At about twenty to four he had every reason to feel that his bowl of glory was about to flow over: Dublin were playing as if determined to get a patent for a new brand of Gaelic football – and Paddy himself was ruling his territory with a style and authority redolent of Bat Masterson.

And the many Kerry battalions in the crowd were as apprehensive as accused men waiting for the jury to return after an unfavourable summing up against them.

And well they might – because in the first third of what was surely the most extraordinary final since Michael Cusack codified the rules of Gaelic football, their team seemed faced not only with defeat, but humiliation.

It looked every bit as one-sided as the meeting of Muhammad Ali and Leon Spinks – and the more it went on, the more the gap in ability was seen to widen.

In their glory-garnished odyssey since the early Summer of '74, Dublin have never played better than in the opening third yesterday.

The symphony of classical football began with Paddy Cullen – he got no direct shot in that period, but his catching of a few swirling lofted balls dropping almost onto his crossbar was as composed and technically correct as if being done without opposition to illustrate a textbook.

And his distribution was as cool and unerring as the dealing of a riverboat gambler.

So was that of his comrades in the rear three – Kerry's infrequent sallies towards the Canal End almost always ended up as launching pads for a Dublin attack.

The drizzling rain seemed irrelevant as Dublin moved the ball with the confidence of a grandmaster playing chess against a novice.

From foot and hand it travelled lucidly in swift triangular movements towards the Railway Goal – Kerry were forced into fouls as desperate as the struggles of a drowning man.

And Jimmy Keaveney was determined to show that crime did not pay: the ball took wing from his boot like a pigeon homing to an invisible loft strung above Kerry's crossbar.

The blue-and-navy favours danced in the wet grey air – the Hill revelled and licked its lips at the prospect of seeing Kerry butchered to make a Dublin holiday.

They roared as the points sailed over – and one felt that they were only flexing their vocal muscles so that they might explode when Charlie Nelligan's net bulged.

And such was Dublin's supremacy that a goal seemed inevitable – by the twenty-fifth minute it was less a match than a siege.

And Dublin, as they have so often done, had brought forth a new ploy for the big occasion – this time the rabbit from the hat was the swift breakdown with hand or fist. It added to Kerry's multitude of worries.

And Kerry's not-so-secret weapons were misfiring: Jack O'Shea was not ruling the air in midfield – and Kevin Moran was playing as if his namesake Denis had only come for a close-up view.

Kerry's map was in such tatters that Eoin Liston, their

lofty target man, the pine tree in whose branches they hoped the long high ball would stick, was forced to forage so far downfield that his marker, Sean Doherty, was operating within scoring distance of Kerry's goal.

After twenty-five minutes Dublin led by six points to one – it did not flatter them. It seemed less a lead than the foundation of a formidable total.

But perhaps it is true that whom the gods wish to destroy they first make mad – the ease with which Dublin were scaling the mountain seduced them into over-confidence.

They pushed too many troops forward and neglected their rear – and then a swift brace of passes from Jack O'Shea and Pat Spillane found a half-acre of green ground tenanted by only Paddy Cullen, and with Johnny Egan leading the race in its pursuit.

Paddy Cullen is a 'modern' keeper – he guards not only the goal but its forecourt. And it was one of the ironies of a game that might have been scripted by the king of the gremlins that now he was caught too far back.

He advanced desperately, but Johnny Egan, scorer of that lethal first goal in the rainy final three years ago, held the big trump – and he coolly fisted the ball over the keeper and into the net.

That goal affected Kerry as a May shower a languishing field of corn.

Dublin were like climbers who had been driven back down the mountain by a rockfall – they had to set out again from a plateau not far above the base.

Soon a few Kerry points had put them at the very foot – then Dublin went ahead with a point. And now came the moment that will go into that department of sport's museum where abide such strange happenings as the Long Count and the goal that gave Cardiff their only England FA Cup and the fall of Devon Loch.

Its run-up began with a free from John O'Keeffe, deep

in his own territory. Jack O'Shea made a flying catch and drove a long ball towards the middle of the twenty-one-yard line.

Mike Sheehy's fist put it behind the backs, breaking along the ground out towards Kerry's right. This time Paddy Cullen was better positioned and comfortably played the ball with his feet away from Sheehy.

He had an abundance of time and space in which to lift and clear – but his pick-up was a dubious one and the referee, Seamus Aldridge, decided against him. Or maybe he deemed his meeting with Ger Power illegal.

Whatever the reason, Paddy put on a show of righteous indignation that would get him a card from Equity, throwing up his hands to heaven as the referee kept pointing towards goal.

And while all this was going on, Mike Sheehy was running up to take the kick – and suddenly Paddy dashed back towards his goal like a woman who smells a cake burning.

The ball won the race and it curled inside the near post as Paddy crashed into the outside of the net and lay against it like a fireman who had returned to find his station ablaze.

Sometime Noel Pearson might make a musical of this amazing final – and as the green flag goes up, that crazy goal, he will have a banshee's voice crooning: 'And that was the end of poor Molly Malone.'

And so it was. A few minutes later came the tea-break. Kerry went into a frenzy of green-and-gold and a tumult of acclaim. The champions looked like men who had worked hard and seen their savings plundered by bandits.

The great rain robbers were first out onto the field for Act Two – an act that began almost as dramatically as the first had ended.

In their cave during the interval, Dublin, no doubt,

determined to send a posse in fierce pursuit – but within a minute of the restart, the bridge out of town had been broken down.

Eoin Liston was about to set out on a journey into folklore – and for the rest of the game it must have seemed to Sean Doherty that he had come face to face with the Incredible Hulk.

Eoin proceeded to leave the kind of stamp on the second half that Mario Kempes left on the final of the World Cup.

People were still settling down for the second half when Jack O'Shea drove a long ball from midfield; Eoin, near the penalty spot and behind the backs, gathered, turned and shot to the net.

Dublin's defence is justly famous for its covering – and the manner in which this score came indicated the level of their morale. Not everyone suspected it – but Dublin had conceded it. From then on only a few of them had their hearts in the battle.

Kevin Moran never surrendered and played magnificently all through that unreal second half. He had good lieutenants in Tommy Drumm and Bernard Brogan.

Kerry's fourth goal was both a finisher and a symbol of their immense superiority.

A high ball dropped into the apron of Dublin's goal. It seemed to be manned by a little man with spikes in his forehead who was shouting 'Take me to your leader.'

The leader, of course, was Eoin Liston, who plucked it out of a low-flying cloud, gave an instant pass to Ger Power on his right and moved on to an instant return.

Eoin's right-footed shot was executed with the panache of one who knew that he could do no wrong. And the remarkable aspect of what followed was that Kerry did not score a dozen goals.

They got only one more – when Eoin Liston raced on to a fisted cross-goal pass from Johnny Egan on the right and palmed the ball in at the far post. And so in the grey drizzle we saw the twilight of the gods.

The Hill watched, as lively as the Main Street of Knocknagoshel on Good Friday. And it all seemed so unreal. The final score was no reflection of Kerry's second-half superiority – neither did it tell the truth about the difference between the teams.

For twenty-five minutes, Dublin were brilliant; for forty-five, Kerry were superb. How come the change? That wry prankster we call luck has the answer. And in the last chapter of the minor final, he had shown his hand.

A fumble by Dublin's keeper gave Tom Byrne the chance to drive home the decisive goal. The mistake that gave Mayo victory came at the Canal End too.

There was a gremlin down there who did not like Dublin. And he was humming to himself: 'What a day for being in goal.'

Evening Press

THE KEANE MUTINY – AND 'THE MOST REMARKABLE GAME IN THE REPUBLIC'S HISTORY'

JAPAN AND SOUTH KOREA 2002

I do not know who perpetrated the joke about Kerry turkeys looking forward to Christmas. All I know is that managers in soccer dread the coming of the Holy Season. For some of them it is a question of how many sacking days remain until Christmas.

Derek Dooley suffered the ultimate hurt in this context. As a player with Sheffield Wednesday he was an icon until he lost a leg in an accident on the playing field.

Eventually he became manager of his beloved club. A time came when it wasn't going so well. He got the dreaded call. And on a Christmas Eve he went to his office and collected his fishing rods.

Peter Reid and George Burley were among the victims this Autumn. There are no more respected men in football. For several years the names of Peter Reid and Sunderland were as intimately linked as fish and chips. The same was true of George Burley and Ipswich Town.

Alas, came the day when relegation threatened; the guillotine was almost inevitable.

Success doesn't guarantee security: David O'Leary kept Leeds United in the top five during the four seasons of his stewardship but he too heard the axle roll of the tumbril.

Art McRory is among the recent victims on this side of the Irish Sea. Tyrone's expectations were so high that somebody had to be fingered – unjustly in this case.

It isn't as sad for managers in hurling and Gaelic football as in soccer. There isn't the same loss of income. And there isn't a similar sense of finality. Soccer managers rarely return to their old clubs. They experience a kind of suffering that is hardly known to their counterparts in Gaelic games.

During their stewardship the club becomes their second home, indeed their first. When a manager is dismissed, it is a kind of eviction. Whether he campaigns out of Anfield or Villa Park or Highbury or wherever, he feels a deep sadness at no longer being captain of the ship.

I worked in several schools in my time as a roving teacher – and though I left them all in a haze of goodwill, I still feel a little stab of loneliness whenever I pass them by.

It is the same with the old *Irish Press* building in Burgh Quay – only more so. It isn't easy to get away from your past self.

Few managers end up winning. Mick O'Dwyer regrets that he didn't abdicate from his post with Kerry after the All-Ireland final in 1986. Kerry lost to Cork in the following season. O'Dwyer's triumphs were forgotten – and he endured fierce criticism.

Those who demand that soccer managers should resign are amusing. How many of them would give up a well-paid job? No manager of The Republic has suffered so many slings and arrows as Mick McCarthy.

Some typewriters were being sharpened against him even before the Finals. In the meantime the criticism has become a light industry.

The Roy Keane affair began as a storm in a thimble; when he attacked Mick publicly, it grew up into a hurricane. Roy's reason for throwing the head didn't make sense: he needn't have trained on hard ground or on soft ground.

He could have pleaded that he was resting his dodgy knee, as Paul McGrath did for years. When Mick convened a meeting of the players, he may have hoped to pour oil on troubled waters. He poured oil on a blazing fire.

It might have been better to confront Roy less publicly – in the company of the senior players. I doubt if it would have mattered: Roy seemed determined not to play in the Finals.

What went wrong with him? My intuition is that he was suffering a form of mental breakdown. Something similar happened to Ronaldo on the eve of the World Cup Finals in 1998.

Roy, like Ronaldo, was carrying a huge responsibility: he was our flagship. The pressure may have proved too much. The affair was not without a tinge of black comedy.

We heard about the plane primed at Manchester Airport to bring back the runaway. Anybody who believed in that is capable of looking for leprechauns at dawn or indeed at dusk.

Even if Roy had returned, he might not have been welcome. The players on whom he had cast the cold eye might not have sacrificed the fatted calf for the prodigal father.

In his absence the band of brothers bonded together and performed magnificently. Would they have done even better with Roy? It is likely that they would. He was the real loser in this sorry mess.

He had played a huge part in getting us to the Far East – he wasn't there for the harvest. I was angry with him – just as I was angry with George Best when I was in Spain in 1982.

George had played his part in getting Northern Ireland to the Finals – he wasn't there when he was most needed. Roy threw away the chance of playing on soccer's greatest stage. It is unlikely that it will come again.

If he could turn back the calendar, I suspect that he would.

I fear that The Republic will not get to Portugal – the ship is holed below the waterline. The defeat by the Swiss will probably be seen as a watershed – or a tearshed.

It was no help that Steve Staunton and Niall Quinn abdicated at such a critical juncture. Thus we went into the game without our most experienced defender and our most experienced forward. And of course we lacked our most experienced midfielder – whether Roy will return I do not know.

There was another factor that should be considered in analysing the recent defeat by the Swiss in the Euro 2004 qualifying campaign. The penalty shoot-out with Spain may have cast a long shadow. I know that the team in general were devastated – and that the players who missed from the spot were inconsolable.

Mick was blamed for his choice of penalty-takers – in Genoa the players volunteered. Jack had no list prepared. Should more time have been spent in practising penalties? In the run-up to the All-Ireland final in 1992 Dublin gave special attention to this aspect. Charlie Redmond was nearing John O'Leary nine times out of ten.

The big day came: Donegal conceded a penalty about the twentieth minute; Charlie's kick was very wide – and so high that the ball was found in the back yard of Gill's pub.

The most accomplished penalty-kickers can lose their nerve on the big occasion. Socrates and Michel Platini and Junior all missed in Mexico in 1986.

The memory of their missed penalties may have affected a few of our players in their games with their clubs at the start of the season. The memory may have affected Shay Given for a different reason. I know that he believed he should have saved the kick that put Spain through. The Republic have never had a better keeper but he has been going through a bad time since the Finals.

One rock of truth stands out in this rather turbulent sea: Mick McCarthy and his little army did us proud in the Far East.

*

If hearts could really break, the World Health Organization would have rushed plane-loads of cardiac surgeons to this country on Sunday evening. As it is, psychiatrists and counsellors and soothsayers will be overwhelmed for the next few weeks, not to mention agony aunts and agony uncles.

In the last half-hour of an enthralling ninety minutes, we saw proud Spain becoming more and more demoralised. They were palpably relieved to see the signal that normal time was up. Now they were down to ten men and were hoping that they could snatch the golden goal.

The Republic looked the more likely to do so – but failed. Then came the dreaded sweat-out. Alas, Mick McCarthy's gallant men gave an all-too-convincing imitation of the gang who couldn't shoot straight.

If William Tell has any Irish blood in him, he must have been sighing and groaning in his grave. And so 'Olé', in this generation almost monopolised by The Republic's following army, went back to its original owners.

The penalty shoot-out is the nearest we have in civilised countries to public execution; while tournaments end in a knockout formula, it is the only alternative to the golden goal.

It is a bad way to go: it puts an albatross for life around the necks of those who fatally miss. It isn't much of a consolation to those who failed on Sunday that they are in a band of three.

When the extra time ended scoreless, many in the crowd and elsewhere recalled Genoa in 1990. Our Jack on that heady evening had made no provision for the shoot-out. It was a question of volunteers; among them was Tony Cascarino.

24

His attempt at a penalty could fairly be described as the worst ever witnessed in serious football – or in any kind of football. His left foot hit the ground before the ball – the divot may have distracted the keeper. The ball rolled gently and ended up in the front of the net.

Soon came the moment when Daniel Timofte shot – and Packie Bonner saved. And David O'Leary, who hadn't taken a penalty since he played with his father Christy on Dalymount Strand, stepped into folklore.

The scenario from Genoa wasn't to be repeated. And so ended a romantic voyage. This was surely the most remarkable game in The Republic's history: all of football life was there.

It didn't begin well for the men in green and white. That early goal was a grievous blow: it was so well taken that it threatened more. And for much of the first half our back four lived on the cliff-edge of offside. They were a very thin green line.

Morientes and Raul, the Bernebau's darling duo, repeatedly threatened to get behind Gary Breen and Steve Staunton. They were too eager and frequently advanced too early. Thus they squandered a great supply from midfield. The Republic were struggling in the middle third of the pitch.

Matt Holland and Mark Kinsella were too busy surviving. They couldn't supply leadership. Gary Kelly and Kevin Kilbane played wide but couldn't find space against opponents who combined sweetly.

Damien Duff and Robbie Keane were forced to forage. Hierro and Helguera let little come through the middle. Steve Finnan was as sound as ever. Ian Harte recovered from a nervous start. Thanks in no small part to Shay Given, we reached the interval only a goal down.

Act Two resembled our restart against Germany: suddenly the Spanish began to look vulnerable. Kenny Cunningham replaced the limping Staunton. Niall Quinn came on for Gary Kelly and brought authority.

Now Keane and Duff were played like lads who had learned their football from schoolboy fiction. Cunningham and Breen reinforced the midfield. The Republic looked more like a team.

Duff set out to give the most thrilling display by anyone in a green shirt since the heyday of Georgie Best. He looks as if he should still be at school – but bemused defenders found that they were dealing with a wolf in lamb's clothing.

In the Ballyboden Butterfly they had a handful, and a legful and a brainful. He forced the penalty that promised a certain equaliser.

Ian Harte is deemed to be in the same bracket as David Beckham as a place-kicker. Alas, his trusty left foot was on the blink. To his eternal credit he put his mistake behind him and played with increasing enterprise. So did all his comrades: their spirit never waned.

When Hierro attempted to deprive Quinn of his shirt, we saw how deep was the Spaniards' unease. Keane stroked the ball past Casillas with all the coolness of a professional gunfighter in the Old West. Then came extra time. Two weary teams strove desperately to break the livelock.

When much of this tumultuous game is half-forgotten, we will remember the shoot-out. It was the day when Matt Holland and David Connolly and Kevin Kilbane weren't spot-on.

They joined an illustrious list of men who missed crucial penalties on the big stage. It includes Liam Brady, Roy Keane, Junior, Socrates, Michel Platini and Roberto Baggio – not to mention Charlie Redmond, Mickey Sheehy, Liam Sammon and Keith Barr.

And then there are those who put away penalties with such seeming ease that you wondered why anyone ever missed. I am thinking especially of Eoin Hand and Denis

Irwin and Jimmy Keaveney. When Mendieta put away the final penalty, there was a collective sigh all over the country.

We had hooked a splendid fish; alas, we saw it slip away on the lip of the landing net and vanish. Now the rest of Ireland know how the people of Kerry felt on a September evening in 1982. We had come within a few minutes of the five-in-a-row and saw it slip from our hands.

And now too the rest of Ireland know how the people of Dublin felt at the end of that legendary saga, when Dublin and Meath played four times in the Leinster Championship. I was close to the Canal Goal when the referee spread his arms – a penalty for Dublin.

Only a few minutes remained: a goal would surely put the game beyond Meath. I had a ringside view as Keith Barr ran up. Mick Lyons was almost hanging out of him. Barr sent the ball low to the left. It went just outside. Meath went away and got the sealing goal.

When my tumult of emotions subsided on Sunday evening, one feeling remained – a terrible sense of loss. A great ship is sailing on without us. We can only watch from the shore as it disappears over the horizon.

Sunday was the end of a remarkable campaign. We qualified for the Far East by playing bold, creative football. We didn't change our philosophy in the Finals, even though thrice we had to come from behind. Especially against Spain, every man had to play up to his best: they did exactly what it says on the tin.

I haven't forgotten our neighbours beyond the Bay of Biscay. Spain played beautifully for about an hour: their one-touch football was good to watch – if you weren't Irish. The lead-up to their goal was simple but brilliant; Morientes' header was a model. And Spain did well to survive the extra time, though without the injured Albelda. Casillas was their especial hero.

The entire voyage was a triumph for Mick McCarthy. I have known Mick since Eoin Hand gave him his first green shirt. He was a good player but underrated by those who cannot see the difference between style and substance.

He is a sound coach and a wise manager. He has endured outrageous criticism. The old Persians have a saying: 'The dogs bark but the caravan passes.' Mick is a decent man. I would go with him into the desert but I suspect he isn't going that way.

Is there a better way to end a tie than the sudden goal and the penalty shoot-out? A tournament in an all-league format wouldn't need a dramatic finale.

The last sixteen of the present World Cup could have been divided into four leagues – with the top teams to go through. Those four would make up the final league. Anything is better than the golden goal or the shoot-out.

What would have happened if the Dublin–Meath saga had gone on and on? It went to four games – it could have gone to another four. What would have been done . . . Does anyone know?

Evening Press

'OLLIE CAMPBELL WAS A CONDUCTOR WHO COULD BRING GLORIOUS MUSIC FROM A SCRATCH BAND'

IRELAND WIN THE TRIPLE CROWN, 1982

On the way out of Lansdowne Road on Saturday evening I rounded Michael Cameron Gibson. It didn't need much sleight of foot since we were travelling in the same direction. But I suspect that it would need extra-sensory perception to know what was at that moment going on in his mind.

He wore the green for more than twice the normal span of an international, playing in three positions – and so well that many deem him the best all-purpose back the game has known – but never enjoyed the satisfaction of sharing in the capture of the Triple Crown.

His neighbours' child, Keith Crossan, was still in swaddling clothes when Mike made his debut for Ireland – and on Saturday he got a place in the gallery of folk-heroes with his first cap.

Such, as the French say, is life. Three words in their succinct language hint at the ferocious irony that lurks in the fates' way of dealing out the cards.

And some people will see in the contrasting fortunes of Mike Gibson and Keith Crossan a particularly dramatic example of that enigmatic parable about the way the workers in the vineyard were rewarded.

But Mike could console himself that he had borne the weight and the heat and the cold of many a day – like the good peasant he had planted and tended the vine but had not been around to enjoy the vintage.

His long-time colleague, Bill McBride, must have taken a similarly wry pleasure from Ireland's first Triple Crown in a generation.

Bill captained the Lions in their storming South

African tour when they went unbeaten through the Test series and was the most respected second-row forward of his day – but the Crown eluded him too.

And Donal Lenihan, one of his successors in the heart of the scrum, enjoyed that glory in his first season in the green. *C'est la vie.*

Paul Dean and Michael Kiernan are also in their first season – and for the two young centres the grey windy stadium at Lansdowne Road must at a quarter to five have seemed like the headquarters of the Promised Land.

Andy Irvine saw the same field and the same stands and terraces and the same sky – but to him the homely stadium in Dublin's most affluent inner suburb must have seemed like a torture chamber left over since the Inquisition.

For Scotland's most glamorous hero since Rob Roy MacGregor tormented the king's men on the slopes and in the valleys by Loch Katrine and Lock Lomond, this was the most harrowing day in a career outrageously inconsistent even by Scottish standards.

Most full-backs have good days and indifferent days – Andy Irvine trades in a dicier market: he is either brilliant or appalling. In his happy mood he can field and find touch with the best, can set up fruitful attacks from the most unlikely situations – and kick goals that seem to defy the accepted laws of physics and geometry.

But when he is under the moon he puts you in mind of a stowaway whom an eccentric captain has made work his passage by taking his turn at the wheel.

His talents seem much more suited to the three-quarter line – yet the Scottish selectors insist on placing him at full-back. It would be as sensible to give a job as fire-prevention officer to a pyromaniac.

Such players as Andy (that is, if there are any others) need an early injection of that potent drug called confidence if they are to bring out their best. On Saturday he didn't get his fix: he fumbled the first high ball that came his way – and Scottish hearts feared the worst. From that moment one felt that a Scots win was almost impossible – they resembled a boxer with a glass chin.

And Ollie Campbell was well equipped to exploit that flaw. To say that this was his day wouldn't be an exaggeration – indeed to date it has been his season. And it was little consolation for the Scots that if surnames mean anything, he is their kinsman.

The king over the water placed dart after dart into the royal blue – do not blame a jubilant Irishman if in the aftermath he said to a Scots friend: 'Ask not for whom Campbell tolled – he tolled for thee.'

The records will show that he put over six penalties and a drop goal – but even if the place-kicking had been allotted to someone else, his contributions would still have been enormous.

That may be illogical: his general play may have owed much to the confidence generated by his early success with penalties – but it is doubtful – he is in such form this year that he hardly needed a fix. On Saturday in his own quiet way he put his name on the ballot paper for the election of the greatest-ever out-half.

If there is a flaw in his make-up, it is part of his genius that he is able to conceal it. On Saturday he did everything that one can expect from an out-half – and a good deal more: he was both artist and artisan, architect and maintenance man. And yet he did little that stamped itself indelibly on the memory.

The mention of great out-halves summons up images of Jack Kyle's outrageous curving breaks and Mike Gibson's brainwaves that left friend and foe wondering what had happened and Phil Bennett's runs that seemed made on a sinuous magic carpet while his opponents floundered on land.

Compared to their poetry, Ollie Campbell's play is

prose – but prose so strong and sensitive that it blurs the distinction. And more than ever on Saturday you felt that his brain had a different clock from that granted to the generality, a clock in which a tenth of a second is ample time for weighing all the factors and making a decision. In that he resembles Franz Beckenbauer – and they also have in common the absence of fuss that is the mark of high intelligence.

Ireland's other especial hero on Saturday was Hugo MacNeill, a young man who plays as if he had read every schoolboy story ever written and believed every word. The contrast with Campbell could hardly be greater: the out-half can go through a game as unobtrusively as a pickpocket – our full-back is the romantic hero forever ready to dash off and rescue the maiden in distress. But enthusiasm, as Hemingway used to say, is not enough – and Hugo has the talents to make his fantasies into solid reality.

On Saturday he may have been at fault for the try – but otherwise apart from one uncostly fumble he was as unflinching as Horatius when he held the bridge against Lars Porsens' army.

And he lost no chance of wounding the enemy with lofted kicks that the Scottish backs welcomed as a mother hen does a hawk.

The difference between the full-backs and the out-halves was the key to this game. Between Andy Irvine and Hugo MacNeill it was so vast that you wouldn't blame any Scot who said: 'Swap full-backs – and we'll play you again.'

Between John Rutherford and Ollie Campbell it wasn't so obvious that a Scot couldn't deny that it was there at all – the big young man from Selkirk scored the kind of try that might be beyond our out-half. But in launching the lofted ball and putting the little teaser behind the mid-field backs Campbell was utterly superior; in football wisdom he was the professor contrasted with the student.

Probably the fairest verdict on the three-quarter lines would be 'not proven': one suspected flaws in both – but they were so under-employed that the evidence was inconclusive.

There was an abundance of evidence on which to judge the scrum-halves – and Roy Laidlaw was one of Scotland's heroes. His passing was quick and accurate: he made one glorious break – and his only fault was a tendency to play as a ninth forward.

Robbie McGrath was not the masterly playmaker we saw at Twickenham – but he is a long time in the game and didn't let his mistakes upset him and all in all he served his out-half well.

In comparing the forwards one must bear in mind an oft-neglected truth: their mental health is bound up with the play of the men behind them – and in Campbell the Irish pack had a conductor who could bring glorious music from a scratch band.

The more confident you are that possession will be well used, the more eagerly you seek it.

On Saturday the Irish forwards saw even the crumbs put to good use – while their counterparts often saw the cleanly won ball kicked so ineptly that it gave Ireland possession.

You could hardly blame them if they felt more and more like election workers taking down the posters of their beaten party.

Technically the Irish pack were better only in driving forward with the ball in the set scrums: they used this ploy expertly – and it paid handsome dividends.

If they looked better in the loose scrums, it was mainly due to Campbell's crafty kicking – they could drive straight in while their counterparts had to run back and turn and thus lose time and impetus.

The Scots were better at getting first touch in the line-out – but what Donal Lenihan won was generally tidier. The line-outs in general were a mess – though in the early stages Ian Paxton and Alan Thomas and Bill Cuthbertson looked likely to achieve command.

Ian Paxton was Scotland's outstanding performer – but obviously they missed David Leslie: Eric Paxton, his replacement, was brave and industrious – but his inexperience was evident. No Irish forward was as prominent as Big Ian – and one is tempted to give our pack a blanket approval. But obviously the solidity of the scrummaging owed something to Phil Orr and Gerry McLoughlin.

Donal Lenihan looks our best line-out man since Terry Moore. And though the claims for Ciaran Fitzgerald's captaincy may be exaggerated, one suspects that he has exorcised his pack of exhibitionism. Fergus Slattery and Willie Duggan and John O'Driscoll and Moss Keane have often been more prominent – but possibly not as effective.

The Irish forwards' brief was to win the ball or force their counterparts to yield penalties – they carried it out well.

They were helped by the fact that whenever Mr Nurling seemed in doubt about whose put-in it was in the scrum, he gave Ireland the benefit – and for once not even the most chauvinistic Irish follower could complain.

They were helped too by Scottish indiscipline – they gave away penalties as if afflicted with an urge toward self-destruction. Ireland gave away their share too – but while Campbell missed few goal-chances, Irvine's unhappiness affected his place-kicking.

It is customary to wax sentimental in wedding speeches – but on this occasion it is perhaps better to tell it 'as it was': the occasion was far more memorable than the match.

Ireland's pragmatic approach had much to do with the colourless textures of the game. But they could not be blamed – the stakes were too high. Oscar Wilde in his trial outshone Edward Carson in epigram and repartee – but Carson got the verdict.

*

Ireland kicked off towards the Havelock End with a lively wind behind them. It was a cold wind too – but at least it lessened the stink of after-shave lotion from the twice-a-year mob in the West Stand.

The Scots were penalised in the first line-out – and Campbell started his scoring spree. After a similar offence in the twelfth minute he scored from fifty-six yards.

A few minutes later came the game's most memorable happening. From a line-out on Scotland's left and near halfway, Laidlaw ran laterally infield and seemed to be going nowhere until he suddenly did a ninety-degree change of direction and sent a lovely pass to Rutherford. The out-half strode majestically through the middle and dived over near the posts. Irvine converted. But soon from a difficult angle on the right Campbell made it 9–6.

And then in the twenty-fourth minute came Ireland's only score from play. On Ireland's right and fifteen yards inside Scotland's half Lenihan won a line-out. The ball was passed across the field – and Campbell looped around his centres and threw a difficult ball to Crossan.

He held it but was tackled. Slattery and Duggan spearheaded the maul. The ball came back nicely to McGrath, who fed Campbell – the deadly right foot hooked over a drop goal.

And with a penalty four minutes later he made the half-time score 15–6.

The second half was mainly a story of solid Irish forward play and steady kicking by Campbell. Scotland could not recapture the attacking brilliance they had shown in flashes in the first half.

Ten minutes after the restart, Campbell defied the

wind with a long penalty – now it was 18–6. Jim Renwick replied in the twenty-third minute – but Scotland were now only trying to save face.

In a quiet last chapter Campbell and he put over penalties – but the crowd long before had bestowed the crown on Fitzgerald and his men. And the windfall of revenue from the celebrations will help the next Taoiseach to bridge his budget deficit.

While all this was going on, Tom Kiernan sat in the stand wondering at the strange workings of the fates: last year they tormented him – this year he was their darling. This game was not a romantic climax to the battle for the Triple Crown – but life seldom obliges in that fashion.

One thinks of the heroine in Liam O'Flaherty's novel *Famine* who for so long had been dreaming of the ship on which she was to be smuggled to America. In her mind it had snow-white sails. When she reached Galway docks, she saw that the sails were old and brown – but it got her away all the same.

Evening Press

'The Tumult that Greeted Him as He Galloped Away from the Last Fence Warmed the Cockles and the Mussels of the Heart'

Desert Orchid

A little after four o'clock yesterday at Fairyhouse I witnessed something I had never seen there before; people were flocking away even though there were still three races to be run. The inclement weather wasn't the cause; those who departed early had come for one reason – to see Desert Orchid.

The wonder-horse lost no prestige at Cheltenham; defeat made him even more a folk hero – it indicated that he was human. I was delighted to see him perform so brilliantly yesterday. And the tumult that greeted him as he galloped away from the last fence warmed the cockles and the mussels of the heart. No doubt some of the acclaim had to do with money – but, believe me, it was only a small factor.

I watched the race with a decent man called Martin Murray from Waterford – we hadn't as much as a penny on the grey-white but we were willing him to win. We all need a little bit of the romantic in our lives – yesterday we got it. Not everybody in this island realises how much Desert Orchid is revered on the other side of the Irish Sea.

Yesterday morning in Tommy Wright's I met two couples who had come from Newcastle-on-Tyne to see him run. They weren't members of the aristocracy or of the moneyed class – they came over on the ferry. At the same time the quay was being swept with rain and sleet – but they were going to Fairyhouse. If only for them I was glad to see Richard Dunwoody and Desert Orchid romp to glory. Richard is one of our own – he and wonder-horse are a kind of Anglo-Irish Agreement.

It can be argued that Desert Orchid had nothing to beat yesterday – don't believe it. He was giving lumps of weight to some very useful horses – and, as they say in the idiom of racing, weight can stop a train. And it wasn't only that he won – it was the manner of his victory.

I cannot see into his mind but my intuition tells me that he loves to race and that he loves to jump. I have never seen a stag jump – but I have often seen hares jump; it is a lovely sight. Desert Orchid jumps like a hare; yesterday it was great to watch him – until he came to the last fence.

For a horrible moment I thought that he was gone – and I was reminded of a day long ago at Fairyhouse when Prince Regent was strolling away with the Grand National when he came to the last. There he pecked on landing and went to the floor.

And his trainer Tom Dreaper uttered an immortal one-liner: 'There should be no last fence.' The same Tom bequeathed another one-liner about the same horse.

Believe it or not, in Prince Regent's time there were handicaps so framed that any horse getting over twelve-seven was ruled out. The purpose was, of course, to keep out Prince Regent. And Tom Draper said: 'The only place I can put him now is in the museum.'

The people who devised such handicaps were woefully out of touch with the racing public. People will come to see a great chaser or a great hurdler even though he has little opposition. In this country, even in these more enlightened times, there are far too few races that give a good horse a fair chance.

How often did the Irish people see Arkle run 'in the flesh'? As soon as his greatness was established, he did most of his racing in England.

Like Prince Regent he carried top weight to victory in the Grand National – that was one of the few occasions we saw him run here.

Yesterday's race is easily described: Desert Orchid as usual went off in front and stayed there.

Bold Flyer, living up to his name, took him on for most of the first circuit; then The Committee took up the challenge.

As they turned down the hill for home, it looked for a little while that Richard Dunwoody would have to get to work on the grey.

Desert Orchid appeared to be tiring – and Brendan Sheridan on Barney Burnett must have felt that he was in with a chance. And when the grey clouted the last fence, the young man from Kildare scented victory.

In some manner best known to himself Desert Orchid kept his feet – or, if you like, his hooves. And his run to the post was like a lap of honour.

Adulation was unconfined – and very few in the multitudes gave a thought to the fact that the wonder-horse is as English as bottled sauce.

Evening Press

THE OTHER FOUR-IN-A-ROW

THE DUBLIN–MEATH
LEINSTER FINAL REPLAYS, 1991

I 'POETS STRUGGLING TO EXPRESS THEMSELVES
IN A BARBARIC LANGUAGE'

Since the draw for the Leinster Championship was published several months ago, we had been looking towards the meeting of Dublin and Meath as a kind of All-Ireland final played in the heat and brightness of June – alas, it didn't work out that way.

For a start the day was grey and windy and cold – the play in the first half seemed to take its hue from the weather.

The opening thirty-five minutes contained hardly a dozen minutes of actual play. And it contained almost everything that is bad in Gaelic football.

The marvellous League Final of some weeks ago seemed to belong to another era and a different planet.

As private battles broke out within the main battle, we were looking at a kind of scrap Sunday.

And the few who attempted to play football were like poets struggling to express themselves in a barbaric language.

The referee seemed to have the same attitude as his counterpart in the recent Wembley final – he had made up his mind that he would send nobody off.

And his six assistants seemed to have the kind of eyesight that hardly fitted them for their task. Most of the action took place off the ball but the umpires and the linesmen seemed to think that it was all part and parcel of the game.

The apologists might blame the wind but the game on

the undercard – the Leinster junior final between Dublin and Meath – had been exemplary.

The half-time signal brought blessed relief; during the break I met several Meath followers, disgruntled because their warriors were five points behind.

And I met several of Dublin's back-up army who weren't too gruntled either. They feared that their team's lead was too skinny – Meath would now have the wind. All agreed that it had been a dreadful Act One, utterly unworthy of two fine teams.

A transformation took place during the tea-break: the sun came out; the wind dropped. The air softened; now it was the kind of day that we had anticipated.

And Meath came alive; hitherto they had seemed content to keep Dublin's score down to a manageable level.

A few positional changes seemed to have a magical effect. Tyro Tommy Dowd had started at full-forward; now he was in the half-forwards; this crouchy tiger was to have a great second half.

And Liam Hayes, who had gone through Act One like a dormant volcano, began to erupt fire and occasionally brimstone. Suddenly he realised that he was the best fielder on the pitch; he began to make a clearing in the midfield jungle. He made several soaring catches which reminded you that Gaelic football can be a game of grace and beauty.

While all this was going on, the wind dropped to a whisper: for the first twenty minutes of the second half it hardly counted at all.

Meath had resumed with two quick points; steadily they whittled away the lead. And when they drew level, ample time remained – and the wind had come back. Their Kop behind the Canal Goal were anticipating a ringside view of the victory run.

It didn't come: Dublin, like their Juniors, battled away fiercely and never lost the lead that they had taken in the first sentence. And when they went a point ahead well into broken time, it looked like being a long, cold Summer for the Royal County.

Sean Boylan was pacing up and down under the Cusack Stand, looking like the proverbial hen that had hatched out ducklings and is watching them struggling in stormy water. And when the US Fifth Cavalry came in the form of a freak point, he must have felt that the sphinx-like gods who favour football had scripted a draw.

All last week people were going around saying that there was only a hop of the ball between these fierce rivals – as it was, a hop of the ball tied the game. And we had the rare experience of a keeper castigated for not saving a point.

If the ball had come down to earth on a worn few square inches, it might have ended up in the net; as it was, it just cleared the crossbar. And so we had a stalemate: next Sunday we hope to experience a fresh mate.

II 'A Kind of Wild Magnificence'

Do you remember the French general who uttered the immortal one-liner as he watched the Charge of the Light Brigade? He said: 'It is magnificent – but it is not warfare.'

Yesterday in Croke Park I was tempted to stand that judgement on its head – but it would be unfair to the warriors of Dublin and Meath. Warfare this game most certainly was but it also had about it a kind of wild magnificence.

The Japanese pilots who bombed Pearl Harbour would have understood – only that they aren't around any more. The old Romans used to say that it is fitting and glorious to die for your country; yesterday we watched young men who were willing to die for their county.

42

This serial could go on running until *Glenroe* is ready to come back. Yesterday we saw the fourth draw between these teams in successive matches.

They ended up level in the League in March and again last Sunday; yesterday they drew again in the first seventy minutes – and again in the mini-match known as extratime. And if this tie is ever to be decided, I hope it will be won decisively.

It would have been a tragedy yesterday if a late score had ended the marathon. Pardon this hoariest of clichés – neither side deserved to lose.

Yesterday we witnessed drama and melodrama. And for good measure we saw a good smidgeon of the romantic. There was a whiff of '83 as Barney Rock came out of the shadows.

He was the first Progressive Democrat to play in a big game of Gaelic football. His performance will give great heart to Dessie O'Malley, not to mention Stephen O'Byrnes and Mary Harney and Bobby Molloy.

Barney did well in the general play – and even if he didn't, his brilliant place-kicking would have paid for his passage. It was a marvellous come-back; Robin Hood and Jesse James couldn't have wished for better.

Ciaran Duff was there too and so by the end of play was Gerry Hargan. And so John O'Leary needn't feel like Oisín after all the Fianna had passed away.

And it was a great day in the young life of a lad called Paul Bealin. It was his first time to start in a championship game: he can be very proud of his debut.

I have often quoted D. H. Lawrence: 'The only tragedy is loss of heart.' He was on the button. I doubt if the sage of Nottingham ever saw a game of Gaelic football – even though he was no stranger to Ireland. If he had been in the Field of Croke yesterday, he would have approved.

There were times when the balance of the battle seemed to have tilted – but the team at the wrong end of the scoreline refused to die. When, for example, Mick Lyons was forced to take early retirement, even Sean Boylan's stout heart must have quailed.

Meath, however, even in less prosperous days were renowned for their stubborn courage.

It manifested itself again yesterday – and at a quarter to six I am certain that Paddy Cullen and his three apostles were glad to be still in contention. And I was glad that the GAA haven't adopted the penalty shoot-out. My heart hasn't yet stopped quaking since that evening in Genoa.

And as we came away from the old grey stadium by the Royal Canal, we were nearly all unusually silent. For a start, we were exhausted – and for a finish, there was so much to ponder.

III 'MEATH NEEDED A GOAL AS BADLY AS A MAN SINKING IN A MARSH NEEDS A ROPE'

It was like seeing a movie for the third time; that was how I felt as I tottered out of Croke Park yesterday evening. I have seen *La Strada* seven times between the big screen and television; I will not be astonished if I witness the Dublin–Meath saga as often.

There is no reason why this shouldn't end up level once again: the script has been written and there is little that the teams can do about it. The wry puppeteer who pulls the strings in Gaelic football will eventually break the livelock. By then we may have grown old beyond our years. And the treasurer of the Leinster Council may have been sent back to school to do a course in higher mathematics.

Of course those people who see all human activity wheeling around money are now absolutely certain that all this is a conspiracy.

Perhaps it is; if so, the men we have watched in Croke

44

Park for what seems like a sample of eternity are consummate actors.

There seems to be no limit to what this drama can produce. Before yesterday's battle ran its course we had seen Ger McEntee and Joe McNally back in action. It was like watching the working of a time machine.

Both are young men in terms of the real world but in football's idiom seemed to have been past-tense in the inter-county scene. All we lacked yesterday was the small brown dog; he would have loved this melodrama.

Yesterday's game was by far the best instalment in the series. The first half was rather turgid; the second went a long way towards compensating for what had gone before.

It was as unremittingly hard as ever but this time we saw flowers peeping out of the rocks. It was akin to watching two heavyweight pugilists who had grown tired of slugging it out and decided to try boxing for a change.

All Gaeldom looks on agog. And as someone said in the Waterloo House last night, the man at the electronic board lost a great opportunity yesterday evening. As the game ended, he should have flashed up the words 'TO BE CONTINUED'. And you will again see a big crowd for the next thrilling instalment.

To find a comparison I have to evoke Leo Tolstoy's *War and Peace*. It is a novel of daunting length. I wouldn't call it a great book but there are great things in it.

Most of Dublin's followers came away yesterday evening in less than gruntled mood. They believed that they had been robbed. The time factor was the source of their grievance.

They argued that Mr Tommy Howard had played thirty-five minutes in the first half – and over thirty-eight in the second.

Meath's equalising point came in broken time – and it

was just as well that it all ended in a draw; otherwise we might have had a case for the Court of Human Rights.

I hasten to add one point in Mr Howard's favour: he kept fairly good order in a battle that threatened to burst its banks.

Most great plays have comic interludes; Keith Barr provided the best yesterday.

He was deemed guilty of a misdemeanour that merited a booking – but the referee couldn't find him. Eventually, acting on information received, he tracked him down. And we witnessed an almost-convincing example of 'Not me, sir.' It was that kind of a day.

Anybody who believes that he can analyse this game has reached the Everest of self-deception. And I wouldn't dare to pick out the man of the match because there were so many. If the words 'ebb' and 'flow' didn't exist, we would have to invent them.

Both sides had such spells of supremacy that they looked almost certain to prevail. That was especially true of Dublin in the middle third of Act Two in normal time. They were territorially dominant in that period and steadily forged a five-points lead.

And a most unlikely prospect loomed – I could hardly believe that this Meath team could be decisively beaten. They needed a goal as badly as a man sinking in a marsh needs a rope – and they got it.

When they got another in the first minute of abnormal time, it seemed that the saga was at last to be ended. Stoutness of heart, however, is not a Royal monopoly.

That goal was quickly cancelled. And from that moment another draw seemed almost inevitable.

The draw was a fair result; as a Dub told a captive audience in the Shakespeare: 'Neither team could embrace the concept of defeat.'

IV 'SEAN BOYLAN HAS TASTED A SMIDGEON FROM THE SALMON OF KNOWLEDGE'

I have long suspected that Sean Boylan has a magic potion which his players ingest on big-match days; after Saturday I have no doubts about it.

And I have long suspected too that he is in league with the gremlins and the goblins and the assorted spirits that lurk in and around the GAA's centre court.

On Saturday the coalition of magic potion and the little people pulled down the best team produced by Dublin since the glorious year of 1977.

As I came away from the old stadium hard by the Royal Canal, an unlikely image surfaced in my tempest-tormented mind. It involved a group or rocks which run their ungodly life a few miles from the southern coast of Devon.

When the sea is agitated, they are hardly visible, and there lies many a tragic tale: the red rocks of Eddystone have wrecked many a noble vessel. They were at their worst in the sixteenth century when trade with the New World was at its peak. It was the ultimate in maritime tragedy to come through over three thousand miles of the Atlantic and end up in Davy Jones's locker within half an hour of Plymouth Hoe.

Tommy Carr and his gallant men will understand; so too will Paddy Cullen and Jim Brogan and Fran Ryder and Pat O'Neill and all those devoted to Dublin's cause. Tommy said: 'It is like a death in the family'; for once the cliché was justified.

Not since the late September of 1982 have I known such a fallout of grief. I will give you an example: a young woman who has never been inside the grey walls of Croke Park but who watched the game on television rang me yesterday morning – she was inconsolable.

And if Dublin had won – as they so nearly did – the

mood in the pubs frequented by the aficionados in blue would have made 'ecstatic' seem too pale a word. As it was, those same pubs were suffused with untempered sadness.

We were in the Shakespeare; the atmosphere recalled the last passage in Carson McCullers's brilliant novella *The Ballad of the Sad Café*. Such speech-fragments as 'daylight robbery' and 'they gave it all away' and 'Meath were poxed' ascended and hovered. And a very strong man who is an old and dear friend was fighting unsuccessfully to restrain the tears.

I kept thinking about Sean Boylan. Do you remember Fionn MacCool and the salmon he liberated from the Boyne? Maybe Sean too has tasted a smidgeon from the Salmon of Knowledge. I believe there is a case for a public inquiry.

I will sign off with a quote from a friend, uttered a few seconds after the end of the 1966 World Cup: 'What will we do for the rest of the Summer?' The people of Dublin will understand.

Evening Press

'THAT RARE IRISHMAN –
ONE WHO MADE THE MOST OF HIS GIFTS'

LIAM BRADY

Small boys and even big boys look on the life of a professional footballer as the ideal existence – little do they know. It is at best an unrealistic life – and at worst a kind of living purgatory. And if you believe that Liam Brady has dwelt for about twenty years in the Promised Land, you must think again. Of course by any standards he has had a fabulous career – but the gods have a wry sense of humour and tend to exact a price for their seeming gifts.

Cast your mind back a few years and remember our scenario for the Euro and World Cups. We had it all mapped out – our team would be built around David O'Leary, Mark Lawrenson, Frank Stapleton and Liam Brady. And when at last we crossed the Red Sea, only Frank, the eternal survivor, was on board.

Injury had guillotined Mark's career; Liam was in the repair shop; David was the victim of selectorial myopia. And young lads who were hardly a wet season in football partook of the glory in West Germany.

Such is life; irony is always lurking around the corner. It wasn't Liam's first encounter with that prankster. In his late career at Highbury he knew a season that promised a rich harvest – and yielded nothing.

Arsenal were chasing a great treble – FA Cup and League and European Cup-Winners' Cup. They ended up all too aware of what Tantalus, the Greek god who was condemned to suffer the ultimate in frustration, had suffered.

Of course Liam Brady has huge entries on the credit side of the book. He is one of the few who has gone into folklore by having an English Cup Final labelled with his name. Everybody remembers the 1979 decider as 'Liam Brady's Final'. And almost everybody deems his display on the momentous day as his greatest ever.

I do not much relish the role of non-conformist – but for once I cannot concur. And I think of a grey windy afternoon at Highbury long ago when Arsenal were playing Everton in the League.

It was a splendid game – and ended 2–2. Liam dominated those ninety minutes as much as an individual can – and for great measure scored an astonishing goal.

It came in the last quarter and was scored at the North End, just below Arsenal's devoted Bank. Liam brought the ball down the inside-right corridor; all the defenders were present and correct – danger seemed remote.

Suddenly, about twenty-five yards from goal, Liam let fly with his right foot – the ball roared high into the net. I can still see the astonishment on his immediate marker's face. Was it Colin Todd?

Until that moment everybody in football and a great many outside it looked on Liam's right foot at illiterate. I remember the heading on my piece on the following Monday – 'LIAM, KING OF HIGHBURY'.

They were great days for the Irish in London or thereabouts. I remember a Saturday when Arsenal fielded seven players from this small island. Of course you can name them – Pat Jennings, Pat Rice, John Devine, Sammy Nelson, David O'Leary, Liam Brady and Frank Stapleton.

I must say in passing that it seemed unreal last Saturday to watch Manchester United playing without an Irishman on board. That's another story; it seems strange now to see The Republic playing without Liam.

Every footballer dreams of ending his career on the highest possible note – it doesn't always work out that way. Liam's international career ended in just about the saddest possible way.

That day at Lansdowne Road I recalled a fragment

from William Shakespeare – 'The deep damnation of his taking off.'

It was a bad way to go; I have no wish to reopen old wounds – but our Jack boobed in publicly humiliating a great player. And his excuse was pathetic; if he had allowed Liam to remain on until the interval, the West Germans might have scored again.

It was, after all, only a friendly; Jack shouldn't have been so worried about keeping his long unbeaten run intact.

And even though I know that Liam needn't worry about the threatened rise in the price of black pudding, I welcomed his testimonial. It provides him with a worthy stage on which to make his farewell bow. I would give more than an old penny for Liam's thoughts as he walks off the pitch tomorrow evening.

He has come a very long way since the day his parents escorted him out to Collinstown and put him on the plane for Heathrow. He was fifteen; it is still a young age; twenty years ago at fifteen you were little more than a child.

I was a few years older when first I encountered London – and I can still remember the fear that smote me as the train from Fishguard neared the gates of the great capital. I soon lost my dread of London and came to love the place – but I didn't start out there as an apprentice professional footballer.

Of course Liam had wonderful talent. And of course he knew it – but talent didn't guarantee that he would survive in that fiercely competitive world.

I have known marvellously gifted players who didn't; I have a neighbour who had such an amalgam of physique and skill that he could have made a good living across the Irish Sea – he lasted only a few weeks.

You need great will-power and infinite patience – and above all you need the mental equipment to fight off man's most insidious enemy, loneliness.

Liam survived – and did a great deal more: he is that rare Irishman – he made the most of his gifts.

We tend to suspect fulfilment; we incline towards those who have within them the Hamlet-like proclivity towards self-destruction.

Liam has always possessed great discipline – he has walked down mean fields without being mean himself.

Some people will tell you that he was – or is – our greatest-ever footballer. That kind of hype is strictly for the birds – if only because no one amongst us has seen them all.

All I will say is that he was a great player and a marvellously entertaining one.

In an age when subtlety is suspect, he cherished the old-fashioned approach; he might have laid the foundation of his craft on a Brazilian beach rather than in the playing fields of Dublin.

That winkle-picking left foot gave us myriad moments of delight – and caused many an opponent to wonder if the laws of physics had been changed overnight.

Evening Press

'ONE OF THE GREATEST MOMENTS IN OUR SPORTING HISTORY'

MICHAEL CARRUTH AND WAYNE MCCULLOUGH
BARCELONA 1992

About an hour ago I recalled that crazy night up in the mountains in the Black Forest above Stuttgart when Kevin Moran said to me: 'I'd love to be in Ballybunion tonight.'

At this moment I would like to be in the Long Mile Inn or the KCR or even in Mulligan's or any pub in Dublin or any pub in Ireland, but most of all in Paddy Hussey's in Castle Island because Paddy was a great boxer himself.

Where were you at the moment that President Kennedy was assassinated; where were you when Mikey Sheehy chipped Paddy Cullen for the goal that launched a thousand quips; where were you when Arkle stormed up the hill at Cheltenham to beat the 'invincible' Mill House and win his first Gold Cup; where were you when Stephen Roche won the Tour de France and where were you when Ronnie Delaney won in Melbourne?

These are all questions that are part of folklore, but after this morning we can add another. Where were you when a red-haired young man called Michael Carruth from Drimnagh in Dublin's southside made pugilistic history by winning our first-ever gold medal in Barcelona this morning?

At the presentation another piece of history was made: it was the first time in a great many years that I have heard our national anthem being played all the way through to the last chord without interruptions.

I know back home for the last few days my neighbours in Dublin are looking forward to winning the All-Ireland; today they won the All-World.

There was a great pool of boxers here from all over the globe – even from Mongolia.

And the standards are very high; it was generally deemed that Michael would do well to win bronze but with the philosopher's stone of legend he transmuted bronze into silver and silver into gold.

There were about a hundred and fifty Irish people in the stadium; the support they gave him was out of all proportion to their numbers – and at the end there was hardly a dry eye among the Irish contingent.

Believe it or not, I saw veteran sportsman and veteran journalist David Guiney weeping unashamedly. And I had to lend Kevin O'Flanagan one of my handkerchiefs.

I knew that the Irish crowd had been augmented because I saw a man waving a copy of yesterday's *Evening Press*.

I feared the worst in the first few minutes for Michael Carruth. Juan Hernandez is at least three inches taller; he moved beautifully; he has a very strange style – he keeps his feet almost level with each other but usually he leads with his right hand.

You could say that he is a semi-southpaw. In the first round for speed of foot and hand he looked in a different league. Michael is full of heart and he kept slogging away, leading with his right and following usually with a kind of straight left.

At the end of the round I thought that Hernandez had a slight lead. Seemingly, Michael's punches began to tell, and more and more the elegant boy from Cuba began to look vulnerable.

Carruth did nothing spectacular; he kept coming forward and throwing punches; several missed but he landed enough to promise that in Round Three he might take the upper ground.

Nothing was going to be easy in this bout; when you reach the final, you are in with the big boys.

Carruth continued as he had started; he became more aggressive and began to land more frequently and twice in Round Three he had the boy from Cuba in some trouble.

And yet at the final bell I was far from convinced that he had done enough. Michael himself seemed confident that he had won; before he went to his corner he waved to the Irish crowd.

When the boxers joined hands with the referee, I felt like closing my eyes as I almost did that night in Genoa when David O'Leary squared up to that penalty.

However, I had the courage to look and when Michael's hand went up, I hugged everybody within reach and some who weren't in reach at all.

I had been privileged to be present at one of the greatest moments in our sporting history.

There is an old husbands' tale in Ireland that you do not win the Sam Maguire unless you beat Kerry in the final.

That, of course, is utter nonsense and yet it was good today to see Michael beating a Cuban in the final because boxing in that island is as much a part of the culture as hurling in Kilkenny or music in the county of Clare.

*

Wayne McCullough also came up against a Cuban, Joel Casamayor. He, too, was a little taller and very elegant and very quick.

It was obvious that the Cubans had done their homework – Wayne loves to fight at close quarters; he loves to get 'stuck in' and punch and punch and punch.

Today the Cuban boy kept him at a distance with a brilliant left hand; the fight would never go Wayne's way.

By the middle of Round Two you knew that he needed a knockout but his opponent is a consummate tactician; he backed away when it suited him and then pounced when McCullough was temporarily unbalanced. At the end of Round Two he had a clear lead.

The third round was amazing; Casamayor seemed to lack stamina. It is McCullough's forte – and he won the last round by a very clear margin, but he knew that it wasn't enough. If the term 'gallant loser' hadn't been so long in existence, we would have minted it today.

The crowd gave him enormous applause when he acknowledged them. He went out with great dignity and shook hands with his opponent's camp and at the presentation even this tough little lad couldn't hold back a few tears.

All in all it was a great morning for Ireland. And I was reminded of a neighbour down in Kerry long ago who took a pig to the fair; when he came home, his wife asked him if he had got a good price. And he said: 'Not as much as I hoped for, but more than I expected.'

Well, with silver and gold we are very happy.

Evening Press

'THE GREATEST RACE IN THE WORLD'

THE GRAND NATIONAL, THE DERBY – AND THE STRANGE CASE OF SHERGAR

I often think of the Greek poet Cavafy: 'In those streets and fields where you grew up, there you will live and there you will die.'

There is a moorland that I cherish. There I grew up. It extends from south-west Limerick and north-east Cork to within about ten miles of the Atlantic – and from a few miles north of Castle Island to within a few miles of Listowel. And thus it is about thirty miles from east to west – and about twenty miles from south to north. The moorland in Dorset that Thomas Hardy christened Egdon Heath is only a haggard in comparison.

A generation ago that moorland in North Kerry was a great patchwork of bog and reclaimed farmland. On an average it was about a thousand feet above the sea.

During World War II and for many years afterwards it teemed with life from early April until September. Turf was king and so was the horse.

The people of the moorland loved horses; of course they were an essential part of the economy, but the love went deeper than that. It used to be said that the cow was the peasant's wife and the horse was his mistress.

On the northern extreme of the moorland a family named Trant have a modest farm. They are a remarkable family: in the worst of times, they managed to live with style.

They have always kept greyhounds and they breed horses for hunting and showjumping. In my youth they kept a stallion called Redwood – he had run in the Derby. It fascinated me that such an aristocrat was in residence amongst us.

Redwood, like all thoroughbreds, was descended from one of the four horses that were sent as gifts to the English Royal Family by an Arabian prince in the seventeenth century. I loved the idea of the Arabian seed being sown in that world of bog and little fields.

The men of the moorland were as knowledgeable about horses as if they lived in Manton or Lambourn or Newmarket itself.

Those men could trace breeding back for generations and were shrewd students of the form-book. In the run-up to the big races, especially the Derby and the Grand National, you would hear discussions that ranged wide and deep.

My neighbours knew horses not as names in the newspapers and the form-books – they knew them as creatures of flesh and blood and minds and spirits. In their thinking, you could say that horses were human.

One Friday morning long ago two friends of mine decided to fulfil a long-time ambition. They took the milk to the creamery, got their monthly cheque, went home and made a peace pact with their loving wives.

They went to Dublin and took the ferry from the North Wall and had breakfast in Liverpool on Saturday morning. They were back home in their local pub on Sunday night and of course were the observed of all observers.

There was a chorus asking had the journey been worthwhile. 'Of course it was.' 'Was the race as good as ye expected?' 'It was far better. Anyone should go at least once.'

That was my experience too after I had first walked on Aintree's dark-brown soil. I think it is fair to say that it is the greatest race in the world. It is dramatic and melodramatic, spectacular and enthralling. All of human and equine life is there. It has the amplitude of a great novel. And no race seems more scripted to show that the gods who govern sport are catchers in the wry.

Such great jockeys as Stan Mellor and Martin Molony and Jonjo O'Neill never even came near to winning it.

Ruby Walsh and Paul Carberry rode to Aintree glory when they weren't long out of school.

Johnny Buckingham was on the point of retirement when he won on Foinavon after almost all the contenders had crashed out in a multiple fall about a mile from home.

Dick Francis was well clear of the field when Devon Loch jumped the shadow of a post and came down a hundred yards from the line.

About ten minutes before the start, you will see the white-aproned women from the restaurants lining the inside rail of the last furlong. The whole world seems to hold its breath as the man on the rostrum attempts to get the milling field in line. At last he gives the signal – and the multicoloured river flows away.

One of the greatest aspects of the National is that a small owner can win it. Roundwood in the hills above Lyrecrompane might have sired a National winner if he had got the right mare.

*

The Derby is almost exclusively the world of the multi-millionaires. Computer breeding gives the small man little chance. The dam of Santa Claus was bought for two hundred and fifty guineas – such a romantic story is now unlikely.

And yet the Derby is the essence of democracy in its own way. Every year over a quarter of a million people take over the Epsom Downs for free.

There was a year away back in the nineteenth century when a 'people's horse' might have made the great race more democratic. The story can bear retelling. It began when a publican in London's East End got a rush of blood to his pocket. He bought a two-year-old and set out to win the Derby.

He had no land but he worked the horse on a nearby common called London Fields. His pot-boy acted as jockey and trainer. He was a semi-retired jockey who had kept his licence.

The Cockney Boy, as he was aptly called, was not raced as a two-year-old. Indeed, the Derby was to be his maiden voyage. As the big day drew near, the interest in the East End was enormous.

Crowds flocked to see the pot-boy putting the wonder-horse through his paces.

There was a mass exodus on the morning of the race. Crowds set out from Whitechapel and Stepney and the Mile End Road and Spitalfields and Limehouse itself. They came from Bethnal Green and Bow and Hackney and from almost every nook and cranny in the East End. An elderly couple set out from Holloway but dallied in a pie ship in Fleet Street and missed the last train from Waterloo. Alas, they didn't miss much.

Horses are very sensitive to smell: the combined aroma of beer and spirits and winkles and jellied eels and shrimps and other edibles proved too much for the Cockney Boy.

On the way to the start the poor horse bolted. He scattered the crowd as he jumped the rails at Tattenham Corner. The gallant pot-boy hung on and brought him to a halt on the road to Reigate. Horse and man spent the night at a nearby inn and next day travelled the twenty-five-odd miles to London.

I wasn't on the Downs that unmomentous day. I was there, however, to enjoy the best performance I ever saw from a horse in the Derby. On that afternoon over twenty years ago the gods once again showed their expertise as catchers in the wry.

Many a fine jockey had gone through a long career

without winning the world's greatest flat race – school-boy-faced Walter Swinburn won it at his first attempt.

And I can still see Shergar's four white socks above the lush green grass as he cruised home like a greyhound running away from collies. I recalled a little verse deemed gospel by the aficionados in the moorland:

> If your horse has one white sock,
> Don't keep him for a day,
> And if your horse has two white socks,
> Sell him straight away,
> If your horse has three white socks,
> You can sell him to a friend,
> But if your horse has four white socks,
> Keep him to the end.

*

No game breeds rumours as fecundly as racing: there is a general assumption that under the surface is a seething, secret world – and everyone pretends to be privy to it.

After his victories in the Epsom Derby and the Curragh Derby a good many people proclaimed Shergar not only the greatest classic horse of all time but a step forward in equine evolution.

His acceleration made him look like an Olympic runner pulling away from joggers – but in the St Leger he looked little better than a jogger himself.

And the strong pace and the extra few furlongs could hardly be the full explanation of his eclipse.

For a few weeks before the race there had been a rumour that all was not well with him. It was – to coin a phrase – categorically denied.

But the race indicated that the rumour was only too well founded.

Whence did the rumour come? The answer perhaps

lies in the relation between upstairs and downstairs.

Racing in these islands is in some aspects a living museum of the past, a kind of Victorian world surviving into the age of the welfare state.

The relationship between master and man is almost feudal – but with this difference: in racing the servants are indispensable.

A lord of old could throw out his serfs and replace them with cattle or sheep – a trainer cannot cope without his lads.

Most of them are meagrely remunerated for hard and dangerous work – but their passion for horses keeps them at it.

And low down in the pyramid though they are, they know more about the horses in their care than do the trainers.

And that is perhaps the explanation of a phenomenon familiar to most people who follow the horses.

It is this: if you get a tip from some little ragged old man to whom you'd given a drive or for whom perhaps you bought a drink, don't be too dismissive of it.

The little ragged old man may have a son or a grandson in a stable – and may be a far better source of information than some stylishly dressed racegoer who is listing from the weight of all the badges attached to his binocular case.

And the rumour about Shergar's ill-being before the St Leger probably came from such a source.

What did the little ragged old man know? He knew that all was not well in the establishment of Michael Stoute.

To the world it presented a formidable face, a superb organisation that was turning out horses as well-conditioned as newly minted coins and making long-founded stables seem as up-to-date as Rip Van Winkle.

And for most of the season the reality corresponded to

the image. But then came a puzzling change – the stream of winners dried up even though the stable was free of coughing or any of the other ailments that afflict finely tuned horses.

The explanation was downstairs: the lads felt that too much of the bonus money from Shergar's victories had been given to those higher up the pyramid – and they were in silent revolt.

They went about their work as usual: the horses were not neglected; technically the lads did nothing wrong – but there is a vast gulf between attention and devotion.

And those hypersensitive creatures suddenly felt unloved. And because Shergar had been the most loved, he now felt the most unloved of all.

The record-book will merely show in what position he finished in the St Leger and how far behind.

It can only show the top layer of the complex entity we call the truth.

As the man said: 'She washed the pot. But did she wash the rag that washed the pot.'

Magill

'I Came Away from the Austin Stack Park Convinced I Had Seen Nascent Greatness'

Mick O'Dwyer

There are war criminals – and there are peace criminals. The faceless people who 'rationalised' our rail system got pensions – they should have got jail.

Thomas Wolfe, the half-forgotten novelist who lived in the early twentieth century, said that the most evocative of American sounds was the whistle of a distant train. The whistle of a nearby train can be evocative too. The train is more than a means of communication: it is a symbol of energy. Its comings and goings are part of the rhythm in the life of a community. The planners inflicted a grievous wound on South Kerry when they uprooted the line to Cahirciveen. Happy is the constituency that has a marginal seat; a generation ago Kerry hadn't. The loss of their train told the people of South Kerry that they were children of a lesser god.

Nature had already withheld some of its favours. For generations Port Magee and Cahirciveen had been thriving on the harvest of the sea. You could buy mackerel from South Kerry as far away as the Rocky Mountains. About 1920, the great shoals ceased to come. Emigration followed. South Kerry declined. This was the world into which Mick O'Dwyer was born in the Midsummer of 1936.

There was no report of a strange star in the sky or three wise men coming from the East. Mick's father, John O'Dwyer, owned a hackney car; his mother, Mary Galvin, worked in the local hotel. Thus the family hovered between the working class and the middle class. Few bothered about such distinctions in those days; it was an age when survival was the name of the game.

Mick was an only child. He went from the national school to the local technical school. Then he served his time as a motor mechanic. From childhood he was playing football in all the spare time God gave him. In this he wasn't unusual: Gaelic football was very much part of the culture in South Kerry. Once upon a time, a visiting philosopher asked Jackie Lyne why football was such a passion in Kerry. My dear departed friend, a star in his own right, said: 'With those bastards of mountains behind us and that bitch of an ocean before us, we have to do something.' Perhaps they sounded like wild and whirling words, but they pointed to a profound truth: we cannot escape being affected by our surroundings.

I have a very clear memory of the first time I saw Mick O'Dwyer play. He was at left half-forward with South Kerry in a county-championship game in Tralee. He wasn't noticeably fast or skilful, but he had a certain quality that, at least for me, made him stand out. He always looked as if he knew what he was doing: whenever he got the ball, he used it well. I came away from the Austin Stack Park that evening convinced that I had seen nascent greatness.

He made his debut for the county at twenty-three and helped Kerry to win four All-Irelands. O'Dwyer didn't look a great player but he was: the sum of his parts came to a total that you couldn't deny. He seldom made the headlines as an inter-county player. His neighbour, Mick O'Connell, was the golden boy in that era. In the Spring of 1974, O'Dwyer retired from the playing fields. Injuries were taking effect. There was another factor: he had married Mary Carmel O'Sullivan in 1962 – now he had a growing family and a thriving hotel to demand his attention. Ironically, he was to become more involved in football than ever.

His boots were hardly a month in the cubby under the stairs when he was asked to manage Kerry. It was a dubious honour. The county had strayed into the wilderness. Cork were now kings in Munster. The reluctant manager brought to his task an alarming lack of experience but the single-mindedness that has marked all his endeavours.

Kevin Heffernan had managed Dublin to win the All-Ireland in 1974 with a training regime that smacked as much of warfare as football. O'Dwyer met steel with steel. He introduced a training discipline that caused deep cultural shock: some brilliant players jumped ship. Payback came on a rainy Sunday in Croke Park in 1975. Kerry, made up mostly of young unknowns, decisively beat Dublin, reigning champions and warm favourites.

Dublin got one back when they beat Kerry just as decisively in the final in 1976. And in the semi-final in 1977, they beat Kerry in a game that is part of folklore. The counties met again in the All-Ireland final in 1978. This game too is deep in the folk memory. Kerry won in sensational fashion. It was the first of the four All-Irelands in a row.

In 1982 the people of the Kingdom were looking confidently to the Promised Land. Kerry would make history by winning five All-Irelands in a row. To mention the possibility of failure was low treason. The number 'five' infiltrated every nook and several crannies in the county. Butchers displayed black puddings, not to mention white puddings, in rings of five. The number was emblazoned on T-shirts and on coffee-shirts and on cocoa-shirts. People greeted one another with five-finger salutes. Hysteria was at large. Nobody would have been surprised if some young woman had announced that she was carrying quintuplets.

Kerry duly got to the All-Ireland final and met Offaly. The Golden Fleece seemed in sight as Kerry dominated the game. Alas, a late late goal robbed them.

It was as if a ship in Elizabethan times, returning richly laden from the Americas, was in sight of landfall, only to perish on the red rocks of Eddystone. Kerry went into mourning, but life went on.

O'Dwyer refused to abdicate – and amazingly led Kerry to Autumn glory in 1984 and 1985 and 1986. His reign with Kerry ended when the county lost the Munster final to Cork in 1987. The team had grown old together. O'Dwyer, the alleged hard, unsentimental manager, had been too loyal to his students. One of them, Eoin Liston, said: 'The circus needs new acts.'

O'Dwyer, without a team to manage, was as restless as Napoleon on Elba. In 1990 he accepted an invitation to manage Kildare, once a great power but then long in decline. With Kerry he had employed orthodox tactics, more or less. With the All-Whites, he embarked on a revolution: at times the ball was passed from goalmouth to goalmouth.

He met with only partial success but he brought the county tangible proof that the gods hadn't abandoned them. Kildare hadn't won the Leinster title since 1956 – O'Dwyer brought it to them twice. He also led Kildare to the final of the National League and to the All-Ireland final – they lost both narrowly.

Why does he do it? Why has he travelled up so often from the bottom of Kerry? Pub wisdom tells of helicoptered ease, courtesy of Sheikh Mohammed. The reality is more prosaic.

What has he to prove? He has a fine record as a player and a phenomenal record as a manager. He has a good wife and four fine sons and a sound business.

South Kerry is hauntingly beautiful and at times can be hauntingly lonely. Jackie Lyne's words recur. It is hardly a coincidence that four sons of South Kerry were so dedicated to football. O'Dwyer and Mick O'Connell and Jack O'Shea and Maurice Fitzgerald were committed to a degree far beyond the normal.

Some people will tell you O'Dwyer is in it for the

money. Mick always knew the value of a pound – but it isn't as simple as that. The truth is he loves football not wisely but too well.

What kind of person is he in the world outside the pitch? With his amazing record you might expect an over-powering personality. Mick, in fact, is disarmingly modest and courteous – and he isn't lacking in a sense of humour. His wife, Mary Carmel, is well known for leading pilgrimages – therein hangs a tale. A neighbour once asked him if he had ever been to Lourdes. O'Dwyer, in the best Kerry tradition, answered the question by asking another: 'Did Kerry ever play there . . . ?'

Magill

'WHAT WILL WE DO FOR THE REST OF THE YEAR?'

THE 1966 AND OTHER WORLD CUP FINALS

Of course you have heard it before – but don't stop me: I am talking, of course, about that marvellous day long ago when England played West Germany in the final of the World Cup.

It was the first World Cup to be broadcast on television in this country – we have never been the same since.

I watched every match that was on the box; I saw the rest in my imagination.

And I looked forward to the final like a small boy about to be taken to his first circus.

And on the eve of that momentous event it seemed that my dream would be snatched away.

A kinsman had taken ill and I was requested to draw his turf out of the bog.

And it was with a heavy heart that I set out that July morning for the mountain country of Ahaneboy. Up there I was to make contact with a grand man called Batt Greaney; he would provide the horse and car.

About half past seven we arrived at the rectangle where our kinsman's turf was high and dry in stooks. The night had rained; the bog was rather soft on top; Batt and I inspected the going – and decided that it was too heavy.

I must confess that it was not an objective judgement; I had often ferried out turf in far worse conditions. And so that day over thirty-seven years ago will go down in history as the only occasion on which I ate a second breakfast. It was with a light heart that I went down into the valley and took to my traditional place in one of my favourite pubs.

Strangely enough, it wasn't Paddy Hussey's, even though I had seen much of the tournament there. I suspected that Paddy's would be all-ticket for the final – and so I adjourned to another pub in the Latin Quarter.

And so it was in Monny McGillicuddy's that I watched what I still consider the second-greatest game of association football that I ever saw.

Castle Island is one of the last bastions of civilisation – and, of course, the television set wasn't in the bar. It was in the living quarters, at the end of a long room that served as parlour and kitchen.

It was crowded, so much so that my old friend, Bertie O'Brien, made a little bit of history. He knelt down near the box and didn't get up until the game was over.

And I will never forget his summing up: 'What will we do for the rest of the year?' In his own simple way he had said it all; it had been a great tournament and it brought a new dimension into our lives. And, of course, it hastened the end of the infamous Ban, the epitome of Green ignorance and prejudice.

In those far-off and not unhappy days I hadn't the slightest suspicion that I might one day be a journalist. In truth I am not – but I work for a newspaper.

And, high and behold, in the Midsummer of 1982 I found myself on the way to Spain to keep an eye or two on the finals of the World Cup.

On that Sunday evening in Gatwick I was more than somewhat uneasy. Somebody with a rather quirky sense of humour had made my travel arrangements – and I was billeted in Segovia, over seventy miles from Madrid.

I can never forget that journey up into the mountains; it was a steaming night and the bus had no air-conditioning. And when we arrived at the hotel, our worst fears were confirmed – the bar was as closed as George Bush Sr's mind.

On the journey I had made friends with an Australian – and Harold and I went into action. We cajoled a young boy to go to the home of the bar manager; he came back with the keys. It was about three o'clock. Never did beer taste so good. The people of Spain may have their faults but they make great ale.

Next day we journeyed down to Madrid and passed through country where a cow would have to travel several miles to fill her belly. The mountains of Castile still haunt me; I would love to go back and walk in that hard brown country, even at the risk of being devoured by wolves – hungry or otherwise.

That Spanish tournament provided some marvellous football; ironically, the best came from Brazil, but they didn't even reach the semi-finals. Their knockout game with Italy took place a long way from Madrid; I watched it on television in the company of Eoin Hand and Billy Young. And we were about equally heartbroken when our favourite team fell out.

One of the shrewdest players in the world was woefully at fault for the fatal goal; Junior was slow to move out after a place-kick had been partly cleared – and put Paolo Rossi onside; the stoat pounced. Rossi was, of course, the hero of the tournament; it was the Everest of irony; a few months previously he had been convicted of throwing games.

A little while ago I spoke about the second-greatest game of soccer that I ever saw – the greatest was in that Spanish tournament. I have vivid memories of that glowing morning when Harold and myself flew down to Seville. I can still visualise the great seas of giant sunflowers that are grown to produce oil.

Seville is a fairly big city – but, believe it or not, when we dropped in to a pub, we met Peter Byrne and Charlie Stuart. And that night we watched West Germany and France in the semi-final; it was the greatest game of football – in any code – that I ever saw. And, as the world knows, it contained the most outrageous example of injustice ever perpetrated.

I can still see Patrick Battiston speeding down the inside-left channel – and Harold Schumacher moving out to meet him. The keeper's greeting was not over-friendly; in fact, he knocked Patrick unconscious – he was near death when the doctor reached him.

And the keeper wasn't sent off: he wasn't even booked – France didn't even get a free. West Germany got through by way of the penalty shoot-out – but they were a weary team in the final.

There was a heatwave that Summer along the Mediterranean; that night in Seville the temperature was 127 degrees. Italy were much the fresher team on that Sunday night in Madrid; they won going away.

I watched West Germany again in the Mexican finals; there Diego Maradona came between them and the ultimate glory.

Next morning I met several of Franz Beckenbauer's warriors in Mexico City's famous craft shop, the Rio. They were the saddest men I had encountered since a Monday morning in Mulligan's in the late September of 1982.

On that occasion myself and John O'Keeffe decided that the only antidote was champagne.

Sunday World

'Galway Hurling Is Like a Dormant Volcano'

Galway Play Tipperary, 1993

Galway hurling is like a dormant volcano: at times you suspect that it is extinct, then without warning it pours out lava, not to mention fire and brimstone.

Aficionados of the ancient game had believed that they wouldn't see a better encounter than the recent draw involving Kilkenny and Wexford; yesterday's match between Galway and Tipperary didn't equal it for purity of hurling but outstripped it for sheer excitement. And it threw up one of the most bizarre goals ever seen in Croke Park or in any park.

It came in the sixth minute and so surprisingly that many in the crowd of about forty-five thousand possibly missed it. Michael McGrath, Galway's right full-forward, got possession about twenty-five yards from Tipperary's goal and in the middle. He seemed to mishit his stroke; the sliothar went like a badly addressed letter towards Ken Hogan.

He had an amplitude of time and space but the ball came off the pitch like an in-spinner in cricket – suddenly it was past his left hand and over the line.

It was Galway's opening score; some people may interpret it as a turning point even at such an early stage – or, if you like, a turning goal.

What may have been more significant was an incident in the first minute: Declan Ryan was seen to be limping after a collision with Gerry McInerney.

He moved into the left full-forward position: Nicholas English went to centre forward and spent most of the game in the middle third of the pitch.

It may have been an unwise move: English needs a little space to express his genius; he seemed out of place in the hurley-burley. He grafted well and won several frees but never looked like scoring a goal – and Tipperary needed one in those desperate late paragraphs.

The Munster champions had started well and for about five minutes it seemed that they might reproduce the extravagance that had devastated Clare.

Michael Cleary pointed a free from far out in the country and into the wind – it seemed a good omen.

In the third minute a foul against English gave Cleary another free; he pointed with seeming ease; now Tipperary's following, who outnumbered their counterparts in flags and in decibels, were in great voice.

Those two dreams of Southern Comfort seemed to herald the expected cruise to the final; then came the goal that will be parsed and analysed for a long time.

It seemed to inspire the men in maroon and white, one of whom picked this occasion to become famous overday.

Padraic Kelly is a young pocket battleship who was nominated at left half-back but who interpreted his brief liberally.

It was as if we were seeing the ghost of Gerry McInerney; the mind's video went back to the final of 1987.

McInerney himself was present in vibrant substance; the man who looks a cross between a Beatle and a gunfighter from the Old West is now a lone musketeer where once there were three.

Tony Keady and Peter Finnerty watched from the sideline; of course they were impressed by the new half-back line – Tom Helebert made up the trio.

It is a badly kept secret that Sean Treacy is unhappy at mid full-back; he looked a master of that difficult brief yesterday.

His curates, Paul Cooney and Murty Killilea, defended with such skill and sagacity that Tipperary's only goal came in the last minute. And it is a tribute to his fellow defenders that keeper Richard Burke was merely a sweeper – he did well.

In the first half we saw Galway laugh at all the predictions of doom, many of which came out of the west. Michael Coleman and Pat Malone ruled midfield despite the heroism of Declan Carr, who strove mightily to the rather bitter end. And though Galway's forwards wasted excellent possession, the western expedition led by 1–9 to 0–5 at the end of Act One.

They had played with the wind into the Railway Goal; nevertheless that lead was daunting. It was a wind that added about thirty yards to a stroke; it breathed a little to the right – and its vagaries caused a string of wides in the early second half.

At last Joe McGrath got a point after a great run; Carr quickly replied; his point started a revival. And for the middle third of Act Two it seemed that Tipperary would make Galway look like brave pretenders.

This was the best part of the game; the texture resembled that of a stampede; men got what seemed clear possession only to see the ball flicked away or blocked down.

The blue-and-gold wave was mounting; Cleary posted four frees in a row; Galway were panicking into silly fouls; at last Joe Cooney punctuated the siege with a point from a fifty-yards free.

Michael McGrath pointed from play; English quickly posted a beauty. Ten minutes remained; now Joe Rabbitte seemed to grow in stature.

He and Cooney excelled in that heart-quaking last chapter. Liam Burke was an able adjutant. Brendan Keogh, who had a fine first half, went off fifteen minutes from the end.

Galway led by five points as thousands of referees blew for time; Pat Cox goaled in the seventy-seventh minute. The last whistle came immediately after the puck-out – it ended at 1–16 to 1–14.

Tipperary went down with dignity. Their best department was the rearguard: Hogan recovered well from his misfortune; full-backs Paul Delaney and Noel Sheehy and especially Michael Ryan were staunch.

Evening Press

A TRIO OF IRELAND MANAGERS

JACK CHARLTON, MICK MCCARTHY AND BRIAN KERR

He was approaching thirty and was going nowhere, either in football or in the world outside. He was thinking of going back to his old job with the National Coal Board. And then the fairy godfather came to Elland Road. Don Revie was dour and mean and dishonest but he rescued Jack Charlton.

The big Geordie got a regular place with Leeds United and went on to ultimate glory with his country in the World Cup. When Jack quit playing, he went into club management. He didn't last long.

The most charitable verdict on his short tenure would be 'not proven'. Once again a fairy godfather came on to the scene, in the form of a hard-headed trade-union official named Des Casey.

The FAI were then a loosely organised body – Des in a moment of inspiration acted on his own. He knew that Jack was out of a job – he invited him to manage The Republic.

I can't forget the first press conference. The venue was the Westbury Hotel in the heart of Dublin 2, far from the gritty terraces and the hot Bovril. Jack came armed with an anthology of Irish poetry.

He wore a very green jacket and an even greener tie. I wouldn't have been surprised if he had produced a clay pipe. What surprised me was that the man who had contained Uwe Seeler in that greatest of World Cup finals was painfully shy.

His second experience of management threatened to be no more exciting than his first. You couldn't but suspect that in picking his goalkeeper he had settled for the one who could kick the ball the farthest.

77

Liam Brady said he often felt like a tennis net as ball after ball flew over his head. This alleged pragmatism didn't pay dividends – or so it seemed.

On a dark dank afternoon in Sofia, the grim soldier-infested capital of Bulgaria, the good ship Republic appeared to have run aground. The home side's win seemed to assure them of a place in the finals of the Euro Cup.

Their remaining game was at home to Scotland. Bulgaria needed only a point. They dominated from the start. The game was televised live but at home few outside the aficionados bothered to watch.

I took up my post in Mambrick's in the living heart of Portobello. My fellow watchers were few, mostly neighbours who had taken time off from work. There was also a little brown dog.

Play was dull; there was hardly any talk; the little brown dog fell asleep. Play went into the last quarter; men drifted back to work.

Then as the four minutes of added-on time began, a fairy godfather sprang up. His name was and still is Gary Mackay. He worked in the family bar in Edinburgh and played for Hibernians.

He won a ball around halfway and got a rush of blood to the head and feet. He set off down the inside-right channel, got within about twenty-five yards of goal and let fly. The keeper was as stunned as the warden when Oliver Twist asked for more – the ball flew into the net. The company in the pub erupted. The little brown dog woke up and began to bark. I was too pitch-wise to celebrate prematurely.

The Bulgarians were as furious and as desperate as a cat that had been playing with a mouse and allowed it steal into the long grass. Three minutes remained. The clock in the pub seemed to have stopped.

Then a second hero emerged: Jim Leighton, a modest

78

underrated keeper, made a brilliant save. And then he made another. An agonising minute remained. Suddenly some of the home players threw themselves down on the pitch. We were in the finals.

Next morning Dublin was aglow. As I went to work about seven, I was accosted by perfect and imperfect strangers. The chorus line was 'Isn't it great . . . ' And it was; on a heady Sunday afternoon in Stuttgart The Republic of Ireland's football came of age.

About the tenth minute, an ethnic Donegal man, Ray Houghton, burgled Peter Shilton's bank. Over the next eighty minutes a native Donegal man was transformed into a magnet. It was Packie Bonner's day.

The Republic's victory over England was a watershed – and a tearshed, tears of joy. Jack Charlton was on his way. He had brought us to our first Euro Finals – he was to bring us to two World Cup Finals.

Followers travelled to our games abroad in numbers never seen or even imagined before. Back at home the streets and the fields and the workplaces were deserted as people watched on television.

One night at half-time in a game, my colleague Colman Doyle took a picture of O'Connell Street from the bridge. That great thoroughfare was deserted except for a lone man standing at a bus stop, blissfully unaware that normal life was on hold.

Jack's luck continued to hold: Alan McLoughlin's late, late goal in Windsor Park was another example.

The time came when luck deserted him – or he deserted his luck. He lost his confidence and that of his players; it was sad to watch this decent Geordie break up like a snowman in the thaw.

And yet in the field of sport – and indeed beyond – in this country, there is no one more popular or respected than 'Our Jack'. He was the first and the deepest Anglo-Irish Agreement.

Mick McCarthy had a daunting act to emulate: he might hope to take The Republic to three finals but he could hardly hope to match Jack's force of personality.

He didn't do too badly; certainly he produced far more attractive football. Indeed the no-nonsense son of Barnsley surprised many by his creative approach.

In his first term, he got The Republic to the play-offs. In his second we were desperately unlucky not to qualify directly. A last-minute goal in Skopje cost us first place in the table. We lost out to Turkey in the play-off.

Mick McCarthy's third term was the best-ever spell enjoyed by The Republic. Our group included Portugal and Holland: they were very warm favourites to gain the first two places.

Bold creative football brought its reward. In the crucial game we faced Holland at Lansdowne Road. The Dutch team glowed with household and pubhold names; our task appeared hopeless when Gary Kelly was dismissed early in the second half.

Jason McAteer snatched a goal about the seventieth minute; the rest was a siege. The Dutch needed two goals; they didn't get even one, although their attack included Patrick Kluivert and Ruud Van Nistelrooy and Jimmy Floyd Hasselbaink.

This was a tremendous performance; it compared with Stuttgart and with our victory over Italy in Giants' Stadium.

Our expedition in the Far East proved to be a mixture of the bizarre and the heroic. The 'Keane mutiny' resounded all over the football world; it didn't make sense for a captain to jump ship.

The voyage went on; the abandoned sailors navigated brilliantly. The Republic drew with Cameroon, the African champions, an achievement underlined by

Senegal's victory over France. A competent display sufficed to beat Saudi Arabia.

It would be hard to overestimate the worth of our draw with Germany. Then came the showdown with Spain – and the shoot-out at the K.O. Corral. That disaster cast a dark cloud over our football.

We could have won the World Cup. We came from behind to hold Germany when they were at full strength. In the final they were without Michael Ballack, the greatest midfielder in the world. And yet they were the better team until a late error by Oliver Kahn gave Brazil the Cup.

The Republic were still demoralised by a penalty shoot-out when they lost to Russia and Switzerland. Even if we had won both games, Mick McCarthy would have been pushed over the cliff. The tongues had been sharpening since Saipan.

The FAI were determined to get Roy Keane back – Mick had to go. The conspiracy failed: the fatted calf was sacrificed but the prodigal father did not return. The good (?) ship FAI lurched on.

*

Enter Brian Kerr. He was welcomed by the casual followers; some aficionados furrowed their brows. He had little experience as a player. They should have known better. He had led St Patrick's Athletic to two championships.

If he had stayed on and led them to a third, he would have qualified for canonisation.

Brian has made a good start. We beat Scotland 0–2 in a not-so-friendly game.

Then we beat Georgia rather luckily. Albania came next – they were more formidable. A draw was a good result.

When I was in Albania ten years ago, it was just recovering from generations of misrule. When their footballers came here for the return game, they couldn't afford to stay in a hotel. One player paid his own way from Paris. Now Albania are threatening to become a major power.

We are at home to them and Georgia and Russia. It will be a short, hot Summer.

Magill

'THE ARMAGH KEEPER BROKE THE WORLD RECORD FOR THE STANDING HIGH JUMP'

ARMAGH WIN THE ALL-IRELAND FOOTBALL FINAL, 2002

Armagh have the ashes of Brian Ború; Kerry have the ashes of a broken dream. Armagh have the Sam Maguire Cup too – and never was it harder earned or more gloriously won.

At about five past five in Croke Park on Sunday evening an old Japanese saying came into my mind. 'The notice in the park says "DO NOT PICK THE FLOWERS" but the wind cannot read.'

The authorities at the GAA's headquarters have a stern rule about keeping off the pitch but the football folk of Armagh wouldn't be denied their half-hour of glory. Thousands of them sprouted out of the pitch as soon as Mr John Bannon signalled full stop.

If there had been a moat around the pitch – as in some stadiums in South America – the delirious people in orange and white would have walked on water.

A decent man from the Kingdom summed up our sadness: 'There will be no bonfires in the hills around Knocknagoshel tonight.' Michael Devane is a farmer from Milltown, a few miles west of Dingle; with a few friends he set out at five on Sunday morning.

He had spent Saturday shearing sheep. Armagh sheared Kerry and kept the wool. And yet the mood in our camp was not low. In Chaplin's friendly bar in Hawkins Street I sampled that mood.

I sampled champagne too. If you are acquainted with the history of bareknuckle boxing, you will know that it is life's chief restorer. I was with Jimmy Deenihan, football immortal, and Gerry Carroll, fabled in the greyhound world.

We agreed that champagne shouldn't be confined to the alleged upper classes – we agreed too that the Golden Apple had found a worthy home.

The All-Ireland football final of 2002 was not a classic, whatever that is, but it was a battle of unremitting fascination. It recalled the opening of a story by Stephen Crane: 'The men were rowing so hard that they didn't know the colour of the sky.'

I know that many Kerry people were concerned with the colour of the sky on Sunday morning. I was down at home from Tuesday evening until Saturday morning – and therein lies a tale. Wherever I went, in pub and café and bog and mountain and town and village and hamlet, I heard the same thing. 'If we get a fine day, we'll win.'

This was spoken as if it happened to be a proposition in mathematics. I did my best to refute it. Kerry, after all, is just about the wettest and windiest county in Ireland.

And Armagh is not inside the Arctic Circle, far from it. I have travelled through that fair county in Spring – it resembles Kent and Sussex. The orchards in blossom are a wondrous sight.

Anyhow, we got a good day: it was dry and fairly bright – the wind was as light as you can expect in a field so near the sea.

Armagh didn't seem unduly bothered by the absence of wind and rain. They began brilliantly. Against Dublin in the semi-final they had shot so wildly that if they were dart players, they would have cleared a pub. In the meantime they seemed to have been coached by William Tell.

It took Kerry about fifteen minutes to settle; then it looked as if all would be well for the green and gold. Colm Cooper and Mike Frank Russell, the Damien Duff and Robbie Keane of Gaelic football, were providing drops of Southern Comfort.

And in the second quarter we saw Kerry pour out the wine that intoxicated us in the games against Kildare and

Galway and Cork. Now they were playing with sleight of hand and foot. The points came in a sweet stream.

Then came the high drama of the penalty – the outcome brought a weird cacophony of cheers and groans. Soon came the sos for tea. Kerry were in a happy position: they were four points ahead – and would have the wind.

The Kerry followers behind the Canal Goal looked forward to a ringside view of a scorefest. Seldom has a prospect been more devastated. If Sean Boylan had been managing Armagh, I would have suspected sorcery. I could imagine him risking all on a potion that he hadn't needed to try before.

The Orchard men resumed as if they knew they were going to win. Suddenly Kerry seemed to be wandering in the land of doubt. And more and more as Act Two went on, it appeared that 'their purse was empty, their golden deeds all spent'.

John Toal and Paul McGrane began to perform as they had against Dublin; the orange-and-white were colonising the middle third of the arena. Then that brilliant goal smote Kerry a blow from which they never recovered.

Now Armagh began to display the inventive touches that had seemed a Kerry monopoly in the second quarter. And more and more they broke the ball – and Kerry hearts.

The last few minutes were almost too much for human hearts to bear. Kerry's followers had enjoyed a bounty of memorable goals; now they would have been overjoyed with the flukiest of points.

It wasn't to be – and at the end I witnessed a kindred reaction from two men who were near me in the Cusack Stand. One is from Kerry, the other is from Armagh – both were dumbfounded in disbelief.

I felt that the Armagh man wasn't convinced his team had won until he saw their keeper, Brendan Tierney, break the world record for the standing high jump.

You can be sure that the pub tribunals in Kerry will be prolonged and profound. They will range from Tarbert down to Port Magee – and from Dunquin to Scartaglen. Of course the management will be blamed. Aren't they always . . .

Paudie O'Shea and his cabinet could hardly be blamed for passes that gave the ball to the opposition or goal chances that were lost. Nor could you blame them for the number of times that Kerry lost hard-won possession by allowing the ball to be knocked from their hands.

They could be blamed, however, for a game plan that depended too much on short passing. The more passes in a movement, the more vulnerable it is to interception.

People who seek deeper causes may argue that Kerry were guilty of complacency. Their brilliance in the second quarter may have deceived them into a sense of superiority.

They came out for the second half in a good position: they had a handy lead – and Armagh had lost John McEntee, the leader of their attack.

The marking was amazingly slack when the movement began that brought the precious goal. It was a wonderful moment for Oisín McConville – it washed away the nightmare of his miss from the spot.

Someone should compile a list of penalty misses at the Canal Goal in big games. It would include Liam Sammon, Colm O'Rourke, Mikey Sheehy, Keith Barr, Kevin McCabe and of course Bill McCorry. Oisín was in good company.

Armagh's victory was due to proverbial team effort. If asked to nominate especial heroes, I would name Kieran McGeeney, the midfield duo, and Ronan Clarke.

Much has been said about the winners' spirit – but remember Ernest Hemingway's 'Enthusiasm is not enough.' Kerry were the most attractive team in the Championship; Armagh were the most effective.

Kerry were the poets but prose has its own high virtues. Patrick Kavanagh has looked deep into the Irish soul. Charles Kickham in Knocknagow looked perhaps even deeper.

During my little stay in Kerry I added to my collection of famous last words: 'This team is good enough and young enough to win the five-in-a-row.'

Most of Kerry's football folk will be glad to win the occasional one-in-a-row. The days of 'handy' All-Irelands are gone forever. Donegal and Derry and now Armagh have broken the old mould.

While I am at it, I must congratulate Joe Kernan and his gallant band and the ultra-loyal followers, not least Séamus Mallon and Paddy O'Hanlon and Jimmy Whan.

Sunday World

HEARTBREAK IN MANCHESTER

BARRY MCGUIGAN IS BEATEN BY JIM MCDONNELL

Here in Manchester in the small hours of the morning it was wet and cold; the foyer of the Portland Hotel resembled a wake-house as a crowd of Barry McGuigan's supporters, many in evening dress, bemoaned the downfall of their hero.

Shock mingled with sadness. And over all hung an air of anticlimax, not so much because the fight had ended so abruptly but because the former world champion had looked so unlike his old self.

In the record-books this fight will be labelled 'referee stopped fight – cut eye' – but any of Barry's admirers who believe that otherwise he might have won are deceiving themselves.

The truth is that he was in trouble long before the referee, Mickey Vann, decided that the cut was too deep to allow the fight to continue; Barry's seconds protested but it was only a gesture. And afterwards the former champion said that he was fit to go on but I believe that Mr Vann did him a great favour.

It was a disconcerting occasion for Barry and his camp; if Jim McDonnell had been picked as a soft touch, someone blundered. He was far from being a lamb for the sacrifice – indeed he was more like the tiger to which Barry is often compared.

In the popular scenario the Irish Cockney would depend on his greater speed of foot and hope to win on points but it didn't work out that way.

It was quickly obvious that McDonnell was prepared to stand and fight; his plan of campaign was clear – he went all-out to deny McGuigan his accustomed dominance of the ring's centre.

88

And as the fight didn't go according to plan, you could sense a growing bewilderment in McGuigan and his corner.

It was hard to believe that we were watching the same man who by sheer strength and determination wore down Julio Miranda in eight rounds at Pickett's Lock last December.

And the submerged truth surfaced again last night – despite his great fusion of courage and strength, Barry is amazingly vulnerable under fire. This was seen in the seventh round of his fight with Danilo Cabrera in Ballsbridge and again in the fifth round of his fight with Miranda.

And it was seen most clearly of all that night in Las Vegas; Barry was clearly ahead after five rounds but suddenly was hit by a flurry in the sixth and almost crumbled before Steve Cruz.

Last night he began with his usual aggression; indeed at the bell he pushed the referee aside – but McDonnell refused to be overawed and at no time did he step back more than two or three paces.

McGuigan perhaps won the first round. He was the more aggressive – McDonnell was cautioned for holding and punching. Nevertheless, it was clear that Barry's corner was far from happy in the minute's break. And his huge following, who afforded the accustomed adulation as he came into the ring, were strangely quiet.

Barry perhaps won the second round too. Again McDonnell was warned for holding and hitting – and midway through the round he buckled under a fierce body blow. His followers, however, were becoming increasingly vociferous and at the bell they chanted 'Here we go! Here we go!' It was a strange reversal.

McDonnell's following numbered about three hundred in a crowd of over eight thousand – the rest were clearly in favour of the Monaghan man.

Round Three began with the usual McGuigan flourish; this time it was edged with desperation because blood was seeping from a cut on the right eyebrow. And you felt that Barry knew that unless he finished the fight soon, he would have to retire.

He never looked like landing a telling blow; this was clearly McDonnell's round. In the second minute he landed a looping left; McGuigan's knees buckled and he almost went down. His followers were silent – and the other crowd were on their feet. Barry was glad to hear the bell.

Obviously his corner men did a good job on his eye because at the start of the round the blood seemed to have been stopped but he made no attempt to guard the cut – and McDonnell's favourite punch, a looping left, got through time and again.

About midway through the round the blood began to flow; Mr Vann took a long look – and it was obvious that all was over.

McDonnell's following surged from their area and surrounded the ring but all was in good order; that was typical of this highly organised occasion.

Evening Press

'IF I HAD A HAT, I WOULD TAKE IT OFF TO MRS HILL AND HER SON'

DAWN RUN WINS THE GOLD CUP, 1986

When Arkle stormed up the hill to his first Gold Cup, few of his myriad admirers realised that nibs of snow had started to come with the wind; yesterday it was very cold in the Cotswolds but in retrospect most of those who were on Cheltenham's racecourse will remember the time between about half past three and four o'clock as a fragment of Summer.

Such was the enormous outburst of emotion that for a little while the thin wind seemed not to matter. And no doubt there are decent men and women who will dip into their imaginations at some distant date and say that they were there – and they will be right.

They may have been away down in the bottom of Kerry taking a break from setting the spuds or on a brief furlough from a factory in Tallaght – but they were at what was probably the greatest ever running of the Gold Cup.

Televisions were scarce in Arkle's heyday; he became a folk-hero – but in his first Gold Cup year, he could have walked down many a street in this country without being recognised. And his background wasn't nearly as romantic as that of Dawn Run.

Charmian Hill might have sprung from the pages of Nat Gould, only he would hardly have had the daring to invent someone so much bigger than what we call life.

She comes from a family that had little interest in racing; she is far from being wealthy – and yet she is now the queen grandmother of National Hunt in these islands.

It is a salutary lesson at a time when it seemed that almost all of racing's big prizes were reserved for the beneficiaries of oil pools or football pools.

Dawn Run was bought for a sum well under five figures – flat racing may be the sport of sheikhs and a few others, but the world of jumping and hurdling is still a democracy.

Yesterday's victory was all the sweeter because it was so hard gained. I am tempted to misquote what Wellington said after Waterloo: 'It was a dawn close-run thing.'

When Arkle cleared the last fence in his first Gold Cup, such was the roar that he almost came to a stop – he nearly met his own private wall.

There was no such wall yesterday: Arkle on that day long ago was coming home on his own – yesterday Dawn Run looked beaten at the last. And it wasn't until Jonjo O'Neill punched the air with his right fist a few strides from the winning post that those not well placed to see the line knew that he had won.

I was about a hundred yards down from the post and next to me a middle-aged man with a Yorkshire accent broke the world record for the standing high jump. He was certain that Wayward Lad had held on – and I was far from sure until Jonjo did his Denis Law act.

That decent Yorkshireman hid his disappointment – and as Jonjo and Dawn Run came back down, he applauded as warmly as if he had been born in Castletownroche or Kildurrery or in Ballyhooly itself.

I understood: on a September Sunday in Croke Park in 1982 I applauded when Offaly snatched the All-Ireland in the last few strides. On such occasions there is no room for begrudgery: tribalism is washed away by the waves of greatness.

Dawn Run will be compared to other chasing heroes, notably Arkle and Golden Miller – but there can be no question about this Gold Cup: it was the very stuff of drama and romance.

And Jonjo's gamble at the second-last fence will be elected to the gallery of great sporting memories. If it had failed, it would have entered a rather different sort of gallery – that reserved for, among other things, notorious own goals.

Dawn Run looked beaten as she came to the second-last – and Jonjo didn't as much ask her for a big jump as command her. Her answer was far from perfect but she landed safely and she landed running. And yet it seemed as if that sweeping jump wouldn't suffice: Wayward Lad and Forgive 'n' Forget looked full of steam.

It is almost unknown for a horse to come again in the Gold Cup: when you lose your place at the bottom of the hill, it is almost always time to say farewell to your hopes.

It is much the same in the Grand National: if a horse makes the running and is passed in the last mile or so, his chance is almost always gone.

Team Spirit was the exception but on that occasion his pilot, Willie Robinson, took a different kind of gamble – he gave his mount a breather.

Jonjo could afford no such luxury yesterday: so hectic was the pace that he had to make up his tactics as he was swept along.

And to be up in front for so long and then fall back must have made even that giant heart quail – but what threatened to be his biggest disappointment produced his greatest victory.

And those who were telling the world on the first two days at Cheltenham that he had lost his nerve were given the perfect answer. I have long deemed him a genius – after yesterday there can be no doubt.

And Tony Mullins need have no regrets: he played a huge part in Dawn Run's education.

This was a collective victory, fashioned by Mrs Hill and the Mullins family and, not least, Dawn Run himself.

And if I had a hat, I would take it off to Mrs Hill and

her son, Oliver: lesser people would have cashed in long ago – they know that there are things which money cannot buy.

And what a blessed change it is from the world of the flat, where as soon as a great horse finishes his second season he is rushed away to stud.

Racehorses are for racing – and Dawn Run will be in action for another season at least. She may not be the best hurdler of all time or the best chaser of all time – but she has shown herself to be the best National Hunt contender that we have seen.

And yesterday fortune favoured the brave: the going came just right for the fleet-footed mare. And when Wayward Lad deviated off a straight line and forced Jonjo to switch to the stand side, it was probably all for his luck – the going was better there.

From a distance it may have looked as good by the inside rails but after fourteen races it was inevitably cut up – nearby you could see that all the gardening done by the staff was little more than cosmetic.

And that smoother corridor on which Dawn Run came home may have made the difference – it was as close as that. And spare a thought for Wayward Lad and Graham Bradley: this was a mighty performance by an eleven-year-old.

I will always cherish the scene at the coming back down the course when all the other jockeys congratulated Jonjo – and Dawn Run. It was typical of their camaraderie – and also a sign that they knew they had been part of a mighty occasion.

And when I could afford the luxury of looking back on this marvellous occasion, I was reminded of a day at home when the world was young.

It was around dawn (there's that word again) and I was fishing in a rising flood. It was windy and cold and when I got the first bite (it is called an 'answer' in Kerry),

94

my coordination wasn't great and I reacted too quickly.

And there in the water near the shore a magnificent trout turned – and was gone. Cursing my stupidity I ran upriver about twenty yards and fished down – he answered again – and this time he ended up on the grassy sand.

And because I was sure I had lost him, the prize was all the sweeter. Although that day long ago continued windy and chilly, I felt no cold.

I will leave the last comment on this historic occasion to a young man not unknown in Larry Fay's pub in Granard. When he was filling in the embarkation card in Birmingham Airport last night, he hesitated when he came to 'Purpose of Visit'. And then he wrote in a very bold hand: 'Enjoyment – to have the pleasure of watching Dawn Run.' Only an Irishman would think of that.

Evening Press

Cork Beat Kilkenny to Win the Three-in-a-Row, 1978

The extraordinary thing about this Cork team who hurled their way to a third-in-a-row All-Ireland yesterday is that the experts who abound in that fair county persist in asserting that they are not a great side – perhaps they are not, but they must be the best middling side of all time.

But this criticism implies that Cork's hurlers need not be great to achieve great deeds – invariably they play with such heart and common sense that they can finish in front of opponents whose collective talents appear more formidable.

After the last two finals, it could be argued that Cork had got the utmost out of their potential and that Wexford had played considerably below their best and yet gone tantalisingly near – that argument could hardly be advanced last night.

Kilkenny – a team that contained at least five young men who, if they were jockeys, would be entitled to the full allowance – need have no regrets; indeed, they far surpassed the expectations of almost all their following.

It was they who were the besiegers in a desperate last ten minutes when, with a little help from the gremlins who control the ball when it bobs around in the goalmouth, they might have snatched a victory that would hardly have reflected the general play.

The siege was lifted a minute from the end – and a typical Cork point put them four clear and the drawbridge up. And that margin was a fair reflection. And the numbers that remained on the scoreboard as the stadium emptied gave a fair indication of how Cork had won.

A goal and fifteen points to two goals and eight points is the kind of score by which Kilkenny all through the years have won many a match.

Yesterday tradition was turned upside down. Cork, who so often have swung a game with smash-and-grab goals, progressed by way of regular points – Kilkenny, for whom the point has long been as the cod to the Icelanders, suddenly found their sea almost bare.

The most remarkable feature of a game that, except for the result, upset the general expectation was that on a day when conditions were a forward's dream Kilkenny managed to send the ball only eight times over the bar.

Cork got their first point in the first minute – a sweet score by Jim Barry Murphy that showed his genius for making time and space into dimensions that suit himself.

A minute later Frank Cummins – from a better, even though more distant, position – was barely wide; these early happenings proved signs of what was to come.

It took Kilkenny a quarter of an hour to get their first point – their efforts up till then were as surprising as a great singer performing off-key.

And when that first point at last came, a Kilkenny voice behind us said: 'That'll give them an appetite now.' One knew what he meant – but the appetite had to do with what must have been the scantiest rations Kilkenny have ever known.

It had been expected that Cork would dominate the middle of the field and that the Kilkenny attack would have to snap up every chance if their team were to stay in contention – but it didn't happen that way at all.

Especially in the first half Kilkenny had more of the flow – but the inaccuracy of their forwards and the unspectacular solidity of the Cork defence kept their score down to 1–4 at half-time.

Cork had only a modest seven points – but apart from a saved penalty had hardly missed a chance. And their forwards too had found themselves up against a defence that was not in a mood to give presents.

And as the teams went in, another voice in the crowd

said: 'So far 'tis only a game of backs.' He was right. Almost every minute had brought a ruck that went on for several seconds as players pulled and poked and shouldered and jostled to get the ball free.

Indeed, so often had the sliothar been hidden between boots and hurleys that one was tempted to say at the interval that the game had not yet got off the ground.

And as the teams took their break in the caverns under the Cusack Stand, one had the curious feeling that the game had not yet begun.

And so it seemed when in the first minute of the second half Michael Brennan sent over the kind of softly struck long-distance point that is Kilkenny's trademark.

And then John Horgan opened up and sent a few mighty clearances soaring towards the Railway Goal as if to announce that Cork were ready for big deeds too.

From then until the referee gave the signals that made one side jump in jubilation and the other feel their limbs fill with lead, the game was gripping all the way.

And so the game changed rhythm like a horse that has been associated with these counties – but the pace was now far faster than in the first half and the play more open.

Even though Kilkenny went ahead twice in the third quarter, Cork looked the more convincing – especially now that they were improving in midfield.

The great surprise in this area was the failure of Tom Cashman, the brilliant youngster who had broken Clare hearts in the Munster final.

He was buffeted out of the game by the far more mature Frank Cummins, was shifted to the wing, and was taken off midway through the second half.

But Cork found the man for the gap in Tim Crowley, their tall left-half forward who moved to midfield and gave what was surely the greatest display of his life.

Two years ago it was Pat Moylan who did most to frustrate Wexford; last September it was Gerald McCarthy; yesterday evening Kilkenny folk were in agreement that Tim Crowley was the man who had done most to deprive them of victory.

And part of Cork's secret in these three successful Summers is that they have so many great players that it is almost impossible to keep every one of them from going walkabout.

Yesterday their forwards, the most alarming band of raiders since the heyday of Ned Kelly and his gang, were fairly well contained by the extraordinarily young Kilkenny defence.

So too they had been in the Munster final – but yesterday, as then, the supposedly suspect defence was always sound and often brilliant.

And the heart and soul of it was Martin O'Doherty, a mobile tower who at times seems to grow walls on both sides of him and gave Kilkenny's front-runners the most frustrating day they must have ever known.

He had a mighty lieutenant in Denis Coughlan, who began the game by giving Kevin Fennelly the present of a fifth-minute goal and then, as if steeled by his mistake, went on to gobble up everything that came his way.

The other four backs were very steady – and Dermot MacCurtain, the youngest and smallest of them, once again showed that he has an early-warning system that makes radar seem out of date.

Cork's most effective forward was Charlie McCarthy – he isn't the best man in the world to win possession, but once he has the ball in his hand or at his feet for a free, the wise scoreboard operator reaches for a number.

Kilkenny's greatest heroes were in defence – and the fact that Cork got only one goal (from a great low shot from the left by Jim Barry Murphy in the fifty-seventh minute) indicates the solidity of Fan Larkin and his men.

Fan himself was marvellous – inch for inch he must be

the best hurler the game has ever known.

In front of him Ger Henderson was brilliant – and it was his early dominance that gave Kilkenny the confidence their young players needed.

Not one of Kilkenny's forwards will look back on yesterday with satisfaction. The best was Michael Brennan, all heart and determination but unable to find the magic touch that a few years ago made him the best forward in the game.

Since then he has known enough illness and injury to put a lesser man out of hurling – and if he failed yesterday, it was only by his own lofty standards.

He helped to make the game's greatest moment when two minutes after Cork's goal he lay behind the defence in the right-hand side to collect a long ball and draw a flurry of backs out to him and square-pass across goal to Billy Fitzpatrick, who slashed the ball to the net.

That left Kilkenny only two points behind with ten minutes to go. Amazingly, it was their last score.

And so Kilkenny opened with a goal and closed with a goal – and in the first fifteen minutes and in the last ten failed to score a point.

It was fitting that Cork should score a point in the first minute – and again in the last.

Charlie McCarthy's sealing score was as brilliant as Jim Barry Murphy's opener – and when all is said and done, the long-range point was the foundation of this Cork team's success.

Evening Press

'NAPOLEON'S POPLARS NOD THEIR DUSTY APPROVAL'

STEPHEN ROCHE WINS THE 1987 TOUR DE FRANCE

Tommy Bracken, the wandering bard from Castleknock, lost no time in bursting into verse to celebrate Stephen's marvellous victory. Yesterday morning he brought me his tribute.

Tommy is in the grand tradition of Zozimus: his brainstorms take little heed of metrical niceties and he never hesitates to bend language to his purpose.

When the emotion is genuine, all is forgiven – and Tommy's integrity is not in doubt; he is a true bard; great events will not let him rest until he has expressed them. His tribute to Stephen begins:

> Let's drink a toast to Stephen Roche
> And keep evergreen the glory,
> And in years to come take out the drum
> And pulsate the story.

He goes on:

> State it well and greatly tell
> That historic win for Erin
> In the Tour de France how he took his chance
> With courage, grit and darin'.

I like especially the sixth stanza:

> Now in the fourth last stage, as if in a rage,
> Roche threw down the gauntlet,
> And all at once the roads of France
> Knew Stephen Roche was dauntless.

Tommy concludes:

> And with arms raised high, Roche sped by
> The finishing line in glory.
> But what gave elation to the Irish nation
> Only Roche knew well the story.

Yes indeed – only Stephen knows well the story and not many in the multitude that greeted him had even a fair understanding of the sport that he adorns.

Television, no matter how expert the cameraman and the commentators, cannot do stage cycling full justice. So much happens unseen; critical moments come – but it is only by chance that they are captured.

The subtleties of teamwork are generally lost to the television viewer and to the crowds who line the roads and streets. The television viewer sees much more than the watching crowds but he cannot know what is going on in the peloton – at best he can have only a general view.

In the last few weeks I heard great arguments about the funtions of the 'domestiques' – some people find it hard to understand that there can be teamwork in bike-racing. Before next year's Tour some expert should write an essay on this subject and enlighten the Irish public.

The domestiques are not confined to tour cycling; they are also in gridiron football, if to a much lesser degree. In that game they serve the ball-carrier by 'taking out' would-be tacklers.

And in horse racing the pacemaker is also a kind of domestique. Now that the shouting has subsided we can ask ourselves what effect will Stephen's victory have on the people of this island.

Charles Haughey spoke about it as if we would never see a poor day again – that was easy to understand; we all experience rushes of blood to the tongue.

We were told that Ireland had got a badly needed lift.

Perhaps it has – but I doubt if the effects will be long-lasting.

Thousands of young lads will take to the bike and dream of glory – it is likely that only a small number will persevere.

There is no glamour in the long haul needed to produce a racing cyclist; few have the capacity to endure the loneliness of the long-distance biker. As Tommy Bracken said: 'Only Roche knew well the story.'

Another possible effect of his victory could be that thousands of people will leave their cars at home and cycle to work – but somehow I doubt it.

Irish people tend to look on their cars as more than vehicles – they see them as an extension of their personalities. And thus the city of Dublin is cluttered morning and evening by drivers who have come from within easy cycling distance. The bike is clean and takes up little room: its proliferation in Amsterdam enhances that charming city.

The Irish preoccupation with the car was seen at its worst at the time when the gardaí appealed to the public to keep their vehicles at home and thus help to defeat the car bombers.

The response was deplorably poor; in this matter of life and death the majority chose to behave irresponsibly.

The truth, I suppose, is that many Irish people would be ashamed to be seen coming to work by bicycle or by bus. And at least in this century I cannot see Dublin humming with the spokesong so familiar in Amsterdam.

There is, however, the consolation that Stephen's victory is almost certain to send a few more of our cyclists into the professional ranks. And there is the possibility that the Tour de France will come to Ireland for a day or two. And that, to mint a phrase, would be a good thing even if the innocent people of this island would be shocked by its outrageous commercialism.

The Irish, just as much as the other west Europeans, love to watch tour racing. I remember fondly the days when a tour would be due to pass through our town.

Usually the cavalcade was due about five o'clock; by about four almost all work had been abandoned; wandering animals were impounded – and dogs wondered why they were being locked up so early.

Of course the race never came on time – and the instant experts could always explain the delay; it was usually a headwind – or a stretch of road that had recently been repaired.

And invariably some local aficionados would drive a few miles up the road and then drive back to Paul Revere the news around the place.

Such-a-one was leading; so-and-so was second; our local hero was at the head of the main bunch – we hadn't then acquired the word 'peloton'. And invariably the race reminded you of the rise and fall of a flood.

At first came a little stream of cyclists; soon came the main bunch; then the water began to diminish; the stragglers came in threes and twos and ones. They were all applauded, even those who could be called 'lantern men' – people admire perseverance.

Those tour races were almost casual in comparison to the great French event – and the commercialism was mild. Such is the commercialism in the Tour de France that the race itself sometimes seems in danger of getting lost.

My old friend Leslie Mallory sent me a little poem yesterday which expresses the intensity of effort that no amount of razzmatazz can conceal. He calls it simply 'Tour de France'. Part of it is like an Impressionist painting:

> Mirages of sweat and rain
> Swamp the eyes;

Dots, bars, stripes blur,
Sun gorges on muscle,
Burns the reserve;
And shins grow
Lead weights.
Pump. Focus. Force the last drop.

Those lines remind me of Tommy Simpson; sometimes I wonder about his last thoughts before he collapsed and died.

Leslie's poem ends with an evocation of the Avenue des Champs Élysées:

Napoleon's poplars
Nod their dusty approval,
Connoisseurs of courage,
They have seen it
Ride those roads before.
In their tongue,
A rock is
Roche.

Stephen's great rival is well named too; Delgado means 'spare and sharp'.

Do not believe that this greatest of all cycling tours is utterly without an element of humour – that couldn't be. My favourite story goes back to 1948, a time when entrants to the Tour were not as rigidly scrutinised as they are now.

The hero of that race was, believe it or not, the man who finished last. He was about seventy and no more than a social cyclist but to ride the Tour was his life's ambition.

He couldn't afford it until he had retired from gainful employment; then he lined up with the men he so admired.

Nobody but himself expected that he would complete the first stage – but he did – and the second and the third and the fourth and the fifth.

It is true that he finished in his own good time – but by the end of the first week he was something of a national hero. And as the Tour went on, his name became more and more a café-hold word.

And long after all the other riders had gone by, you could see crowds lining the road and the streets. And if you asked the reason, you would be told: 'We are waiting for Godot.'

Evening Press

WATERFORD WIN THE ALL-IRELAND –
AND BRAZIL WIN THE WORLD CUP

Three times three cheers are due for Waterford: they won their World Cup on Sunday – or if you like, they won the Cup of the World.

I regret that I was in Pairc Uí Chaoimh only in spirit. Not only did they win the Munster title – they did so by defeating the All-Ireland champions.

Tipperary walked a tightrope on their way to Autumn glory last year – but when a team wins the League and the Championship, you cannot quibble. Indeed I believe that the ship captained by Nicholas English could compare with the best.

Thus Waterford's achievement has a special gloss. Justin McCarthy can be proud. My affection for Waterford's hurlers goes back a long way, back to the days when I was imprisoned in a school in the woodlands of east Cork.

We were released occasionally: I saw Waterford play Cork in the league in Midleton in 1941. In later life when I was a freeman, I lived in the fair city of Cork and saw Waterford play on several occasions.

Hurling in those days wasn't always a beautiful game; what I admired about Waterford was their sporting attitude. And I rejoiced when the county at last won the All-Ireland. That was in 1948; they beat Dublin decisively in the final.

I would have been in Croke Park but I was in the throes of examinations. My especial heroes on that team were John Keane and Christy Moylan. John was deemed the greatest centre-back of his generation. I remember Christy as a fast and stylish half-forward.

I was in Croke Park when Waterford got their second taste of Autumn glory. That was in 1959. They beat

107

Kilkenny in a replay. It was a game that left no doubt about their superiority. Tom Cheasty was my especial hero on that team. He was my 'man for all seasons'.

Their worst day came in the Midsummer of 1982: they lost to Cork by a margin I have chosen to forget. Life went on: Waterford seemed to have been granted only two days in the sun.

Waterford in the bad days had a succession of dedicated and competent managers who failed to strike water from the rock. At last one of my favourite people, Gerald McCarthy, brought hope to the blue-and-white.

In his stewardship he had everything except luck. You needn't tell him the difference between success and failure can be a single puck . . . 1998 was the worst year of frustration.

Every team needs a flagship, a man who can inspire by his very presence. Tony Browne was Gerald's talisman; I was glad for him on Sunday. I regretted that I wasn't present to see his ship reach that harbour. I watched on television.

He was in and out of the game in the first half – in the second he was seldom far from the heart of the action. His goal midway through the half was surely a signal that Waterford were on the way.

I haven't forgotten Fergal Hartley: for several years now he has been exemplifying Joe Sherwood's theory that centre-back is the most important post in hurling.

Waterford's young stars now have the roof provided by Browne and Hartley over their heads. Ken McGrath and Paul Flynn, among others, can go out and play without feeling that too much depends on them.

On Sunday several 'unknowns' contributed handsomely to what was the proverbial team victory. The dark horses proved to be very bright horses indeed.

Most small boys and no doubt most small girls love the concept of the comeback. So do big boys and big girls and those of their elders who are fortunate enough not to have too much sense. Alas, some of the most celebrated comebacks never happened at all.

Jesse James is an example: when he rode again, it was in Hollywood fiction. When he had done enough murdering and robbing, he settled down to a quiet life in Kansas City.

He seemed about to live happily ever after until his best friend, a nice young man called Robert Ford, shot him very dead.

Muhammad Ali did come back – but compared to a young man nicknamed Ronaldo, he merely went around the corner to buy a bottle of milk or an evening paper.

Ronaldo was Brazil's ultra-golden boy in the World Cup Finals in 1998. On the eve of the final he went down with some mysterious ailment. Speculation was rampant: food poisoning was blamed; somebody was supposed to have put a sleeping drug in his wine – and so on and so on.

Anyhow, Brazil lost to France. The natives were not amused – the hero became the anti-hero. In the intervening years he has suffered a misery of injuries and spent more time in the repair shop than on the bench.

He was like a king in exile: though not fully fit, he was recalled for the Finals – last Sunday his second goal put honey on the icing on the cake.

One aspect of Sunday's game confused those experts who were never done preaching that Germany were a dull team. You may not be tempted to call them poets but prose has its own virtues.

The texture of Germany's play in the first thirty minutes on Sunday was intelligent and precise and nicely speckled with touches of imagination. They dominated that period: they were the more creative and adventurous – Brazil's attacks were confined to the occasional foray.

In those breakouts, however, they were ominously dangerous. And in the last fifteen minutes of the half they began to play as had been expected. The writing seemed to be on the pitch.

It seemed by the interval that Brazil had mastered Germany's attacking force and would go on to impose their brand of poetic football.

The Germans had other intentions and resumed boldly. The suspect Brazilian defence continued to be remarkably resilient – and their keeper, Marcos, didn't put a small finger or a small toe astray.

Brazil's first goal came against the run of play – and it was the kind of score that you didn't expect Germany to concede. Dietmar Hamman had plenty of time to clear but he dallied and was robbed by Ronaldo, who sent a quick, short pass to Rivaldo.

His low shot from twenty-five yards went straight to the keeper. He made a mess of what should have been a routine save. Ronaldo pounced like a stoat on the loose ball. It was a horrible moment for Oliver Kahn, who a few hours before had been judged the best goalie in the Finals.

Germany had twenty-five minutes to equalise. They seemed to despair of finding a path through the middle and resorted to shooting from outside the penalty box.

Brazil's second goal was all Ronaldo's own: he wove a carpet of space for himself and gave Kahn little chance.

I watched West Germany come back with two goals in the final of 1986 – this time Rudi Voller's bravehearts knocked at a bolted and barred door.

Few can begrudge Brazil this World Cup: they were the most creative of the thirty-two expeditions in the Finals. No doubt the celebrations in Rio de Janeiro and Nova Brasília have been shown on screens all over the world.

I would like to see the cameras visit some of the villages on the Amazon. The people of the rainforests were economically secure for countless generations, mainly through hunting and fishing. Now their way of life is under relentless threat. Their heroic leader, Chico Mendes, was assassinated a few years ago. Capitalism is not sentimental.

The victory in Yokohama last Sunday means more to those good people than we in this country can understand.

Back in Germany in the pubs and the cafés I can hear people saying: 'If only we had Michael Ballack.'

Sunday World

'A BAD GAME OF FOOTBALL
BUT A GREAT GAME TO WIN'

DUBLIN BEAT GALWAY IN THE 1983
ALL-IRELAND FOOTBALL FINAL

Mick Holden summed it up: 'It was the worst game of football I ever played in – but it was a great game to win.' From a Dublin point of view you could hardly disagree.

It was a sour end to what all in all was a good season – but it would be unfair to lay the blame at the door of any individual.

In many ways it was a day of reckoning, long postponed but certain to come – this travesty of Gaelic football was rooted in the folly of those who govern the game.

It has been clear for many years except to all those who do not, to see that Gaelic football is degenerating: the lusty ballad has become the doggerel in the manger.

Last year's final managed to rise above the common textures – and fools, some of them in high places, went around telling us that there was nothing, whatsoever, wrong with the game.

One pheasant doesn't make an Autumn – and in looking back now that match between Kerry and Offaly seems to belong to a different planet.

There was no reason why yesterday's final shouldn't have been a game to warm the cockles of the soul – and anybody who blames the conditions is deceiving himself.

The day was windy and occasionally wet – but we have seen good football served up on worse days. The fault lay in the attitude of some of the players – and in the casual system of appointing referees.

Let me make it clear that I do not blame the referee, Seán Mac Eochaidh: he was the victim of the system. He was by far and away the most important man on the pitch yesterday – but there was little space devoted to him in the papers last week. Nor did I hear his name mentioned in the RTÉ programme about the game on Saturday night.

I would like to have known about his career as a referee – and why he was considered qualified to take charge of an All-Ireland final.

In other games a referee has to work his way up through the ranks. He is watched regularly by referees senior to him – and they report on his performances.

Before he reaches the highest grade he will have served a long and rigorously scrutinised apprenticeship and practice – I doubt if this is the case in Gaelic football.

Seán Mac Eochaidh was saddled with another difficulty yesterday: some of the rules in the book are more often than not ignored – and some of the rules that some referees invoke aren't in the book at all.

And so in at least two major games this season we saw the fictitious 'advantage rule' in operation – the man with the whistle and, presumably, his assistants allowed blatant and dangerous fouls to go unpunished.

Seemingly the object was to allow the game to flow – and seemingly it didn't matter very much if in the process the pitch was strewn with injured warriors.

The referee's first duty isn't to the spectators – his first duty is to protect the players. And in that duty most senior referees in modern Gaelic football fall down.

They ignore existing rules and invoke rules of their own creation – and pat themselves on the back for allowing the game 'to flow'. Flow on, unlovely river . . .

You didn't need to be a relative of Old Moore's to know that yesterday's big game carried the seeds of trouble. Dublin – rightly or wrongly – has got the name of being a 'physical' team. It is a curious word – it is hard to see how a team could be anything else. In the current debasement of language, 'physical' is a substitute for 'dirty' – it is a cowardly way of avoiding the truth.

I don't look on Dublin as a dirty side – but after the replay with Cork the word was out that they had 'softened up' the Munster champions. And the word was out too that Galway were determined not to turn the other cheek.

These pre-match rumours are usually pub rumours – this one seems to have some foundation.

For whatever cause, the opening passages of what should have been the showpiece of the Gaelic football season brought shame on the game.

I have no idea who started the ugliness – possibly it was a kind of spontaneous combustion. All I know is that it was sickening to watch.

I had looked forward to an enthralling battle, a test of hardihood and skill and intelligence – and what we saw for most of the first half was an exhibition of man's base nature.

The referee seemed stricken by surprise – and before he took action the poison had infiltrated the system.

His first big decision was dramatic. The sending off of Brian Mullins may have been technically justified – but it was morally harsh.

Brian's action appeared to be in retaliation – and certainly it wasn't in cold blood. How his absence affected the game we can never know – it is possible that it harmed Galway.

And certainly it destroyed one myth – the belief that if you stop Mullins, you stop Dublin. It had become clear in the course of this campaign that some of the younger players – notably Pat Canavan and Tommy Conroy and John Caffrey – had come of football age.

And I feel that yesterday's game provided further evidence that an outnumbered team can have an advantage. You cannot prove this theory – but it is hard not to suspect that it is true. All I know is that from the moment yesterday that Galway got a 14–12 advantage in the numbers of players I felt that they were doomed.

Dublin now had everything to fight for: victory would be doubly sweet – and defeat wouldn't demand an excuse. Galway's position was the reverse: victory would be gravely flawed – and defeat ignominious.

Yet this mental disadvantage cannot excuse Galway's display after the dismissal of Ciaran Duff – they seemed to have forgotten the basic tenets of the game.

And you couldn't begrudge Dublin their victory: courage alone wouldn't have sufficed – they showed great common sense.

This was most evident in the way they went for the clean catch – well aware that the breaking ball would favour those with the spare men. And their great talent – their ability to find one another – was never more precious.

Thus they diminished their tactical disadvantage – and it wasn't until about the last quarter of an hour that Galway were able to set up something like a siege.

And then another Dublin talent raised its head: in this year's championship run they have benefited from many last-ditch saves – the pattern was maintained yesterday.

And so we saw the remarkable sight of a team playing into a strong wind, two men short and with only a small lead – and winning.

Inevitably in the aftermath there was talk of the twelve apostles – but when the crisis came, there were only eleven. Dublin had no shirkers yesterday – and I'm sure that the balladeers are already making verses to immortalise them.

For Galway's followers it was the bitterest day in modern times – but they should temper their criticism by allowing for the bizarre circumstances.

Galway played their best football when both teams were at full stretch and when they were facing the wind at its stiffest.

And yesterday's shambles revives a familiar argument: should you allow a substitute for a dismissed player? I believe you should. It is fairer to the opposing team and fairer to the crowd.

It can be argued that Galway's lack of football sense was the biggest cause of their defeat and that they didn't deserve an All-Ireland – but it should be remembered how Offaly failed to use their seeming advantage after Jimmy Keaveney was dismissed early in the 1979 Leinster final. And yet on paper they are much the same team.

It must be admitted, however, that they made a woeful blunder even before any sending-off could affect the game. It was bad enough for Padraig Coyne to attempt a short free with a big space unguarded behind him – but in that space lay Joe McNally. Seemingly he was injured – but there was nothing to prevent him from getting up.

That he was left unmarked was beyond understanding. As it happened, his presence had no effect – but the incident hinted at a strange lack of wisdom.

If someone had remained to keep an eye on the recumbent player, the goal might have been prevented.

Dublin have benefited from some strange goals in their voyage to the title. There have been times when it was as if a man had fired a shot to frighten a flock of rooks – and seen a fine fat cock pheasant come down at his feet.

Fair play to Barney Rock – he took the chance sweetly. And if Dublin have had their share of luck this season, they made the most of it.

For Padraig Coyne it was a terrible moment – generally he is the soundest of keepers. And indeed for all the Galway team it was a day they will hope to exorcise.

It would be unjust to lay the blame on any individuals – lest it be deemed a collective failure. And so I will not single out any Galway players for praise – lest it be deemed a condemnation of the rest.

Once again the Dublin half-backs played magnificently. P. J. Buckley and Tommy Drumm were masterly – and yet Pat Canavan looked the senior partner in the firm.

The full-back line was reduced by the dismissal of Ray Hazley – he went off with Tom Tierney in the second quarter.

After an uncertain start Gerry Hargan and Mick Holden gave little away. Jim Ronayne was his usual self, honest and unspectacular and effective. Barney Rock's total of 1–6 speaks for itself. Tommy Conroy played a great first half.

John Caffrey emerged as a midfielder, first class. His catching was superb – and it is no exaggeration to say that he did the work of two.

For most of the second half Anton O'Toole and Joe McNally were like modern soccer front-runners – outnumbered but battling away hopefully and often causing alarm. John O'Leary was blameless for the goal – and did his routine work well.

Dublin, above all, were a team – Galway in that strange second half were a collection of desperate individuals.

It was a pity that it didn't end in a draw – the replay might have been worthy of the occasion. That, of course, is a neutral view.

I understand Mick Holden – for Dublin it was a great game to win.

Evening Press

'A Man Who Has Done More Than His Share of Running Away'

The Tragedy of George Best

One day a few years ago on a flight from Belfast to Glasgow I sat next to a man from our northern capital – and understood a little better the tragedy of George Best.

My neighbour was a deeply intelligent man. He was also highly articulate (aren't they all in Northern Ireland?) – and in that short journey gave me an insight into the Belfast soul.

I have always found Belfast a wonderfully warm-hearted city – but had feared that my image of it owed more to the tavern than to real life.

My neighbour on that trip over the North Channel confirmed my impression: he was in his forties, had travelled far and wide, but was as near heart-broken as an intelligent man can be – because he was going into exile.

The exile was only temporary: it was April – and his business in Canada would be finished by Christmas.

He was perfectly sober – but by the time we passed Alisa Craig he was already desperately homesick. And he was leaving a Belfast where life was fearfully constrained – and where the chances of being killed or maimed were by far the highest in western Europe.

I do not wish to pose as an instant psychiatrist – I will leave that to the runners-on in Croke Park – but I cannot help suspecting that George Best has been in exile for almost all his adult life. And like Brendan Behan he came from a family whose closeness made the arrows of exile all the sharper.

It is something I have often observed in Britain: city people (and especially those from Dublin) make unhappy exiles.

They miss the intimate life of their heartland, whereas a lad or lass from the mountains around Knocknagoshel – or Cahirciveen for that matter – can settle down in London or wherever like cows in fresh grass.

Brendan Behan was the kind of child on whom grannies and aunts and assorted oul' wans dote – so seemingly was George Best.

Such indulgence makes for a pleasant childhood – but when eventually you sail out into the open sea, you may find the going a bit rough.

It is the ambition of a great many young lads in these islands to be summoned to Old Trafford; George Best was – and returned home next day, even though he was accompanied on that first venture by his neighbour and fellow-hopeful, Alec McMordie.

In the years between he has done more than his share of running away. Perhaps he has now stopped – but I doubt if any bookmaker would be in a hurry to oblige if you wished to bet that he hadn't.

And I must confess that I find the misadventures of Mr Best about as fascinating as the marital tribulations of Princess Anne and her unfortunate spouse.

And I have a particular little cause for being ill-disposed towards him (George, that is – not Mark whatever-his-name-is).

It concerns a Christmas week some years ago when I was spending a well-earned holiday in the bosom of my family (the 'well-earned etc' part is what local correspondents in the *Kerryman* say about some dosser home for a few weeks from England).

There I was on Saturday night, 28 December 1975, eating a little piece of Christmas pie and drinking a mug of lemonade, when words arrived over the electronic wire ordering me to be in Cork on the morrow.

The reason for this dramatic message was the rumoured appearance of wee Georgie in the colours of

Cork Celtic at Flower Lodge in a League of Ireland game.

At that stage of wee Georgie's career everything was rumour. But I turned up – so rather amazingly did he.

And so the greatest gaggle of small boys and indeed small girls seen at large since the Pied Piper of Hamelin turned debt-collector. The winding little lane that leads down from the city to Flower Lodge was almost bursting its banks.

I find it hard to forgive George Best for his display that day.

Lo and behold – George was back for the next match (against Shelbourne at Harold's Cross). A big crowd came to that game too – and went away less than gruntled.

George appeared one more time for Celtic – and people stayed away just because his name was on the teamsheet.

An old truth had been illustrated – you don't pay twice to see the same fat man in the circus sideshow.

How Best squared his conscience over that Cork venture I don't know.

If one takes his autobiography (written by someone else) seriously, the conclusion is that his conscience has been a long time in deep freeze.

It is a dreary book – and I can only hope that some time he will be mature enough to tell the real story.

And his book contains far too much about drinking and lying about on the beach in Marbella or wherever. Such activities require no special talent.

About the texture and the mental ambience of the many great games he experienced we learn very little. Nor does he make a serious attempt to evaluate himself as a footballer.

Perhaps he believes the popular myth (originally promulgated by Parkinson) that he was the greatest ever. I have heard otherwise sensible people repeat it – and it is, of course, utter nonsense.

George Best was one of the most exciting players ever – that is a different thing. But he was essentially a forward – even though he could perform well in midfield.

But if you agree that the concept of greatness implies all-round ability, you cannot bracket him with such as Franz Beckenbauer and John Charles.

There was also a man called Pelé who was no slouch in midfield or up in front – and who could have played in the back a little bit too.

And for the title of 'most exciting forward' George would not lack rivals. They would include Bobby Charlton, John White and Denis Law.

Football lovers older than I would throw in a few more names, including those of one or two who never left these shores. And they would probably argue that George Best – at least on the pitch – was a throwback to the days when coaches had wheels under them. And they wouldn't be far wrong.

George was special not only because of his marvellous balance and devastating acceleration – but because he was tactically unspoiled.

He was an outrageous romantic who believed in the comic-strip hero that took on a dusty street full of baddies and laid them all low. In his early career every Saturday beckoned like 'high noon'.

But the drinking and the absences from training ate away at his genius – until eventually his play became a thing of bits and fragments.

The fault was not all his. There are those who believe that Matt Busby is ripe for canonisation – they can include me out.

Busby was the supremo of Old Trafford in Best's great years – and he indulged him amazingly.

This hard puritan (a Catholic can be a puritan too) forgave him repeatedly for lying in bed while his colleagues were out training.

The petting that started in Belfast was continued in Manchester – and I suspect that the waters of adulation are still lapping around wee Georgie.

He was a victim too of Jimmy Hill's master-stroke. He might have lived happily if the maximum wage hadn't been abolished.

At an age when many of his contemporaries were still at secondary school, George Best was getting about two hundred pounds a week. And he was at large in Manchester, a city second only to Glasgow in the British drinking league.

A generation earlier he might have found fulfilment. He was part of an age when entertainers were rewarded too much for their own good. And he became not part of life but of a lifestyle, a term that signifies the caperings of the bored rich.

George Best lost a great part of his Belfast heritage – he didn't appreciate the value of work.

Evening Press

'YOU COULD SEE THE CROWD EBBING; THE DESERTERS MISSED FIVE MOMENTOUS MINUTES'

IRELAND WIN THE TRIPLE CROWN, 1985

When Bill Shakespeare wrote about a divinity that shapes our ends, he was hardly referring to the late minutes of sporting events – but around half past four on Saturday his words seemed remarkably appropriate.

And as all paradise broke loose and strong women wept, a few more lines from a long-abandoned school book surfaced: Alexander Pope believed that genius and madness are such close kin that only 'thin partition' divides them – Michael Kiernan will understand.

If his drop-kick had missed the target, he would have been accused of momentary madness, by those who believed a try was 'on'; as it was, his act was deemed a stroke of genius.

And the young centre joined two other Corkmen – J. C. Daly and Jim McCarthy – in the sparsely populated club reserved for those whose dramatic scores have won Triple Crowns.

Alexander Pope didn't live to see rugby become an organised game; it was a pity; he was ideally placed to enjoy it – he lived by the river in Twickenham.

Bill Shakespeare missed that pleasure too. I passed by his home town the other day – and an old, old thought recurred. This man of mighty imagination came from a people who have long prided themselves on their solidity and common sense. His West Country neighbours were well represented at Lansdowne Road on Saturday. Nine of England's squad play for clubs within cycling distance of Stratford-on-Avon.

West Country rugby is famous for its fusion of physical and mental toughness: it is no arena for flash or faint

123

hearts. And therein lies a piquant little story: it concerns England's quest for a full-back.

There are men old enough to explain why so many of our financial institutions are crumbling like sandcastles in a bank-holiday tide who have yet to see a reliable full-back sport the red rose.

And this season the selectors looked to the west and called up a man who would at least be dependable. Chris Martin has no pretensions to imitate Serge Blanco: he is an old-fashioned full-back who is content to gather and find touch. He excelled last season in Bath's winning of the John Player Cup.

At three o'clock on Saturday he was the man about whom England had the least worry; a few minutes later the image of the West Country was shattered.

And the oft-quoted dictum from Dick Fitzgerald's book *How to Play Gaelic Football* sprang to my mind: 'A goalkeeper may get little to do but he must do that little well.'

Martin's first touch of the ball had resulted in a woeful blunder: he had deliberated over a simple clearance and suddenly was hit by a bolt from the green – Brendan Mullin blocked his kick and easily won the race for the touchdown.

On Tuesday night at Wembley we saw Gary Bailey perpetrate a semi-own-goal – but it came only a few minutes from the end and he was able to hide with his misery.

Poor Martin had to soldier on and long before the final whistle it was painfully clear that his place was not the pitch but the psychiatrist's couch.

It recalled that night in Leon when England were cruising past West Germany until Peter Bonetti allowed a harmless-looking shot from Franz Beckenbauer to go under his body.

For the rest of the game he looked like a man who

would welcome an earthquake so that he might have a hole in which to hide.

Martin's experience in the second half on Saturday was as near to public execution as most of us are ever likely to see. The effect on his team-mates must remain incalculable – it was hardly beneficial.

England will ponder too the loss of Nigel Melville: this notoriously unlucky scrum-half lasted only eighteen minutes.

He had played with authority: his replacement, Richard Hill, took a long time to settle. And so England found themselves without their Moses and by the end of the first quarter seemed in for a crushing defeat.

Toughness of spirit had been their most notable trait this season: they put the early disasters behind them and settled down to erode pre-match fantasies of an Irish run-over.

This was a game that made the predictions seem as out of touch with reality as the tips for the Grand National.

And it reminded you that Napoleon wasn't altogether jesting when he said that the most formidable opponent he had encountered was a general called Luck.

It would be churlish to say that Ireland were fortunate to win on Saturday: an overall look at the season persuades you that Mick Doyle's crusade deserved such a climax.

But despite Shakespeare's suggestion, I doubt if there is some divine department entrusted with rewarding boldness.

And the real truth is that but for the outrageously romantic finish, those who were loudest in praise of Ciaran Fitzgerald would have been loudest in condemnation.

Ireland fell far below their previous form this season. And to blame the shower that fell around three o'clock is a feeble excuse: it wasn't a Summer day at Murrayfield.

And it was hard not to suspect that the Irish players had been affected by the mental climate, as fish are coloured by the water in which they live.

The general opinion – and it was almost impossible to find a dissenting voice – was that it would be less a contest than a triumphal procession.

We had conquered on two foreign fields and now thanks to the January snow and ice would have England as sparring partner for an exhibition.

The public mood was like that which suffused Kerry in the weeks before the expected five-in-a-row. Ciaran and his warriors had to put their talent where so many were putting their mouths – and found themselves in territory that did not correspond to the general picture.

That gift of a try may have been a malediction in disguise: it seemed to confirm the view that England were a soft touch. And as Ireland found the opposition unexpectedly stubborn, their composure seemed to ebb.

The passing lacked the smoothness we saw at Murrayfield; the tackling wasn't as decisive as against Wales; the forwards were not as aggressively confident in the loose as against France. And the temptation to kick towards Martin led to the waste of some clean possession. His trauma delighted the sadistic element in the crowd but didn't yield scores.

England had a weakness that was less obvious but no less perncious: Rob Andrew is primarily a kicking out-half – but he didn't kick well.

They had two much more subtle out-halves on the bench – Huw Davies and Stuart Barnes.

Seemingly Andrew had been preferred on the 'all things being equal he is a better place-kicker' basis.

But all things are seldom equal and this season has thrown up an interesting question. What is a recognised place-kicker?

Patrick Lescarboura and Mark Wyatt carry the tag; so,

of course, does Rob Andrew – Michael Kiernan doesn't. And the Irish selectors were wise in not picking someone whose biggest talent was his place-kicking.

In an attempt to analyse a strange game all I can say with confidence is that Ireland had an advantage in two positions – at full-back and out-half.

Huge MacNeill fielded cleanly and kicked well. Paul Dean has an old head on young shoulders – he played with quiet authority.

Michael Bradley's passing was as uncertain as ever; his work 'around the field' was splendid.

The Irish three-quarters didn't always show the cohesion we expected from men who have been so much together.

Keith Crossan was the soundest of the four. Trevor Ringland had some bad moments.

The Irish set-scrum was again in trouble – and Fitzgerald did well to win his put-ins.

Those who know – or pretend to know – say that the weakness was in the front row. It didn't seem to demoralise Phil Orr and Jim McCoy: they did very well in the broken play.

The line-outs were a mess to which Donal Lenihan and Brian Spillane and Wade Dooley brought some order.

But not even all the firm catches resulted in clean possession for the scrum-halves: the binding patented by the All-Blacks was not copied. This was all too obvious to Lenihan: wherever possible he peeled off – and made a few mighty surges.

Willie Anderson was lucky that his dicing with offside didn't prove costly but he worked hard, if almost anonymously.

Nigel Carr gave Andrew little space. And his clubmate, Philip Matthews, frustrated Hill's ambitions to break.

Spillane's covering was again brilliant – both in

appearance and in play he is a throwback to the years when a lock was expected to be a footballer.

The display of the English pack confounded their critics – and especially Fran Cotton.

Their scrummaging power was expected. Their quickness to the breakdown was not – and they did well in the loose scrums but saw much fine possession kicked away.

David Cooke was outstanding – but possibly because of his flaxen hair.

English opinion, however, is that most of the pack are only standing in: missing for one reason or another were Maurice Colclough, Steve Bainbridge, John Scott, Nick Jeavons and Peter Winterbottom.

The English three-quarters looked formidable and certainly in left-wing Rory Underwood they have found a chariot of fire. And it was they who provided the only 'created' try of the day. It was a score of sweet simplicity.

It came fourteen minutes after the restart. England had lifted a siege – and won a set scrum about forty yards from the Irish line and in the middle.

The ball was moved left and Paul Dodge sent a lovely kick towards Ireland's right-hand corner. It slithered over the line – and Underwood's amazing acceleration brought him the try.

This left the score 7–7: Andrew had kicked a huge penalty in the second minute. Kiernan had added a thirteenth-minute penalty to Mullins's try.

England's try inspired a long spell of dominance by their forwards but it brought only a penalty goal by Andrew midway through the half.

Kiernan got the equalising penalty in the seventy-third minute. And as the packs visibly tired after what had been a tougher battle than that between Ireland and France, a draw looked all too likely.

Indeed through the opening between the East Stand and the South Terrace you could see the crowd ebbing.

The deserters missed five momentous minutes.

Andrew got the chance to put England ahead but missed a middle-distance penalty. The escape seemed to inspire Ireland – certainly it inspired the crowd.

The drop-out was accompanied by an enormous wave of sound. And Spillane soared up as if on a thermal and made a mighty catch. And then came the green stampede that seemed to catch most of the English unawares.

Spillane and Lenihan and Kiernan were the immediate heroes of the melodramatic climax – but over the eighty minutes no Irish forward did more than Fitzgerald: he was seldom far from the thick of the battle.

A few years ago an English journalist referred to him as a leprechaun. I doubt if he is – but on Saturday he found a crock of gold at the foot of the rainbow.

And I found out how the good people of Offaly felt about a quarter to five on a Sunday evening in the September of 1982.

Evening Press

JACK DEMPSEY

Hurling is our oldest field game but remains a minority sport. Nevertheless, if you asked a hundred Irish people to name our greatest sporting hero, I believe that many would go for a hurler.

Christy Ring and Mick Mackey would be strong contenders – you could hear Tipperary voices speaking for John Doyle. I know many Wexford people who wouldn't look beyond Tony Doran – and I have never known a hurler more cast in a heroic mould.

Some aficionados would point out that these heroes hadn't been tested in the world's arenas. The debate would widen. Pat O'Callaghan and Bob Tisdall would get a strong mention. Voices, not all feminine, would make a case for Sonia O'Sullivan.

Some of the younger generation would nominate D. J. Carey. Gaelic football and soccer would produce an array of candidates. Jack Kyle would be on his own from rugby.

And yet I feel that the honour would go to a hurler. It is the more dramatic game: its heroes are more romantic. We see them as warriors.

I do not know of any footballers in Irish mythology – because of course football is a modern game – but we all know about Cúchulainn. In our school books he was the brave wee lad who hurled his ball all the way from the Cooley Peninsula to Ulster's Royal Palace.

As hurlers come on to the pitch, you feel that you are about to witness a battle. Sometimes it can be moderate or indeed dull – but on the good days it has no equal. And even though it isn't an international game, I would vote for an icon from hurling to be our hero of heroes.

The English might elect Stanley Matthews. The Welsh

would probably go for Cliff Morgan. Our Scots neighbours might waver between boxers and footballers and end up with some self-destructive comet such as Benny Lynch.

Who would the Americans elect as the sporting hero most symbolic of their country? They could begin with Babe Ruth and come down to Michael Jordan. Both reached peaks of excellence of which others would hardly dare to dream. And of course Tiger Woods is still ascending.

Yet I feel that the man who most typified America wasn't deemed the best in his own sport. He was part-Irish, part-English, part-German and part-Cherokee – it wasn't a bad start for a lad whose ambition was to be heavyweight champion of the world.

He had, however, an obvious handicap: his father was a farmer and his mother was a teacher – great pugilists are not supposed to come from the middle class.

The caravans had long ceased rolling westwards – Jack Dempsey went eastwards. He ate and slept in hobo camps. He earned the odd few dollars as barman or short-order cook, sometimes even as a long-order cook.

Ernest Hemingway and other budding writers did so too – to give a romantic flavour to their potted biographies on the back cover of Penguin books.

With Dempsey, however, it was 'for real'. On his pilgrimages he often lived off the thin of the land. He acquired the rudiments of his profession in mining towns, in fights that earned him little more than the price of his supper. As he moved eastwards, his fame, such as it was, went before him. Boxing had its own grapevine.

In time he was taken in hand by a man whose name may have been Jack Kerins. Kerins was streetwise and ringwise and wise in any other way necessary for survival in the rough world of America's adolescence. He wasn't noted for honesty or generosity, but he guided

Jack Dempsey with the expertise of a riverboat pilot.

He kept most of the prize money and gave Jack just enough to keep body and spirit in one piece. And so when Jack challenged Jess Willard for the world title, he was truly a hungry fighter.

That evening in Toledo he weighed only a few pounds over twelve stone. The rest is folklore. His manager rewarded Jack with a down payment out of the purse. He went away and enjoyed his first decent meal in weeks.

When he awoke next morning, the man who had been more at home in hobo camps than in hotels could hardly believe that he had won the greatest prize in the sporting world.

Most experts now agree that Muhammad Ali was the greatest heavyweight of all time – the comparison with Jack Dempsey could hardly be more marked.

Half a century later Jack might have hitched his way across the vast continent. He stowed away on the baggage cars of trains to combat what Thomas Wolfe called the cruel distances of America.

Ali was a home boy. He had a loving mother to safeguard him from the terrors of white American cuisine. His ascent could hardly have been more orthodox. He came up through the amateur ranks and was crowned as Olympic light heavyweight champion.

He was at all times shrewdly managed and expertly coached; Dempsey too was shrewdly managed but got no coaching at all. Thus in the popular image he is seen as a fighter rather than a boxer – but it wasn't so simple.

From the films of his fights with Gene Tunney you can see that Jack was more than a brawler. He looked slow on his feet but he moved with catlike grace. He had beautiful hands – they were like cobras' heads.

Dempsey became a national hero after his victory over Willard, but his fame waned when it was revealed that he had not gone to war. When he defended his title against

Georges Carpentier, the challenger was announced as 'Soldier of France'.

Dempsey's popularity made a remarkable comeback when he fought Gene Tunney. Tunney came out of the war with honour – and yet the people, or at least those who followed boxing, disliked him. He was too correct, too far above what Scott Fitzgerald called 'the hot struggles of the poor'.

The belief that he had been cheated in the second fight with Tunney increased Jack's standing. He hadn't – but it was a bonus.

He became a folk hero, on the same shelf as Kit Carson and Paul Revere and Davy Crockett. He was seen as a symbol of a young country's raw energy and epic ambition and above all its restlessness.

Jack's heyday coincided with what was called the Jazz Age; it was America's last era of innocence that imploded on an October day in 1929.

As the Americans became more and more urbanised, they saw Jack as part of the old world – with the hot dog and the cracker barrel and Mom's apple pie.

He appealed to the frontiersman that lingers in every American, not least in George W. Bush, who regrets that he was born too late to be the hero of shoot-outs in dusty streets.

Jack Dempsey's life story should have made a great film – it didn't. Indeed the films about famous boxers are almost all outrageously sentimental and melodramatic. Only John Huston in a short film came anywhere near expressing the essence of the profession.

There are miles of American writing about boxing – good and honest but rather lacking in deep insight. The English essayist William Hazlitt wasn't a sports writer: his principal fields were politics and drama – but he wrote memorably about boxing.

When you read his account of the battle between Tom

Sayers and John Heenan, you realise why neither ever fought seriously again and why both died before they were forty. His account of the fight between Tom Hickman and Bill Neate is perhaps his most famous passage on the Noble Art.

He evokes the waiting for the fight: 'This is the trying time. It is the time the heart sickens as you think what the two champions are about and how short a time will determine their fate.'

The fight ends when Hickman is knocked out. His first words on awakening are: 'Where am I? What is the matter?' His second says: 'Nothing is the matter. You have lost the battle but you are the bravest man alive.'

Hazlitt's especial gift was his creative imagination. It made him a brilliant writer in several fields. Sometimes I think that he is my hero of heroes.

Gene Tunney was well educated and highly intelligent. But in his life story he didn't capture the essence of his epic battle with Jack Dempsey.

Incidentally, when Tunney quit the ring, he threatened to tour the United States and other fortunate places lecturing on Shakespeare.

A reporter asked Jack for a comment and he said: 'If it suits this racket, it's OK by me.'

Magill

'A GRAND MAN FROM DUBLIN WATCHES THE CHELTENHAM FESTIVAL IN THE PUB BUT DRESSES AS IF FOR THE RACES'

TALES FROM CHELTENHAM

On the plane to Birmingham on the Tuesday morning of last week a sweet-faced hostess introduced herself to me: 'My name is Breda. I think you know Paddy Freeman . . . ' Indeed I do. Who doesn't know the original Ginger Man . . .

I was relieved to hear that he was fit and well and up and running; he hasn't been seen in his old haunts for ages.

Rumours abounded; Paddy is as intimate with the world of gambling as Lester Piggott is with the ups and downs of Epsom racetrack – it was being whispered that he had been employed by the Football Association to help untangle the alleged match-fixing conspiracy.

Perhaps it is true; anyhow, we hope to see him back soon in Mulligan's – politically correct or not.

In the little station bar in Cheltenham Spa I missed the small man with his white hair combed into a fringe; I have no doubt that he was – and hopefully still is – an authority on the growing of leeks.

Missing also were the two dear little ladies with their red-ribboned straw hats; I hope that we will see them back; the bar was in the hands of a pleasant young man who spoke with the cider-apple accent of his native heath.

Across the road there was little change: the Midland, the pub nearest to the station, has long been familiar to Irish racegoers.

For years it was about the scruffiest tavern in the west of England – or the west of anywhere; now it has been slightly refurbished but remains as homely as ever.

A glowing coal fire greets the traveller; you can get an excellent pint of Stella Artois for one pound sixty.

They (whoever 'they' are) say that if you stand for five minutes on O'Connell Bridge or in Charing Cross Road or anywhere in Manhattan, you will meet somebody you know: if you spend five minutes in the Midland on an evening after racing, you will meet too many.

One day long ago I decided to see what the Midland is like when not populated with racegoers. And so I went down from Birmingham on an early train and found that homely pub crowded.

Most of its denizens were in their working clothes and many were railway men; I had almost forgotten that Cheltenham Spa is a major junction.

Thence you can voyage to the extremes of the south-west or away to Fishguard or over to London or beyond or, unless you have more sense, up to the north-east of Scotland.

Two doors from the Midland there is a Tote betting shop; I know local men who have never been out to Prestbury Park; they watch on television – and, of course, every decent pub has a runner to take the bets and bring back the money.

I know a grand man from Dublin who has lived for almost forty years near Cheltenham; he watches the festival in the Midland but with a difference – he dresses as if for the races.

The turf – and especially the world of hurdling and chasing – continues to abound in stories. The amazing progress of Alderbrook from the flat to the hurdles is an obvious example.

When he was sent to Kim Bailey, only about two months remained before Cheltenham: Alderbrook was and is a very smart horse on the flat, a winner at such prestigious tracks as Goodwood and Longchamp – but hurdling is a different race game.

136

. The trainer thought that he had been given an impossible brief: the Champion Hurdle is not for novices.

Some horses take slowly and reluctantly to the hurdles; some do not take at all; some take as readily as seagulls to the slipstream of the plough – Alderbrook was such an apprentice.

In the race at Wincanton which we spoke about a few days ago he was having only his second trip over hurdles; he ran and skipped with the zest of a novice and the expertise of a veteran.

I was mightily impressed; so were those connoisseurs of reality, the bookmakers; his price for the Champion Hurdle had been a derisory fifty to one – next morning it was forty-two points less.

Alderbrook's rise was liberally etched with romance; the ascent of his partner at Cheltenham, a young man named Norman Williamson, would make Nat Gould's highest flights of fancy seem prosaic.

Until the day of the Champion Hurdle he had never ridden a winner at the festival; by Thursday afternoon he had landed the big double of hurdle and chase and piloted two other winners for great measure. And he had proven that our poor backward little island hasn't lost its facility for producing brilliant riders.

We down in my part of Kerry will look on Norman as one of our own: he comes from near Mallow; we are so intimately acquainted with north-west Cork that we regard it as part of our spiritual territory – we thought nothing of cycling to Mallow Races in leaner times.

He is a graduate from the point-to-points, a *dura matrix*, a hard school.

In his Irish incarnation he worked for a trainer in east Limerick, a guru who was famous as just about the shrewdest judge of horses and men in the business – now read on . . .

One day at a point-to-point the young Corkman came

137

to grief on a hotly fancied mount from the stable and broke an arm in the process; worse was to follow – the famous judge of horses and men told him not to come back.

Jonjo O'Neill had a similar experience in his green youth: while working in a stable at the Curragh, he was involved in a fall; it cost the horse his life and Jonjo his job. It isn't only prophets that aren't recognised in their own land.

Success is a great elixir: horses are extremely sensitive; if you have confidence, it rubs off on them.

Norman Williamson went to Uttoxeter on Saturday; there he got a leg up on a horse called Lucky Lane in the Midland Grand National; his mount had no great form and at twelve years of age was unlikely to improve; Norman adopted bold tactics and brought him home at twelve to one.

And Martin Hourigan followed up his great victory with Dorans Pride: at Limerick on Saturday he saddled three winners – King's Cherry and Lisaleen River and Queen of the Lakes. It was a good week for the Deep South.

Sunday World

'THE GAA IS A DEMOCRATIC ORGANISATION, KIND OF, BUT IS CURSED WITH MEN WHO ARE TERRIFIED OF CHANGE'

THE GAA BOARD

Most people love to be in at the birth of things. I am quietly happy to know that the Dodder rises out of a bog-hole on the western slope of Kippure.

The French love their rivers and have a special affection for the Loire, the last wild river in France. They go on pilgrimages to its birthplace: it comes out from a wooden pipe in a farmer's yard away in the east of the country.

I love to see racehorses being worked, especially in the very early hours. The riders, buttoned up to the neck and with woollen caps over their helmets, are almost anonymous.

And so are the horses unless carrying some distinctive mark such as Florida Pearl's badger's blaze. Thus as you watch a string of horses in the very early hours, you feel that perhaps you are experiencing a triple birth.

The day is being born and perhaps in that Spring in the mist there is a young horse or a young lad destined for greatness.

I would love to turn back the calendar and be in at the birth of the Gaelic Athletic Association. It provokes a question: do great movements spring from a collective or from an individual urge?

Ernest Renan, the leading French philosopher of his day, said at Ivan Turgenev's graveside that the silent spirit of the people is the source of all great things.

Leslie Stephens, his English counterpart, tended to believe that the scholar in his ivory tower could create a ferment which surprised him and of which he became fearful.

The British Museum is hardly an ivory tower but Karl Marx's long hours there helped to usher in the modern world.

Michael Cusack, that pragmatic dreamer from the haunting landscape known as the Burren, would seem to exemplify Leslie Stephens's intuition; of course several others were involved in the formal founding of the association, but it was Cusack who seemingly single-handed gave us hurling and Gaelic football.

In 1884 when Cusack began to exert influence in the infant GAA, hurling was not only in decline – it was almost extinct. The decline began with the Act of Union. Dublin was no longer a capital city. Many landlords moved to London.

It was this class who had been the mainstay of the ancient game. They kept teams of hurlers just as their counterparts in England kept teams of cricketers. In their absence the game lacked a framework; the effects of the Great Famine caused further decline.

When Cusack set about a revival of hurling, he faced a tormenting problem. Two forms of the game existed: they were distinguished as Summer hurling and Winter hurling. The former was that favoured by the landlords; it was played with a broad-bladed camán.

Winter hurling, as the name indicates, was played mainly in the 'idle times' – when work on the land wasn't too demanding. It was played with a camán like a hockey stick – and generally by the working classes.

Cusack, after long cogitation, chose the Summer version as the official form for the GAA. (Incidentally, in my youth in Kerry we played our own version of hurling. The road was our pitch; the camáns were improvised; the ball was the bottom half of a small polish tin.)

When it came to choosing a form of Gaelic football, the sage from the Burren had no problem – the game didn't exist.

140

It couldn't come into being without the invention of pneumatic rubber. This of course is also true of rugby union and rugby league, Australian rules, soccer and American gridiron football.

Gaelic football is as traditional as the bicycle pump. And the form known in the early days of the GAA was very different from what we know today. In P. D. Mehigan's excellent book, *Gaelic Football*, you can see this for yourself: 'Masses of men drove into each other while the fleeter of foot watched on the outskirts.' This of course was rugby before it was distilled into the form we know today.

Cusack took what he deemed the better parts of soccer and rugby and fused them into Gaelic football. His brainchild was an almost instant success: the new game spread into almost every nook in the island, not to mention the crannies.

Its popularity was easily explained: it wasn't too difficult to play and it was easy for spectators to understand.

Rugby was strong in Kerry before the birth of the GAA but the new game diminished its appeal. This was not surprising: rugby, even when played by competent and honest exponents, is the most dangerous of all field games – and to most people its laws are revealed truths that they cannot comprehend.

If Michael Cusack multiplied Rip Van Winkle's little nap by six and came back, would he be pleased by the state of the association which he did so much to foster?

Hurling, the truly traditional game, is not flourishing: only two new counties, Waterford and Offaly, have won the All-Ireland since 1948.

The situation is much healthier in Gaelic football. Offaly and Down and Derry and Donegal and Armagh have battled their way to the Round Table since 1948. Nevertheless, fourteen counties have yet to win the football All-Ireland.

Recently, Peter Quinn, former president, in a rare outburst said the association was in need of radical reform. Indeed it is: 'The hungry sheep look up and are not fed.'

The natives are getting restless, all the more so since the introduction of the back-door format. It is no more than a stumble – but in the right direction. In the previous system a county faced the prospect of being cast into exterior darkness after one game. It wasn't much of a reward for a training regime that began in January. Now every county gets to the second-chance inn. It shouldn't be the journey's end.

One bold leap would bring the association out of the twentieth century. A proper league with promotion and relegation, as in every county where soccer is played, would turn up ground that has long been fallow.

The All-Ireland based on the provincial pattern is ludicrously lacking in logic. There have been long periods when Kerry had no opposition in Munster. To win the All-Ireland they had only two rivers to cross.

Ulster has long been daunting territory: to emerge from it can demand five stern ties. It is little wonder that so few counties from there have captured the provincial title back to back – most are happy to win one in a row.

The case for the open draw is obvious. In 1984 we had the Centenary Cup; it was based on an open draw. It was a success: thirty-five thousand watched the final in Croke Park. I watched it in a marvellous atmosphere.

The experiment was abandoned because it succeeded. I would love to see a League, in both games, preferably in three divisions. Then the so-called lesser counties would get a chance to grow.

Can Kerry ever prosper in hurling while there are landlocked in Munster? Can Kilkenny ever prosper in Gaelic football in the midst of powerful neighbors?

These are simple and honest questions. They should be asked loudly and clearly at every annual convention of

142

the association. The GAA is a democratic body, kind of – but it is cursed with men who are terrified of change.

If their counterparts had prevailed since the birth of man, we would still be living in the trees and dining on fish and wild berries. These 'traditionalists' seem able to coerce the radicals.

The Germans have a saying for it: 'The strong blind man carries on his back the lame man who can see.'

I am confident that the leagues would grow in prestige until in time they would be seen as championships. They could be played between March and August: the knock-out competitions could be run off in September and October.

The new leagues would bring far-reaching benefits: every county would have at least twenty meaningful games in the better months, plus the games in the knock-out tournaments.

Defenders of the All-Irelands as we know them can hardly claim that they are based on fair play. Dublin has, for instance, a population of well over a million; Leitrim has about thirty thousand people – and most of them are in Dublin.

The early All-Irelands were not based on counties but on county champions. It made more sense. Now the All-Ireland club championship is growing in stature by the year. It is a healthy regression.

And so the wheel in turning backwards has turned forwards.

Sunday World

'A Manager Who Practised a Brilliant Philosophy of Football'

Brian Clough

There was little or no organised football in the heyday of the Roman Empire but those who were employed to mint one-liners in those distant times might have foreseen the trauma of Brian Clough: 'Whom the gods wish to destroy, they first make mad.'

If we are to believe most of what we read and hear, this modern version of Robin Hood is now a lost soul without even a Little John or an Alan-a-Dale to stand by him.

He seems the victim of a cruel paradox; he is freeman of a lovely city but is trapped in his home, inhibited from venturing out lest he suffer the slings and arrows of outrageous criticism.

A few years ago while undergoing interrogation by a certain Joe Duffy, I was asked to name my favourite football manager. I didn't hesitate: 'Brian Clough.'

Matt Busby and Bill Shankly and Bob Paisley achieved an abundance of success with clubs that were 'natural' members of the Round Table; Clough achieved this with clubs that seemed destined to be onlookers at football's feast.

And he did so by producing adventurous football; Clough grew up in a woefully deprived part of Britain but emerged from it as a poet; it was as if a rose tree sprouted out of a slag heap.

Those of us who are older remember him as a brilliant 'goalador', an old-fashioned centre-forward with a gift for snapping up unconsidered chances and turning them into goals.

He seemed all set for football's higher plateaus – the First Division, as it was then, and the international arena.

Then came the proverbial shears of fate: injury grounded the soaring eagle – he would never fly again.

His second career brought him fame and glory and the kind of money that he could hardly have made as a player – and yet I cannot help suspecting it didn't bring him satisfaction.

No matter how much success a teacher achieves, he remains prey to a niggling doubt; he cannot help feeling that his disciples might have done just as well with someone else.

And of course no matter how much Clough resorted to positive thinking, he couldn't but ponder on what might have been, on the pitch as distinct from the bench.

Clough's players, especially in the later years, sometimes didn't see him between one match and the next; this suggests that he didn't enjoy teaching; yes, I know, there is a more popular explanation. And perhaps the latter explanation is nearer the mark.

We have been hearing for years that Clough has a drink problem; seemingly rumour is now accepted as fact. I suppose we shouldn't be surprised; Tommy Docherty's words come to mind – 'In this business you either drink or go mad. And I have no intention of going mad.'

Brian Clough is intelligent but he is hardly an intellectual; I doubt it he takes much pleasure in reading or in contemplation. He lives in a part of the country where there is great angling water but I doubt if he is a follower of Izaak Walton. And when a man has a surplus of money and time, you shouldn't be too hard on him if he seeks refuge in fantasies.

You could, I suppose, argue that Clough's quiver of trophies should be a great solace in middle age – seemingly it isn't. He lost his last war; two years ago he threatened to retire – he went the proverbial ford too far.

When Nottingham Forest were ravaged by injuries,

even Clough's genius – or what remained of it – couldn't arrest the spiral. It was a bad way to go out.

In the end he couldn't articulate his little spiels for the local electricity board and Shredded Wheat. The tabloids have had a beano.

Now you might say, if you were in the mood for clichés, it's time for all his friends to rally around – and so it is, only that he seems to have no friends.

Believe it or not, he never had a drink with Peter Taylor, the man who for so many years was his Sancho Panza; seemingly their wives never even met.

Perhaps it isn't true to say that Clough has no friends: many of my colleagues claim to be close to him – but that to me is a dubious kind of friendship; it is rather like that between Albert Reynolds and Dick Spring.

A dear friend of mine, a brilliant player who was a member of England's squad for the finals of the 1966 World Cup, will tell you that Brian Clough is eminently equipped to write the inverse of Dale Carnegie's handbook – *How to Make Enemies and Not Influence People*. He played under the great man and didn't especially enjoy the experience.

Brian Clough is still a comparatively young man; he seems 'magnificently unprepared for the long littleness of life.' Last Monday's *World in Action* hardly made enjoyable viewing for this modern Robin Hood. It suggested that he robbed the poor to feed the rich – in this case, himself.

The charge was not new: we remember the accusation of embezzlement when he was with Derby County. And of course there was the case of Paddy Mulligan's benefit and the brown paper bag.

And there is the story told by Graham Alston, a director of Scunthorpe in the eighties; he alleges that Clough demanded fifteen hundred pounds to take Forest to Scunthorpe for a friendly in 1982.

The receipts came to a meagre ten thousand pounds. Clough, accompanied by Forest's chairman, Maurice Roworth, took his money and said 'Thank you very much.'

And yet I prefer to remember Brian Clough as a great judge who bought shrewdly and practised a brilliant philosophy of football.

I will allow the last words to Geoff Boycott: 'If Brian Clough walked into the dressing room before a game, I would score a century every time.'

Evening Press

'Limerick, You're a Lady – in Waiting'

Offaly Beat Limerick in the All-Ireland Hurling Final, 1994

I have never known such an evening for comparisons – in the Shakespeare and in Mulligan's and in Hourican's they floated in the air.

We heard about Kerry and Roscommon in the All-Ireland final in 1946 – that too had a melodramatic climax.

The western champions led by two goals with four minutes to go: twice Kerry put the ball into their net – and drew. They won the replay.

And of course we heard about Kerry and Offaly in the All-Ireland final in 1982 – the year of the five-in-a-row that never was. Kerry led by five points with about that many minutes remaining – the rest is history.

And of course there was the All-Ireland semi-final in 1977. Kerry seemed to be coasting to victory: two goals in as many minutes wrote a new scenario.

I remember all those romantic codas – but for me yesterday afternoon's score-quake recalled a game not far from Croke Park but in Anfield. It happened on a May evening a few years ago, in the last game in the topmost division of the Football League.

Arsenal came to Lancashire in what seemed a hopeless position – they needed not only to win but to win by two goals to take the title.

With five minutes to go their cause seemed hopeless: Liverpool were coasting home. And then came a goal; within a minute there came another goal – the home team hadn't time to recover.

Next to me a little girl of about sixteen put her head between her hands and wept hysterically. She might have lost her family in one fell swoop – or, if you like, in two fell swoops.

Yesterday evening I heard that same kind of sobbing again – a little lass bedecked in green and white was inconsolable.

Most of my neighbours on the Canal Terrace were from Limerick – their collective trauma brought me back to the All-Ireland final of 1982.

The green-and-white army shuffled up to the Canal Bridge in almost total silence. They were goal-shocked and point-shocked and heartbroken and mind-broken – this was sport at its most cruel.

On the way down to the city centre I met some Offaly folk – they too were almost silent. For once I fully acknowledged what it is to be dumbfounded.

And in the long nights in the run-up to Christmas this amazing game will be parsed and analysed whenever hurling people meet.

You could feed all the relevant data into the most sophisticated computer and end up no wiser. The All-Ireland hurling final of 1994 will defy the microchip – and even the microfish.

It will not explain why Limerick were dominant for all but two spells amounting to little more than fifteen minutes and yet lost. And not only did they lose – they lost by a goal and three points. It passed understanding.

Folklore will say that Kerry were Darbyed in 1982 – yesterday you could say that Limerick were Dooleyed.

When Johnny stood over that free in the sixty-fourth minute, the logic of the juncture demanded that he go for a point. Matt Connor in a similar situation in 1982 had twice chosen to put the ball over the bar. Johnny cast logic to the wind and drove the ball low into the net.

Suddenly Limerick's lead of five points was down to two – the rope had become alarmingly thin. A minute later that rope was in shreds. Limerick fought back bravely – but for them Offaly were the Fateful County.

And you couldn't help feeling that it had all been scripted by those pranksome gods who sometimes seem to preside over sport.

Those late five points seemed the stuff of dreams; for Offaly they were like manna – for Limerick they were like arrows piercing the soul.

And followers of the green and white will – when they recover their minds – argue that Offaly's three goals were tinged with good fortune. And perhaps they were – many goals in hurling are.

The first came in the fourth minute. Joe Quaid parried Johnny Dooley's penalty; Joe Dooley pounced like a hawk on a chicken too far from her mother.

The twenty-one-yards free that brought goal number two was not a rocket in the style of Nicky Rackard – it stole in between two camáns.

The third goal came after a long ball that bounced twice before Pat O'Connor cut it to the net from twelve yards.

Spare a thought for Damien Quigley: he scored two goals and two points – and ended up in the losers' enclosure. As Shakespeare said: 'There's a destiny that shapes our end, rough-hew them how we will.'

And yet when all is said and done (that'll be the day, not to mention the night) you must give credit to Offaly. A lesser team might have lapsed into ragged despair as Limerick pulled away into what seemed an unassailable lead in the last quarter.

The Midlanders kept their shape, more or less – they owed much to Johnny Pilkington and Brian Whelehan. Martin Hanamy is an inspiring captain but even he seemed resigned to playing out time doggedly.

I had a ringside view of him in the second half – as the clock on the Canal Terrace showed a quarter to five, his face seemed devoid of hope. And then Johnny Dooley's moment of inspiration made Offaly's garden flower – soon it became the Promised Land.

When Limerick's tragedy is coolly analysed, two factors will stand out. They perpetrated eighteen wides, many from very good positions. And they overdid the passing: sometimes they passed when a shot would have made more sense.

And yet if you wished to name a man of the match, you would look through the ranks of the losers.

Davie Clarke would be the choice of many; Mike Houlihan and Ger Hegarty and Ciaran Carey would be strong contenders; you could find backers for Damien Quigley and Gary Kirby.

The game of coming up with counterparts of this disaster will be a boon for the licensing trade.

And we remember how Jersey Joe Walcott was cruising past Joe Louis but ran into a late punch-storm.

You could go on and on – but I doubt if you will find a real counterpart to the collective trauma suffered by Limerick and their following yesterday.

Yes, 'Limerick You're a Lady' – but, I fear, a lady in waiting.

Evening Press

DAVID CAMPESE

Kerry didn't take part in the All-Ireland of 1935; they withdrew for a reason which was palpably dishonest – the stated reason was to protest at the detention of certain prisoners; the real reason was that most of the great team of the late twenties and early thirties had retired.

Kerry could have fielded a team but they wouldn't have been contenders – and so the county board made a virtue out of necessity.

Perhaps they felt that the competition would be devalued without them; the All-Ireland of 1935 was one of the best ever. It reached its climax when Cavan beat Kildare in a great final and thus got their first taste of the Golden Apple.

The United States withdrew from the Moscow Olympics; their reason was even more dishonest than that of Kerry in 1935: the Soviet invasion of Afghanistan was the pretext. It was all right for the US to have a dirty paw in almost every state in Latin America . . .

The Olympics went on and were a great success; the medals weren't devalued by the absence of the greatest athletic power on earth.

South Africa didn't take part in the inaugural World Cup in rugby, nor in the second; they had no choice. The exclusion of the Springboks was another example of dishonesty; racial discrimination wasn't confined to South Africa. Those invited to the tournament in the Antipodes included Zimbabwe and Fiji.

Mr Mugabe is hardly a model democrat; a little while before that first World Cup a reputable London paper had provided convincing evidence to prove that his soldiers were engaged in genocide in Matabeleland.

And a few weeks before that competition the democratically elected parliament of Fiji had been overthrown because it contained a majority of Indian origin.

Fiji went on playing in the finals; nobody objected despite daily reports of physical violence making life horrendous for the Fijian Indians.

The exclusion of South Africa from the Olympics was monstrously hypocritical. There are degrees of evil; athletes from far more oppressive regimes competed without a murmur of dissent. The hounding of Zola Budd was particularly vicious; never did we witness a worse example of guilt by association.

I am glad to see South Africa back in the mainstream; their absence took from the two World Cups; unlike Kerry and the US they hadn't opted out.

In a sense the 1995 World Cup will be the first World Cup; I need hardly add that the Springboks will leave no pebble unturned to win it.

Their display in Sydney last weekend was a declaration of intent; they beat the official world champions on their own battleground.

The ecstasy of their little travelling Kop was a joy to behold; they had witnessed their warriors vanquish a great power in a mighty battle; for good measure, it had been a marvellously sporting encounter.

The Australians will point to the absence of injured stars Michael Lynagh and Willie Ofahengaue, and with excellent cause.

Lynagh is a superb out-half and a place-kicker of whom William Tell would approve; Marty Roebuck took over the place-kicking last week; he planted the first three penalties but then seemed to lose his touch – he missed a few crucial kicks.

Australia's deputy out-half, Scott Bowen, came trailing clouds of glory but didn't seem to be on the same wavelength as his inside partner, Nick Farr-Jones, generally deemed the best scrum-half in the business.

Ofahengaue's deputy, Garrick Morgan, also came with a great reputation but looked what he is – a second-row forward who has been cast as a wing-forward.

Ofahengaue is already a legend; he is from one of the southern islands but the Aussies have embraced him to their hearts; he is a mobile giant whose bursts take a great deal of containing; appropriately enough, he drives a bulldozer in his spare time.

The Springboks have made amazing improvements since they came out of bondage; a year ago the Australians beat them 3–26 in Cape Town.

Incidentally, they failed twice recently to defeat France – even though playing at home; the French were short seven regulars in both games – that for us here in Ireland is a rather alarming fact of football life.

I do not know if someone was named man of the match last weekend; there was a very obvious candidate for a new honour – non-man of the match.

If anyone ever tells you that David Campese is the best winger in the world, try to keep yourself from exploding into ribald laughter and say a prayer for the poor devil or deviless.

Campese is one of the wonders of the rugby world – and for two reasons; his virtues are as remarkable as his failings. As a ball-carrier I have never seen his equal; he makes the flight path of a snipe seem utterly predictable.

When he sets off, nobody has the ghost of a notion whither he is going, least of all himself; some day someone will chart one of his longer try-scoring runs – it will mesmerise the known world.

Alas, the most famous Italian–Australian reminds us of the ancient joke about the priest who gave a reference to an emigrating parishioner: 'I have known Paddy Murphy all his life and can guarantee that he is capable of anything.'

There is no such thing as an own try in rugby but the bould David is working overtime to create the concept. He handed – literally – South Africa a try last weekend; he was equally guilty when he helped the Lions to a victory over Australia; he was helping in the enquiries after France knocked the Wallabies out of the World Cup in 1987.

And you may remember that he would have been the villain if the Aussies had lost to us in the World Cup in 1991 – as they nearly did; as it was, he ended up a hero.

Sunday World

'THE GREATEST CROWD-PULLERS SINCE GENE TUNNEY AND JACK DEMPSEY'

MEATH AND DUBLIN IN THE LEINSTER FOOTBALL FINAL, 2002

Dublin and Meath are the greatest crowd-pullers since Gene Tunney and Jack Dempsey. Sunday's game was not sudden death, but Croke Park was crowded. When those neighbours meet, it is always sudden life.

Meath are fierce competitors. Perhaps it is something in the grass – they would turn a Communion breakfast into an eating contest. When Dublin take the field against the men from the Royal County, it is less a game than another battle in a long-continuing war.

Sunday's meeting couldn't have had a better setting. The new Hogan Stand was being unveiled – and for good measure we got our first view of the new pitch.

The weather came right: the afternoon reminded us that we were in Midsummer. The pitch looked well. How it will stand up to heavy rain is the question. The experts who put it down are confident. We hope that they are right.

The Hill was an ocean of blue; I surveyed it with mixed feelings. How long more will it be with us? Seemingly its days are numbered. We are told that it is due to go the way of all concrete and steel.

I had a good seat on Sunday but I occasionally looked towards the Canal End with nostalgia. I more or less grew up there. I was part of a little community. Our meeting place is gone forever. A stadium without a terrace is like a living room without a fire. Terraces are like the yeast in the loaf.

I have happy memories of the Kop at Anfield and the Stretford End at Old Trafford and the North Bank at

Highbury. I could go on and include the terrace in Barcelona's Nou Camp.

There is a common belief that because something is modern it is better.

It isn't too long since the Hill was torn down and replaced by a better and safer version. Seemingly it is to be demolished again and a terrace put in its place. How long will it remain a terrace?

People may feel that Sunday's game was overshadowed by the World Cup – it wasn't that way at all. Indeed the heady tournament in the Far East enhanced rather than diminished the afternoon in Dublin 3.

I felt that I was sitting down to a plate of black pudding and fried potatoes after weeks of dining on haute cuisine.

And, not for the first time, a curious question invaded my mind: isn't it unnatural to see men using their heads rather than their hands to control the ball . . . Women in Africa use their heads for carrying things – and thus walk with wonderful grace. That is another story.

Heading the ball rather than handling it hardly makes sense. And yet it is the most distinctive part of the game that is played in every nook and cranny of the earth.

Another stray thought ambushed me on Sunday. We watched thirty-two countries from all five continents over the last few weeks – and yet apart from their varying colours of skin they all looked the same. They all play 4–4–2 or 4–3–3 or 4–5–1 or 3–4–3 or 3–5–2.

The reason of course is simple: most coaches all around the globe are from Europe and South America. They all preach the same true faith: such apostates as Brian Clough and Malcolm Allison are not invited to manage national teams.

Dublin, I am told, have changed managers eight times in the twenty years. Can you argue that there is any significant difference between them? Paddy Cullen favoured the long ball more than the rest – I cannot think of any other difference.

Tommy Lyons is the latest to be cast in the role of rain-maker. He made his debut recently in Carlow's Dr Cullen Park. The game against Wexford couldn't be used in evidence against him: it was played in the afterglow of our game with Cameroon – Matt Holland's goal was still reverberating.

Last Sunday was the real maiden voyage; this was the First Chance Inn. The consensus was that Dublin had slain the dragon; no longer will they look to Meath as their bogey team.

I recall what used to be said about a certain politician: you could bury him at a crossroads and drive a stake through his heart and he would spring up. Well, eventually he didn't; nevertheless, I deem Sean Boylan and his bravehearts as still a power in the land.

They were almost at full strength on Sunday. Only Ollie Murphy didn't start. Dublin had Paul Curran and Dessie Farrell nursing injuries.

If Tommy Lyons is a revolutionary, it wasn't obvious on Sunday. If asked to advance one word to sum up Dublin's approach, I would invoke 'sensible'. They played a limited form of the possession game; they didn't pass for the sake of passing.

When they transferred the ball, it usually went to a comrade in a better position. Their general plan seemed to be clear – work the ball into space.

Meath were upset when they lost midfielder John Cullinane at a moment when the game had hardly settled. They won enough possession but wasted much of it. They played their best football in the second half; helped perhaps by a maverick wind, they encamped for spells in the railway half.

Point by point whittled the lead down to a goal – then Dublin's second and furiously disputed goal sealed the game. The final tally – 2–11 to 0–10 – exaggerated Dublin's superiority.

The texture of play was fairly good. The pace was fast. The level of skill wasn't too bad – except for the shooting.

We saw the usual pulling and dragging, but no more so than in the World Cup, where this type of play was far above the international average.

Dublin were desperately unlucky not to beat Kerry in their first meeting last year. Maurice Fitzgerald's point that robbed them is already part of legend. They played with great fire in those two games in Semple Stadium.

We saw the same fire last Sunday. Meath of course always meet fire with fire – and sometimes with brimstone. If Dublin's approach differed from that of last year, it was in the way their forwards interchanged positions.

Even Darren Fay, Meath's brilliant full-back, was at times caught in two minds – and sometimes in three. Meath, inspired by Graham Geraghty, fought back with typical tenacity, but it wasn't their day.

Sunday World

'JOHN ALDRIDGE SALMONED UP AND KNOCKED THE BALL INTO RAY HOUGHTON'S FLIGHT PATH'

IRELAND BEAT ENGLAND IN EURO 1988

One day when I was a small boy, I ventured far beyond the approved limits with my greyhound and my terriers and for a little while had the alarming and exciting experience of being lost.

I found myself in what at seven Winters and six Summers I thought was a forest. Now I know it was only a wood. And when I came back home, I tried to tell my elders about the wonders I had experienced but I couldn't find the right words.

Long after that marvellous day I read a passage in the letters of Vincent Van Gogh in which he expressed his frustration at experiencing visions which he couldn't depict. The great painter spoke about the wall between what you can see and what you can express. I understood.

In Stuttgart yesterday as I came across the yellow river called the Neckar, I recalled the trauma. I had experienced a momentous occasion but I knew that nothing short of an epic symphony could capture it.

There have been better games of football but never in our sporting history has there been such an occasion and such a fallout of emotions.

Ron Delany's gold nugget was sweet but less widely celebrated. Communications are infinitely better now.

The country rejoiced when Barry McGuigan won the world title but it was expected. Yesterday's result was all the more heart-expanding because few if any foresaw it.

In time people will ask one another: 'Where were you when Ray Houghton scored the goal that gave us victory over England in the Euro Cup?' And otherwise honest people will persuade themselves that they were in the Neckar Stadium; it will replace the GPO of 1916 as a place of harmless dreams.

Word came to us here last night that in Dublin they were dancing in the streets; I wouldn't be surprised that in Donegal they were dancing on the water.

The All-Ireland has never gone to Tír Chonaill but yesterday provided a huge compensation; our especial heroes have deep roots in that fair county.

Ray Houghton, whose father is from Buncrana, scored that precious goal. Paddy Bonner from the Rosses prevented several.

In a way it was Goodison Park in 1949 all over again; England had far more chances but a mixture of bad finishing and superb goal-minding cost them the day.

Pat has gone into folklore with Tommy Godwin. It was his day, so much so that his only mistake led to his best save.

A swallow would have been hard put to it to fly through his goal-space; so big an object as a football would have needed a mind and a will of its own to elude him.

Before this tournament began the experts were saying that the three best keepers were in our group – Peter Shilton, Rinat Dasayev and Hans van Breukelen. Now they can make it four.

And if ever you say to Peter Beardsley and John Barnes that a goalkeeper can destroy you, they will surely agree; for them it was like the recent Cup Final all over again.

The difference was that England had far more time to recover; this game could be divided into two parts – the first six minutes and the remainder.

The Irish began with a confidence and a creativity that belied their status as seven-to-two outsiders; their goal came after six minutes of bold and intelligent tactics.

From the moment that England restarted play, we witnessed a new game; more and more the Irish conceded midfield until at times only Frank Stapleton and John Aldrige looked like attackers, and even then only remotely so.

For long periods in the first half England stroked the ball around in movements that contained a dozen or more passes – goals seemed inevitable.

Bryan Robson was dictating play – and in those multi-pass movements he often figured two or three or four times.

The Irish defenders looked vulnerable, especially Mick McCarthy; he was wonderful in the air but dangerously impulsive when the ball was on the ground.

Both he and Kevin Moran were often beaten for speed but always there was someone to come to their assistance. And yet at the end of the day the two mid-backs could be proud; their fierce courage and their will to win inspired their colleagues.

It was a harrowing day for the Irish supporters; the ecstasy engendered by that marvellous goal soon turned to gnawing apprehension as wave after wave flowed towards Bonner's posts.

Chris Waddle was exuding ideas; Gary Stevens and Kenny Sansom were making deep inroads; you felt that Gary Lineker would surely get a few of those chances which usually he ravenously snaps up. But for this brilliant goal-smith it was to be a tragic day; he snatched at some great opportunities – and when he was on target he saw Bonner had seemed to shrink the goal-space.

The Irish supporters were mightily relieved to hear the half-time whistle or at least to see the referee's signal. This game was played in a sound-storm.

And those I met during the interval shared my fears that our warriors couldn't hold on – it needed only one slip for our lead to be wiped away.

Bobby Robson at the press conference said that one

score might have brought several; it was hard to disagree.

But he must take some of the blame; the English attacks recalled a famous dictum beloved of Irish navvies: 'It isn't how high you raise the pick – it's how deep you sink it.'

Their movements were pretty but predictable; the ball was being striked gracefully in short passes but more often than not going back and forth rather than forward.

Paul McGrath and Ronnie Whelan powerfully augmented the mid-backs; Houghton scurried here and there like a little Dutch boy with several leaking dam walls to mend.

In the frenetic excitement you had little time for analysis but I believe that a video would show how effective were Chris Morris and Chris Hughton. Both kept house quietly and tidily. Barnes gave Morris a relentless examination but the young Celt passed with honours.

Houghton is generally deemed to be one of yesterday's men but he played with a mixture of dash and wisdom; this was the Chris of five years ago.

As England's multi-pass movements began to look more and more like misguided tours, Bobby Robson must have felt the need for a public confession. It took the form of calling Neil Webb ashore and sending in Glenn Hoddle.

And thus the last half-hour became more and more agonising for the Irish supporters; the reprieved man played brilliantly.

Before his advent the great danger to The Republic had come from the ball played into the space behind the back four. Hoddle is famous for the long lifted pass; he excelled at it yesterday in his little stint.

As time went by and England's score stood at zero, Bobby Robson's mind seemed to go on the blink; eventually he sent on Mark Hateley for Beardsley and thus took out the greatest menace to the Irish.

Despite England's territorial dominance this game could have ended with the same scoreline as that at Goodison Park on that famous day long ago. Twice in the second half the Irish almost went two up. Aldridge risked life and limb to get in a flying header that went just over. And Whelan with a close-range shot grazed the bar with Shilton stranded.

And yet but for Bonner's brilliance we might have had to be content with a draw or discontent with worse. He was great all through – in the last ten minutes he brought off two miracles.

When Lineker got inside the back four and closed in from a little to the keeper's left Bonner kept the shot out with his legs. Then in the eighty-eighth minute he made his only mistake in this tumultuous day.

From a free-kick on the left and near the corner flag Hoddle curled the ball in the direction of the penalty spot; Bonner advanced but knew he couldn't get to it – and as he back-pedalled, Lineker got in a powerful header; somehow the keeper got a touch and turned the ball over the bar.

About ninety seconds remained – they gave the Irish camp a sample of infinity. And when at last Siegfried Kirschen signalled full time, the supporters were so exhausted that they could hardly express their joy. It had seemed an eternity since that header had found the net. It was a goal worthy of this historic victory.

Tony Galvin hooked the ball so that it came down about ten yards from goal. England defender Kenny Sansom made a mess of his attempted clearance and Aldridge salmoned up and knocked the ball into Ray Houghton's flight path as he came in from the right; his angled header put the ball between Shilton and the far post.

Once again a goal from Jack Charlton's team had come from a player outside the front-runners but you couldn't fault Aldridge or Stapleton. They were isolated so much at times but could hardly have played better. And Galvin silenced his critics with a brave and skilful display.

Jack Charlton was remarkably quiet at the press conference: he knew better than most that Lady Luck had taken us by the hand.

Bobby Robson looked almost serene; he reminded me of the old mother in Synge's *Riders to the Sea* after her last son had been drowned; the worst had happened him – the future could bring no greater disaster.

In the aftermath of this marvellous victory, I heard many wild and whirling words. One eminently sensible man said that our inferiority complex had been buried forever – and he was talking about more than football.

My colleague, Chris Dooley, was working at his first big assignment of this kind and I said: 'You brought us luck.' Chris is from Offaly – he said: 'It makes up for Seamus Darby.'

And someone else said: 'Jack has landed his biggest fish.'

I will leave the last words to Kevin Moran. They were uttered in a hotel deep in the forest: 'I'd love to be down in Kerry tonight.'

Evening Press

KERRY PLAY DUBLIN IN THE SEMI-FINAL OF THE ALL-IRELAND FOOTBALL CHAMPIONSHIP

Do you remember the fourth Sunday of September two years ago? Do you remember how Kerry beat Dublin in a manner that left no room for argument?

And afterwards everyone (well, almost everyone) said that Dublin could never match Kerry – the lads in green and gold were 'born footballers'.

And Kerry were, according to popular opinion, to go on and farm the All-Ireland for five or six or seven years.

And some of the Dublin team were too old and would have to retire from the fray and take up gardening or the fretless banjo or whatever and ask for free travel from CIÉ.

Well, it didn't happen that way at all. At Croke Park yesterday much the same Dublin team, including all those senior citizens, shattered myths that like Humpty Dumpty can never be put together again.

This was a day that will live forever (well, for a few thousand years) in folk memory by Liffeyside. And even though this Dublin team has won two All-Irelands, Croke Park has never known such ecstasy in blue as it did about a quarter to five yesterday afternoon.

Then as Dublin stole Kerry's formula and came from behind with a marvellous goal, the roar carried up the canal to Dalymount Park.

And there those that preferred to listen to the rock than watch the Blues went mad when the good news came through and gave a new version of the Dalymount roar.

This was a game that the wildest writer of sports fiction would not dare to invent. Simple figures give an indication: Kerry were two points ahead with only six minutes remaining – and yet were comprehensively beaten.

And how did it happen? The answer is that in an

166

astounding last paragraph Dublin proved beyond doubt what many have long suspected – that they are the greatest goal-smiths in the modern game.

A goal is worth only three points in cold figures – its psychological value is incalculable.

One remembers Anton O'Toole's great drive to the net that so rattled Cork in the semi-final in 1974.

That was the declaration that Dublin had come of age. They have scored many a great goal since then – but none greater than the three they sank yesterday. The first was the least spectacular but the most important.

Dublin had gone in at the interval three points in arrears and rather lucky to be not irrevocably behind. They came out as if reborn. Kevin Moran within seconds of the restart declared war with an eighty-yard run and a shot – Paud O'Mahony saved.

From the clearance Dublin roared back – Tony Hanahoe with a sweet flick put John McCarthy clear – and he put the ball into the net under the noses of the folk who live on the Hill.

And that started the greatest thirty-odd minutes of football seen in Croke Park since the days when you could buy a pint for nine old pence.

Suddenly both sides put aside the messing that had made the first half so ragged and began to play as if they enjoyed football. And Dublin, who had stuttered for the first twenty-five minutes, now articulated with golden tongue. This was the day when for their forwards at last it all came right.

For a long time now most of the front six have been living uneasily on their names. The greatest compliment one can pay them on yesterday's display is to say that Jimmy Keaveney played his typical game – and yet was the least distinguished. The other five played splendidly – the fact that they put three goals and twelve points past a vaunted defence is proof of that.

Anton O'Toole repented of his sins – and was the one Dublin forward who from first to last did not put a foot or a ball astray.

Bobby Doyle, who has spent most of the Summer running into nowhere, suddenly decided that the ball has a part in the game too.

He played with his old alarming simplicity – and the single point he had to his credit at the end gives no indication of his contribution.

Dave Hickey had an untidy first half but was always working with the fury that made him so valuable three years ago.

Six minutes from the end he had what was surely the greatest moment of his career.

Kerry were two points ahead and the Hill was silent as Brian Mullins sent in a line ball from midway and under the Hogan Stand.

Anton O'Toole fielded it and shot – the ball hit a defender and bounded to Tony Hanahoe.

A swift pass gave Dave a little space and he unleashed a tremendous shot that left Paud O'Mahony holding air.

Tony Hanahoe's part in that goal was typical – he played all through with great intelligence and total unselfishness.

The remaining forward, John McCarthy, did little spectacular – but he forced Jimmy Deenihan to stay at home when he was needed badly to bolster a leaky half-back line. Here only Denis Moran, who had a magnificent game, gave nothing away.

Tim Kenneally was obviously the worse for a few knocks he got – and should have come off. Ger Power once again gave evidence that by instinct he is poacher rather than gamekeeper. And Kerry failed too at midfield – Paud O'Shea was grossly miscast. He is a deputy, not a sheriff.

Brian Mullins held the stage here – though it was hard

to know whether he was playing the villain or the hero. But about one thing there could be no doubt – his fielding was not the least of Dublin's assets.

One was reminded of a maxim uttered by John Dowling, Kerry's midfield hero of yesteryear. Once when he was on the fringe of a debate about the modern game, when the talk was about running off the ball and all that, he said: 'There are a lot of high balls to be caught in Croke Park yet.'

Bernard Brogan exemplified that maxim too – why he was only called in as a substitute is a mystery. He played immaculately – and his late goal that put Kerry over the cliff had long been invoiced.

Dublin's backs all had their moments of glory – but for consistent brilliance the honours must go to Robbie Kelleher and Pat O'Neill.

The talk among Kerry folk after the game was not unlaced with criticism of their warriors – you would not have thought that they were in front with only six minutes to go. But no one could deny the worth of the full-back line – and when we say that Ger O'Keeffe was the best, it is high praise indeed.

Most disappointing and disappointed Kerryman was Pat Spillane. In the Munster final he had roamed the field – yesterday he was like a cowboy who had lost his horse. Sean Walsh was brilliant in everything he did – and that included a typical goal and the best point of the match. Afterwards we heard it said that Kerry would have been well advised to cut out their pretty football and pass to him direct. We agree – but that is the wisdom of hindsight. Do you remember the Ancient Mariner?

> A sadder and a wiser man,
> He woke the morrow morn.

Evening Press

Cork Play Wexford in the All-Ireland
Hurling Final

There is something I long desired to see and never will – an account by John Rafferty of a big hurling match.

We tend to take this remarkable game too much for granted: a fresh eye would more sharply perceive its blend of bravery and hardihood and delicate skills.

John went across his final river last Friday: his shrewd and humorous and quietly passionate pieces will brighten our Sundays no more.

He would have enjoyed Croke Park yesterday: when a man's understanding of one field-game is deep – and his knowledge of soccer was unsurpassed – he has an intuition of all.

He would have enjoyed too the craic in the pubs on Sunday night – 'craic' is a word as Scottish as John was himself.

The early swallows from Cork and Wexford were in town – mostly lads and lasses who fraternised freely in an intermingling of red and white and purple and gold and whose thoughts were more on love than on war.

What matter that tomorrow was Waterloo: there was drink to be sent down the red lane and songs to be thrown into the air and hearts to be assailed and conquered if only for a few hours.

But not all was gaiety. The hard facts of life are not suspended for an All-Ireland – and we met an old acquaintance whose most fervent hope was that Sunday would yield a few showers of rain.

And he estimated that about two o'clock it would do most good. From this you will gather that he was not a farmer worried about his parched acres but a seller of tickets who knew well that a threat of inclement weather would turn people's thoughts from terrace to stand.

His prayers were not heard but he did quite nicely and is looking forward to a few weeks in Spain after the bonanza of the Kerry and Dublin epic.

It is strange that Croke Park is not tight with people for the hurling All-Ireland – part of the reason is the faint interest in the ancient game in the capital itself.

Croke Park yesterday was awash with accents from distant streets and fields – in a way it was not unlike being at Wembley for the final of the Rugby League Cup.

That sensation is familiar – it is so long since Dublin have been in a hurling final themselves.

Yesterday there was an added dimension of strangeness: Wexford had beaten Kilkenny by seventeen points on their way to the final, a feat approximate to Norwich beating Liverpool by five goals in the English Cup, and yet their right to be there was in question.

However the famous non-goal that was a goal did not unduly worry their followers; they felt that if fortune had smiled on them, it was not before its time.

Early comers yesterday saw a very solid Tipperary minor team defeat Kilkenny comprehensively by a tactic that has long seemed almost a black-and-amber copyright – the point from far out.

Conditions at three o'clock when the seniors came out were excellent: the light came diffused through white clouds – there was no glare; there may have been some breath of wind but it was imperceptible.

Cork's young commandos had made a minor Kop of the Hill and were hand-dancing with red-and-white scarves and chanting extravagant promises about never walking alone.

Across the fence under the scoreboard was a less coherent Wexford counterpart.

As Tony Doran went to his position in front of the Hill

171

goal he got a hero's welcome: he seemed a Horatio not on the bridge but at the helm.

From the very start one was inclined to believe that the new-style sliothar is changing the game: in the third minute Denis Coughlan hit a left-hander wide from ninety yards – within seconds Ned Buggy pointed with a similar effort. And then in the fifth minute came Wexford delight: Tony Doran made a great high catch and sent an overhead hand-pass into the goalmouth – Martin Quigley cut it into the net.

After only six minutes Wexford were eight points ahead and playing as if the best was yet to come: their followers were settling down to bask in glory.

But Cork's hurlers are nothing if not big-hearted: Gerald McCarthy and Pat Moylan began to put things together in midfield and suddenly red-and-white waves swept towards Wexford's goal.

There was more fury than method in those early Cork attacks – but it was obvious that Ray Cummins had recaptured his old sharpness and Willie Murphy would not own the front of goal as he did against Kilkenny.

Cork began to nibble away point by point at Wexford's store. And in the twelfth minute their full-forward created a clear chance for a goal.

Cummins went out to his left to gather a lobbing ball and then sent a great hand-pass to Charlie McCarthy, who had circled inside him – he shot on the run and just over the bar.

Point by point Wexford's lead diminished. Just on the half-hour Cork got their first goal: a huge puck-out from Martin Coleman found Ray Cummins behind the defence – his hurley was hooked away from him but he kicked the ball to the net.

The teams went in at half-time level on scores and warmly applauded. The atmosphere during the interval was of quiet tension.

Wexford started the second half as they had the first: Tony Doran put up his hand in a thicket of ash, brought down the ball, and with a full swing of the hurley sent it to the net.

But two minutes later Cork got an even greater goal: Gerald McCarthy first-timed a ball to Brendan Cummins, who sent it into the path of Charlie McCarthy – a lovely half-volley angled it into the net.

Now came a period when the dominance of Cork's midfield slackened – and Wexford again had the winning look.

The loudest roar from their followers came in the twelfth minute of the half, when Ned Buggy sent in a long sideline ball that Tony Doran fumbled but that ran on for Mick Butler to collect and palm past Coleman.

Cork at this stage looked on the ropes: Colm Doran and Mick Jacobs were at once defenders and auxiliary midfield – but Wexford's abundant possession produced too few scores.

The great winged points that had dethroned Kilkenny did not come; it was Cork that sent over most of the long ones yesterday and thus kept in touch even when outplayed.

Wexford in this period of dominance could never get more than two points ahead. Time and again pucks from scoring distance dropped short, possibly due to an obsession with goals.

No more goals came. Mick Butler had one great chance when he was through, ball in hand, but somehow fumbled. And both he and John Murphy might have had penalties – but the referee allowed play go on in dubious application of the advantage.

After Butler's miss one sensed desperation in Wexford's attacks. Even Tony Doran seemed affected: his earlier subtlety deserted him and he charged at goal like a man who had lost the key and was trying to batter down the door. And most surprising of all at this stage was the fading away of the Quigleys – there were times when Tony Doran must have felt alone.

And yet at that juncture when watches are being looked at, Wexford were still two points ahead. And then Mick Butler missed the simplest of frees.

From that moment Cork sprang back. Jim Barry Murphy, up to then almost unseen, began to show his sweet skills. And in the last ten minutes Cork swept over six points without reply.

Wexford were left to bemoan lost chances. They were the heroes of this season's championship campaign, but not the winners.

Yesterday they could not maintain the magical flow that had swamped Kilkenny. Cork fought too fiercely all the way for that. Between them they fashioned the best final in twenty years.

Evening Press

'YOU KNOW WHO WOODY IS – HE DOESN'T MAKE MOVIES'

MUNSTER RUGBY

There is a carefully nurtured myth that implies that when Limerick rugby players get up as far as the Red Cow or pass through Ballyfermot on the way to Kingsbridge, they lapse into the language of the nursery and go: 'He, haw, he, hem, we smell the blood of Dublin men.'

We have been brainwashed to believe that the warriors from Limerick are physically and mentally harder than their Dublin counterparts – and Saturday's games at Lansdowne Road and Donnybrook seem to bear this out. A little journey down the coast, a Limerick treble was completed by Young Munster.

You can be sure that the rail journey to Limerick on Saturday evening was a lively voyage; it was much more than a train of thought. I have never been a party to this myth or, if you like, to this mystique.

The grand finale to last year's All-Ireland League should have at best shaken it; Young Munster pride themselves on their hardihood – but St Mary's met fire with fire – and brimstone with brimstone.

I watched Old Wesley and Garryowen on Saturday; the Light Blues won clearly but not because they are a different species to the men who fight out of Dublin 4.

The main source of their win was far greater experience behind the scrum and comprehensive tackling by all sections of their team.

Add in the support of their travelling army; the coaching from the sidelines was unremitting.

Garryowen are now level at the top of the table with Blackrock; the Dublin club have a game in hand and a much better points difference.

Garryowen's aficionados – that means every man and woman and child in their following – cannot be happy about their warriors' performance.

Their backs – and especially Dan Lackin – were not as steady as usual when the ball was kicked deep into their territory; the pack were surprisingly ragged in the line-out. And Old Wesley could claim that luck didn't ride postilion with them.

They lost Niall Farren, their most experienced back and best place-kicker, after twenty-five minutes. Then a few minutes after the interval they lost right-wing Michael McArdle.

Scrum-half Des Jackson was posted to replace him. It seemed a strange move; he had been playing brilliantly – and was Wesley's most likely creator of a try; on the west wing he was in exile.

Wesley suffered another frown from the gods; midway through the first half they might have had a penalty try for obstruction; seven points might have made a great change in the game's texture.

It must be stressed, however, that from kick-off to Mr Stephen Hilditch's final blow, the Limerick team were the more convincing.

Wesley played with an admirable sense of adventure but such was Garryowen's tackling that most of the moves initiated by Adrian Hawe did little more than go across the pitch.

You felt that their scores would have to come from penalties or drops or from a kick and chase! It was from such a ploy that Nick Johnson was impeded when he looked certain to score.

Garryowen began with a light wind behind them as they played towards the church goal and went ahead in the tenth minute.

Wesley failed to deal with a high kick into their right-hand corner and conceded a scrum; as it broke up, prop

Ciaran Ronan struggled over for a try; Kenny Smith failed to convert.

Then came two bad moments for Wesley. First Mr Hilditch failed to give the penalty try; a few minutes later, just a little past the middle of the half, came a try that gave Garryowen's followers uninhibited delight.

Wesley were lax in allowing Philip Danaher to make a little break from his own ten-yard line; he gave to Richard Wallace on his right.

He rocketed away close to touch and got to within ten yards of the try-line! Keith Wood took a short pass and touched down. Smith's kick failed but ten points was a good lead.

Hawe reduced it with a penalty; Smith restored it with the last kick of the half. The two exchanged penalties in the same order in the second half – and so it ended at 6–16.

Garryowen in this period lost three clear try chances by bad judgement – and, in all fairness to Wesley, through good tackling. Wesley battled to the end but Garryowen's defence frustrated them.

The Limerick team must worry about the line-out; Richard Costello and Mick Coghlan brought off some good catches but there was far too much untidy tipping down.

Wesley did fairly well in that department, mainly Dave Bursey and Greg Duffy and Johnson; Henry Hurley did much good sweeping.

Wing-forwards Robbie Love and Chris Pim often essayed to set up attacks from the scrums but found little room around the flanks.

Garryowen's half-backs, Steve McIvor and Pat Murphy, were neatly competent; Danaher was the best midfielder back on view.

Paul Hogan was Garryowen's best forward; he excelled in the hidden agenda. Wood was in his element, sometimes in the heart of battle, sometimes acting as an extra back.

If you happened to be in the midst of the Garryowen Kop on Saturday, you would have heard a few old-fashioned nicknames, kind of. Hoagy has nothing to do with the man who gave us Stardust and Buttermilk Sky – it refers to Paul Hogan. Danier is Philip Danaher, Skiver is Steve McIvor. And of course you know who Woody is – he doesn't make movies.

Incidentally, Ulster has produced the last three All-Ireland champions in Gaelic football; Munster has produced the three All-Ireland champions in rugby. Can Pat O'Neill's warriors and Blackrock make it a Leinster double in 1994?

Sunday World

'A Day of Magic for Edel Byrne, the Sprite from Magheracloone'

Monaghan Beat Waterford in the Ladies' All-Ireland Football Final, 1997

About half-past two on Sunday I was in the cavern under the Hogan Stand and experienced a heart-warming spectacle: about thirty young girls in blue and gold were embracing in a wild circle and chanting: 'Campiones, campiones, campiones! Olé, olé, olé!'

This was a nice example of how cultures influence one another. Longford had just won the All-Ireland Junior Football final; it was the county's first.

It is a long time since the heart of the Midlands had been in the sporting headlines – not since Brendan Barden and his merry men won the National League in 1966. That was a great team: they might have won the All-Ireland if they hadn't shown Kerry too much respect in the semi-final.

That was in 1968. Longford made a woeful start but made a marvellous recovery and lost by only two points. The victory of the girls was all the sweeter after that long absence; the celebrations were ecstatic. Longford beat Tyrone by 2–12 to 1–11.

Thus they completed the League and Championship double. Next season they will be in the senior ranks. Monaghan and Waterford sent out a message on Sunday that it will take a very good team to displace them from the upper branches of the tree.

In the senior game we saw a fair degree of skill and a high level of fitness. I have missed only one final since the first in 1974; in 1991 I had to cover the Finals of the World Cup in rugby – Sunday's game was the only one that ended in controversy.

The second half lasted for more than eleven minutes beyond normal time. This was a record for any game that I've ever seen in hurling or Gaelic football or ladies' football.

That stint of broken time seemed unreal: as it went on and on, I got a crazy idea that perhaps there was a new rule to get rid of a draw and that we were waiting for a clinching score – as in the final of the Euro Cup last year.

I might as well add that I hadn't a watch; I was depending on the clock above the Canal Terrace; this is hardly a precise chronometer – a colleague who was better equipped told me that the broken time extended to 11 minutes and 52 seconds.

I am sure that there is a full video of the game; it would be interesting to find out how much time was lost. There should be an independent timekeeper. This problem is not new: in the hurling final in 1996 full time was not played.

It was a pity that even the slightest smidgeon of controversy should be attached to this final – it was a memorable game. I wouldn't call it great because the first half was too one-sided – the second compensated in excitement and eventually in drama.

This final will be remembered for many reasons, most of all perhaps for the display of Edel Byrne – it was a day of magic for the sprite from Magheracloone, a townland near Carrickmacross.

It is a resounding name and, as far as I know, it means 'the Meadow on the Plain'. I might as well add that politicians needn't bother to ask Edel for her vote – she is only fifteen.

I know many able girls who have tried and tried for long and laborious years to win All-Ireland gold; Edel has achieved it in her first season as a senior – I can hear my friend Jason Sherlock laughing to himself.

Seemingly Waterford won the toss and chose to play

into the wind and the Railway Goal. They may have regretted their choice as Monaghan made a brilliant start that was crowned with a goal in the tenth minute.

As a ball bounced about ten yards from Waterford's citadel, it became a race between the keeper, Annalisa Crotty, and Edel – the forward got her hands to it and it rolled into the net.

Waterford compensated within a few minutes: a long high ball from Gerladine O'Ryan deceived friend and foe and floated into the net. The best goal came in the twenty-second minute.

An attack began in midfield; almost inevitably young Miss Byrne had a hand; she gave the final pass to Niamh Kindlon, who found a small parcel of space about eighteen yards from goal and gave the keeper little chance.

Monaghan led by 2–9 to 1–3 at the break; I was almost certain that the contest was over. Waterford would now have the wind; it was breathing diagonally from the Nally Stand and didn't seem of great significance.

Perhaps its effect was mainly in the mind; for whatever reason, Waterford now began to show why they have been such a dominant force since Kerry won their fabulous nine-in-a-row between 1982 and 1990.

Their revival resembled that of Mayo against Kerry in the recent final; there was a difference – they were translating their territorial superiority into scores.

Geraldine O'Ryan put Monaghan a point ahead in the fifty-ninth minute; their followers began to cheer them home but play went on and on in broken time and Jenny Greenan equalised in the sixty-fifth minute.

Most people expected Mr Finbarr O'Driscoll to signal full time but play went on – and when Edel put Monaghan ahead with a point, hundreds invaded the pitch.

It was cleared with little difficulty. Edel added another point. Now Waterford's case seemed hopeless; they needed a goal and obviously there could be only seconds left.

However, the final drama was to come; a long low ball went behind the back three and ran to Mary O'Donnell, in the middle and thirty yards from goal; she lost a precious fraction of time in picking it up and the posse cut her off at the pass. Thus it all ended at 2–15 to 1–16. Most of the Waterford girls were almost inconsolable.

Jenny Greenan and Linda Farrelly gave Monaghan midfield dominance in the first half; Martina O'Ryan and Noreen Walsh compensated in the second. Angela Larkin was Monaghan's leading forward; Geraldine O'Ryan was her counterpart.

This game emphasised two truths for me. The first is rather obvious: although soccer has penetrated into almost every nook and cranny in this island since the tel-evised World Cup Finals in 1996, it has had little effect on Gaelic football or on ladies' football.

The other truth may not be so obvious. It concerns the pick-up. The girls may pick up with their hands but there are times when a clean lift with the foot would be more profitable – some day some coach will see this.

Over fifteen thousand people paid into Croke Park on Sunday. The attendance is growing year by year. The best is yet to be.

Sunday World

'HERE ARE THE INGREDIENTS OF A THRILLER'

THE IRISH GRAND NATIONAL

'I left at half-time. Afraid I'd fall asleep. Went for a walk up the canal and had a few pints.' It is Easter Monday morning in a pub within sound of the machines that print this paper. Words are swarming.

The speaker who feared he would fall asleep at Dalymount is a countryman, long domiciled in Dublin, though by the way he kept referring to Dundalk's missed chances we doubt if he was at the game at all.

'Soccer,' he says, 'is too slow. Now take Hurling – the fastest game in the world.' The inevitable man in the corner says: ''Tis only the second-fastest. Now don't get me wrong – I have nothing against the GAA. But ice hockey is the first-fastest.'

A co-adjudicator adds: 'What use is Hurling? Can't see the ball half the time. All right if you grow up in some place like Tipperary. But we can't all be born in Tipperary.'

And so the ragged symphony goes on, soon to be superseded by speculation on the big event at Fairyhouse.

How the Irish Grand National has come on. Not too long ago it was a topic for only aficionados. The field was usually small and rather colourless – today's is nearly as full of characters as a Russian novel.

Its fascination is reflected in the pub talk. Ten Up's ailment is elevated into a major mystery. And there is extremely learned discussion on the state of the ground and how it affects some horses.

The man who nearly fell asleep at Dalymount again holds the floor. His rural background gives him status. ''Tis the horse with the high action or the horse with the small hooves – one can't act on hard ground or the other on soft.'

The man in the corner says: 'I don't know, I think a lot of it is only to cod the likes of us, if you know what I mean.' But for once the man in the corner is wrong.

We remember in our own green years when we were involved with a different kind of turf how some horses could hardly work at all in soft bog while others could almost swim through it. And a big horse that jumps boldly is not likely to relish the jarring of hard ground.

On the bus to Fairyhouse senior citizens and their wives wear holiday faces. A gaggle (or should it be 'giggle'?) of young girls behave as if they had invented laughter.

The heavy brigade studies the racing pages and makes guarded pronouncements, all the while emanating an air of profound wisdom and secret knowledge.

A woman aims a question at an acqaintance a few seats away: 'Who did you back in the National?' 'Prolan – and that eejit Golden Rapper brought him down.'

Outside is the yellow-brown of tilth, the bright speckling of dandelions, the bare armature of ash, that tardiest of trees to put out leaves.

The sun is radiant – but yard-pumps are still swathed in straw. We are passing through Ratoath. It is little more than a hamlet but has two betting shops – the significance is clear.

From there the road to the racecourse is narrow and thronged. Buses and cars inch forward sporadically – cyclists go past like free spirits.

While we are temporarily becalmed, a youth walks past with a transistor. The bus driver opens his window and says: 'Any football news?'

The youth, suspecting some urban joke, turns away his head, unaware that just about now Queen's Park Rangers and Arsenal are ending a game of great moment.

Today Fairyhouse seems the capital of the world. The area around the parade ring is almost impenetrable. Sardines, by comparison, seem to live in houses standing on their own ground.

The sky is thinly clouded; the sun comes through diffused. There is a light wind; it comes from the north-east – yet out in the more open spaces the day is balmy.

The course is very well grassed: the turf is springy – officially and accurately the going is described as good.

As we stand at the rails watching the finish of the Percy Maynard Hurdle, a young man next to us gets very excited as Bobby Coonan brings Bold Charlie with a late run.

As his fancy hits the front he shouts: 'Best bloody hurdle jockey in the world! He'd lose Carberry.' These are wild and whirling words, my lord.

Half an hour before the big race we struggle towards the parade ring. By various stratagems we get within viewing distance. Next to us a little girl is perched on her father's shoulder. She says: 'Daddy, where is Rag Trade?'

Women are talking about Prolan as if he were a pop star. He is threatening to become the most popular white horse since Tom Mix made coffee and fried beans under the stars. A girl says to her boyfriend: 'That's a lovely horse, number sixteen.' 'She's a mare,' he says, 'and she hasn't a hope. The bookies aren't even quoting her.'

Flashy Boy seems determined to live down to his name: he is the only restive horse in the ring and his green blinkers and white noseband make him seem even more an exhibitionist.

Brown Lad looks as if he would be able to plough single-handed, if that is the word; now and then he stops and stares deep into the crowd, observed and observer.

As the horses are led past the stands in the ceremonial parade, the bookmakers' raucous symphony rises to a frenzied crescendo.

Down at the rails near the winning post a well-dressed citizen lies asleep in blissful unconcern. Crowds have gathered at every fence – the testing time is nigh.

The horses are released by their handlers; they turn and canter down to the starting place. The handlers walk back self-consciously carrying straps and covers.

Soon the white flag is up and almost immediately the fifteen runners are away, climbing the hill in a compact huddle.

The most-repeated name in the commentary is that if April's Canter, as topical a tip as Royal Frolic if one were given to such logic. Most people have to look at their cards to learn something about the leader.

There she is listed as a bay filly – a rather surprising description for an eight-year-old. But filly or mare, she runs a great race, despite the young man who said she had no chance.

Passing the stands at the end of the first round she is going with tremendous zest. Prolan is very nicely placed; so is Brown Lad. But indeed all are there with a chance.

They go up the hill again almost as compact as before, but as they turn across by the ash trees towards Ballyhack the field is beginning to lengthen.

April's Canter is going as well as ever. So is Prolan, as easily picked out as Bobby Charlton. Brown Lad is obviously full of steam. But so is Ten Up – here are the ingredients of a thriller.

But five fences out Ten Up goes down – his old trouble has recurred. Prolan too is out of the race – he has made a mistake and lost ground that at this stage cannot be recovered.

Now it is Flashy Boy upsides with April's Canter. But as they turn for home Brown Lad is galloping like inflation and at the jumps gains ground in a way that shows what chasing is all about.

His handler has remained at the rails halfway between

the final fence and the winning post; now as his charge lands safely over the last he runs up to the finish, delight blossoming on his face.

After the big race the day loosens. The bars are overflowing. Soon come the statutory announcements about lost children. The surprise is that there are so few.

All over the great fields we see abandoned infants wandering at will and turning Fairyhouse into a kind of Tír na nÓg.

Evening Press

THE GRAND NATIONAL

As a people we are slow in banishing our feelings of inferiority. And we tend to look on some of our neighbours as better in certain ways, especially in the context of art.

The issue of the euro currency should exorcise our doubts forever. The notes are inexplicably ugly; a great opportunity was lost. Ours were infinitely better but none of them was as good as that popularly known as 'the Ploughman'.

That was the pound note that first appeared late in the 1920s. When it ceased to be, I do not know. It was a splendid note: it showed a stalwart man, a Matt the Thrasher of the new century, ploughing with a pair of powerful horses.

I got one in the course of my job, unpaid and unpensionable, as letter-writer and form-filler for my neighbours, including the travelling people.

One of those, a newcomer to the locality, put me in my place one day: 'They tell me you can write . . . but can you spell?' I assured her and so took down a varied list to be sent with a postal order to good old Hector Grey.

That's another story. Writing out betting slips was also part of my duty. This activity reached its peak on the day of the Grand National.

Most of our neighbours, like ourselves, hadn't much in the way of money. They distrusted banks. You could hardly blame them for that.

It was a civilised era: burglars were few and far between – if only because they had so little to burgle. And so people kept their money in their houses. Thus in the run-up to the Grand National I got notes from many kinds of private banks.

Biscuit tins were a great favourite. Old stockings and even young stockings served too. Thus I came by the Ploughman. One night when my float was very low, I tendered it in Pat Hourican's pub in Dublin's Leeson Street. When I came to redeem it, one of the barmen asked me to allow him to keep it – I did.

The Grand National is the greatest sporting event known to man; even the final of the World Cup in soccer doesn't come near it.

I couldn't even make a wild guess at its television audience but I suspect that even the shepherds below in the bottom of Chile watch it.

I know that at home on the big day I met people from the heart of the mountain whom I might not see again until the occasion of Duffy's Circus.

It is something that everybody should try to experience at least once, like the Rhine at Cologne Cathedral and Manchester United on a good day and Michael McDowell in full flow.

If you ever see the jockeys coming out from the weigh room for the big race, you are unlikely to forget it. Most are palpably apprehensive: they are acutely aware that within half an hour they could be heroes or playthings of fate. Some, the kind of men who would laugh on the gallows, are making jokes.

It is an awesome sight: some come on their own; most come in a multicoloured huddle as if trying to protect one another.

No event has such a capacity for defying logic: surprise – and indeed sensation – are its lifeblood. Horses that on known form couldn't be rated even as no-hopers have won it.

Stan Mellors, a great jockey who never knew glory at Aintree, had a theory to explain this. He believed that horses whose working lives have been spent in such modest courses as Plumpton and Newton Abbott and

Market Rasen become somewhat mad when they experience Aintree.

The aroma of hot dogs and burgers and cold dogs and beer and cider and spirits can cause some animals to lose the run of themselves – or perhaps to find the run of themselves.

I could sing out a litany of famous jockeys who never tasted success in the race over long careers – Bruce Hobbs won it at sixteen. For good measure his mount, Battleship, was the smallest horse that ever won the National.

That race caused bitter debate: the Irish contingent were certain that Royal Danieli had won. There was no photo finish then; the two horses finished far apart on the wide track. The judge gave the nod to Battleship by a head.

Dan Moore on the Irish horse was certain that he had won; the photographs in the newspapers seemed to bear him out.

Many years later at Aintree I mentioned the controversy to Dan – he wasn't the slightest bit embittered. I was.

Caughoo's win left a debate that hasn't yet died out. Whenever the great race is being discussed in a pub, you can be sure that it will surface. Caughoo, you will be told, went around only once. It was a misty day; he spent some time hidden behind a fence.

It was a lovely story; at least one person believed it – Danny McCann, who rode the runner-up, Lough Conn. In his telling he took the lead a mile from home – and nothing passed him afterwards.

One night many years later the two jockeys met in a pub in deepest Meath. Danny called Eddie Dempsey a cheat. They were fighting words. The affair ended up in the district court and was dismissed under the Last Offenders' Act.

Two factors militated against Danny McCann's claim: there is nowhere to hide in the Aintree track; the radio commentary had Caughoo in the race all the way. The story, however, will go on and on – some people have no time for facts.

Devon Loch's fall about a hundred yards from the winning post will always be a source of debate. His rider, Dick Francis, couldn't offer an explanation.

There he was, coasting home to win the greatest prize in steeplechasing – and suddenly his partner was sprawled on the floor. I have seen the video many times. I believe that Devon Loch was tiring and losing concentration and jumped the shadow of a pole.

You had a feeling that this could happen only at Aintree: the gods that preside over it seem to delight in dealing in the bizarre. There was, for example, the day of the false start.

The man on the rostrum couldn't have been more experienced; he had been doing the job for many years – it was his last day.

There was the usual milling around and the usual admonition – the tapes went up, most of the horses started – sufficient didn't to justify a recall.

Much the same happened again. On the third occasion it seemed that the race was on, even though several horses were left.

To add to the confusion the television monitor kept flashing: 'Race is off.' This could have meant two things – that the race was on or off.

A man ran onto the track and tried to wave the runners down. The jockeys thought that he was one of the animal-rights people and carried on. Eventually John White on Esha Ness was first past the post – alas, his joy was soon guillotined.

Sport can be cruel, very cruel. The starter lived to tell the tale but I doubt if he lived happy ever after. It was a bad way to go.

Now I will give you a marvellously useless piece of

information: no matter how unlikely the winner of the Grand National is, you will meet someone who has backed it.

A friend of mine who worked for our Electricity Supply Board backed ESB, who became the beneficiary of Devon Loch's downfall.

That night in the pub I didn't tell him that in many roadside cafés in England those letters signify eggs and sausages and bacon.

There is another thing I will tell you about the great race: don't count any runner out.

I dismissed Caughoo; so too did no less a judge than Aubrey Brabazun, even though he was owned and trained by his friends the McDowells.

He had ridden the little horse to victory in two Ulster Grand Nationals but deemed him too small for Aintree. He was bigger than Battleship. And there is an old saying: 'A good horse was never of a bad colour.'

Aubrey's own mount fell at Beecher's first time round – and left him unconscious. He awoke to find Charlie Weld pouring brandy into him – and to hear the tannoy hailing home Caughoo.

And so not for the first time the gods of sport, those expert catchers in the wry, had a good laugh at Aintree.

Sunday World

'You Can Run, But You Cannot Hide'

Muhammad Ali and Joe Frazier

It was fitting that Frank Sinatra should this morning pre-
cede Muhammad Ali on our television screens – one of
the great egotists of our day was precursor to one even
greater.

Both are quintessentially American products; each in
his way pursues Gatsby's dream. You might say that both
have long since overtaken that dream and passed it out –
but in that territory there are no Everests.

We all hunger to be the greatest, and that hunger never
dies, no matter how cruelly life lays naked our fantasies.

Sinatra should by now be in mellow harbour – he is
still in the marketplace, left with only tattered shreds of
dignity and growing old disgracefully. Increasingly he is
substituting power for art.

Ali has the advantage in that he moves in territory
where greatness can be more satisfactorily measured – yet
he, too, knows the rack of uncertainty.

He can demonstrate consummately his superiority to
all his contemporaries – but he cannot fight with ghosts.
Always the doubts will remain – in the minds of others, if
not in his own.

Always there will be those to say that he would not
compare with Joe Louis and Jack Johnson or perhaps Jack
Dempsey and Gene Tunney. And Ali can never disprove
it. That he wishes to put his argument beyond all doubt is
obvious – he is concerned not only with winning but with
his manner of doing so.

Combined with this vast ambition is the prudence of
an insurance broker. He prolongs fights not to parade his
wares but to reduce to almost nothing his danger of
knockout.

Of all the great heavyweights he is the most glamorous – yet he is the least romantic. 'Chance' is the dirtiest word in his vocabulary. And in his own brilliant way he is a cheat.

He allows even such vastly inferior opponents as Joe Bugner and Chuck Wepner to spend their capital while he hoards his own. There were long periods last night when he was so inactive that he would have been disqualified in a village hall.

But he was not in a village hall but on a plateau of power that no boxer has ever known. And that eminence when combined with genius makes him nigh-invulnerable.

The game needs him and so his infinitely cunning eccentricities must be condoned – and when these ploys have exhausted his opponent, he moves in like a banker foreclosing a mortgage.

Never was this cunning eccentricity more manifest than last night. There were times, especially in the twelfth round, when he seemed to be acting not only the hedgehog but the ostrich.

As he half-crouched with the great arms covering head and body he seemed to be like a child hiding in a corner to avoid his father's wrath.

He seemed even to be pretending that the great big bad world outside was not there at all – in fact, he was saving while forcing Joe Frazier to spend.

That generally was the pattern of the fight. Frazier came forward almost all the time, crouching, hooking, working feverishly to find a solid target, very occasionally succeeding.

Ali had built up some capital by unusual aggression in the first few rounds and this he hoarded like a Shylock, spending a little energy only to wipe out Frazier's fragmentary gains.

And it was eminently predictable that Ali would

attack in the fourteenth: Frazier was a near neighbour to exhaustion and it was time to leave no margin for the eccentricity of the judges.

The verdict will go into the book as a technical knock-out – it was misleading. The end was reminiscent of old-style fights to the finish. Frazier simply could not carry on.

It reminded one also of the second fight between Tunney and Dempsey. There is a good film of that much-discussed contest and the similarities are many.

Dempsey's style was like Frazier's – and Tunney's was rather akin to Ali's, though of course without the stiff extended left arm and the long squirrellings.

Dempsey too experienced the frustration of fighting against a man bigger, faster and more skilful than himself. Frazier's task was similar but more enormous.

His hopes lay in his ability to be able to take more punishment than his opponent and to bludgeon away his brilliance as he had done four years ago.

But Ali's fighting brain seems endlessly fertile: since that first meeting he has expanded his vocabulary – Frazier uses the same language but with less force.

There were moments last night, especially in the middle period, when Frazier must have been hopeful of regaining the old moral ascendancy. But hope soon turned to fantasy.

Long before the end he must have known that only an act of God could bring him victory but he battled on with bitter dignity. Again one was reminded of Tunney and Dempsey.

In the fourteenth round even Frazier's enormous courage began to leak from him and almost subconsciously he crouched lower and lower as if seeking to burrow down into the ground. At the end his face was a desert of bewilderment and sadness and weariness – and it was the window of a scathed soul.

The ring is still the severest testing place of all. You cannot fake the answers. You can run, as Joe Louis said, but you cannot hide.

The moment comes when all publicity has to stop. When the first bell goes truth takes over.

You are back again with Tom Sayers and John Heenan and with Dan Donnelly and George Cooper. And despite all the vulgarity and chicanery that surrounds it, boxing retains a bruised dignity.

Evening Press

Roger Bannister Breaks the
Four-Minute Mile, 1954

It was known as the British Empire but essentially it was the English Empire, even though the Scots and the Welsh and the Irish contributed hugely to its making.

It is quite some time now since it could be called 'the Empire on which the sun never went down' but the mentality it created is still lurking around. And it takes centre stage whenever some son or daughter of Albion does well in the world of sport.

England has been doing very well of late in athletics and pugilism: indeed you could say that in both sports our neighbours are enjoying a golden age.

In other spheres, alas, all is not so rosy. The failure to qualify for the Finals of the World Cup was a grievous blow to the people of the land where soccer originated. Last Saturday at Twickenham the chariot ran off the course and the rose wilted. In cricket the picture is gloomy.

All those disappointments would have been washed away if Torvill and Dean had come up trumps in a little town in Norway. Their comparative failure had at least one compensation: it boosted the sale of paper hankies.

I took no pleasure in their relegation to third place; they seem to be a nice couple, the kind that you would take home to your mother – even if you were sure that she was there.

I am old enough and was young enough to have a lucid memory of one of the greatest occasions in English sport.

Very soon it will be the fortieth anniversary of Roger Bannister's immortal run. It was in the Spring of 1954 that the young medical student ran a mile in under four minutes for the first time.

I must qualify that last sentence: it was the first recorded occasion. For all we know, someone might have broken that four-minute barrier in a field outside of sport. He might have been running for his life as he retreated from the field of battle.

There is a famous story about a private in the British army who was courtmartialled for desertion after a battle in Flanders in World War I. His defence was simple: ' I didn't run until I saw my captain running.'

The chairman of the tribunal was indignant: 'How dare you suggest that your captain deserted . . . '

'Indeed he did. And he ran very fast. When we were going through a field, a hare jumped up – and the captain said "Come out of my way."'

That's all another story; what concerns us here is that Roger Bannister ran that immortal mile in 3 minutes 59.4 seconds.

I was then living down below in the south-west of Ireland; I remember feeling a little quirk of sadness when the news came through.

I was then even more of a chauvinist than I am now and had hoped that my great hero, John Joe Barry, would have been the first to reach that goal.

He was eminently capable of doing so, a fact well known to Bannister, who greatly admired the Ballincurry Hare.

John Joe sent him a telegram next day and got a telegram in reply: 'It should have been you.'

That too is another story but I will say in passing that people tend to judge John Joe not by what he achieved but by what he didn't achieve.

His record glows with great achievements but such was his potential that people believed he should have achieved even more. George Best would understand.

And if you said that the difference between Bannister and Barry symbolises the difference between two peoples, you would be exaggerating – but not much.

Bannister was self-assured to a degree which seems beyond an Irishman. He was picked for the 1948 Olympics but declined the invitation: he felt that at nineteen he was too young.

This astonishing decision was to have a sequel which suggested that he had incurred the wrath of the gods: he competed four years later in the metric mile in the Helsinki Olympics but finished only fifth.

It was a bitter blow to this fiercely ambitious young man: he knew that he might be too old to take gold in Melbourne in 1956. And so the mile in under four minutes became to him as the South Pole had been to Captain Scott.

There was another parallel with the ambition of the Antarctic explorer. As Scott prepared for his journey southwards, he knew that Amundsen was also getting ready.

And as Bannister prepared for his goal, he knew that the great Australian John Landy was on a similar quest. That was why he bought forward his plans to go for his private gold at a small meeting in Iffley Road, Oxford University's track.

Seemingly he hoped for a quiet atmosphere but the word had passed along the grapevine of athletics. Oxford was invaded by hordes of the media – before that silly term was minted: their presence alerted the public; Iffley Road was crowded.

Indeed such was the crush and the hysteria that Bannister might have failed to reach the line – as almost happened to John Treacy on that momentous day in Limerick Racecourse.

It all ended happily: Roger Bannister ran into folklore. Purists may argue that his achievement was diminished by the fact that it wasn't a real race: Chris Chataway and Chris Brasher acted as pacemakers.

And those who delight in puncturing English chauvinism will point out that Bannister's coach was the legendary Austrian Franz Stampfl.

Even back in the fifties the drama we call life abounded in ironies. Brasher was deemed less gifted than Bannister and Chataway but was the only one of the trio to take Olympic gold: he did so in the three thousand metres steeplechase in Melbourne.

John Joe Barry, by the way, is alive and well; we have the odd drink together in deepest Portobello.

And while I am at it, I must congratulate another hero of mine, Eamonn Coghlan, on his over-forty mile.

Evening Press

'IRELAND HAVE SUCCEEDED
WHERE NEW ZEALAND FAILED'

IRELAND BEAT ENGLAND IN THE FIVE NATIONS, 1994

Seldom has an Irish rugby team gone into battle with such a burden of criticism, printed and spoken; the condemned men ate a hearty dinner on Saturday night.

Ireland exemplified my private definition of intelligence – common sense in action. Ireland won the battle of the minds; they kept England guessing.

England's congenital weakness, an utter lack of imagination, has seldom been so palpable. Their every move was clearly signposted; when their game plan failed, they were reduced to improvising, a business at which they are not great.

The short-head margin didn't tell the full tale; in the late paragraphs England all but surrendered. And we were left to ponder an amazing and marvellous truth: Ireland have succeeded where New Zealand failed.

Some of our savants will have a great deal of writing and talking to do, as they attempt to wriggle out of their nonsense.

Eric Elwood can hardly be blamed if he goes around this week smiling to himself. Several typewriters and at least one mouth had been primed to compose his obituary.

There is, of course, a tacit belief that you shouldn't expect a good out-half to come from west of the Shannon. Elwood is an iconoclast; he is getting better with every appearance in the green – he was superb on Saturday.

I wasn't in the least surprised at our victory; I set out my stall very clearly on Wednesday. I said that if we tidied up our line-out, we could win.

The cats in the alleys, not to mention the dogs in the

streets, knew that England were grievously limited. They haven't had a good out-half since Richard Sharpe – and he plied his trade in the days before decimalisation.

Rob Andrew looked on Saturday as he had always looked: he is an honest journeyman. His midfield partners, Will Carling and Philip de Glanville, hadn't a smidgeon of creativity between them.

Rory and Tony Underwood have exceptional pace and little else; if you called them footballers, you could find yourself accused of putting on a misleading label.

Jon Callard is a full-back who has little to offer in attack.

Rather ironically, England's most creative back – indeed their only creative back – is as Irish as the Hill of Howth.

Kyran Bracken's inexperience surfaced at times on Saturday but at least he was capable of surprise.

I have no doubt that Simon Geoghegan was well toasted in many a hostelry on Saturday night; he has established himself as the best winger in the Five Nations.

He took his only clear chance yesterday; even better was that run and kick and chase that devoured an acre of ground and led to a penalty. Richard Wallace was less spectacular but he had his best game in the green.

Maurice Field had never before been inside Twickenham; that fact didn't seem to unnerve him – firemen, especially in Belfast, know that rugby is only a game.

Tackling played a big part in this glorious victory. Philip Danaher would be a useful man to have on the scene if a horse bolted.

Michael Bradley threw the occasional wild pass – we wouldn't recognise him if he didn't – but he had a fine game both as warrior and general. He varied his play shrewdly and kept England's loose forwards guessing.

Conor O'Shea didn't kick as well as he can but he

should be happy with his display and especially with his part in the try.

Neil Francis, the Captain Dreyfus of Irish rugby, surprised almost everybody by playing better in the second half than in the first. He won little in the line-out – but a few of his catches were invaluable.

England as expected won the battle in the air; the count was about two to one. Figures, however, mean little in themselves; much of their possession wasn't possession at all.

It was almost incredible to watch grown men using the ball so crudely. Geoff Cooke and Dick Best have a case to answer. Martin Bayfield soared far above everybody sent to mark him but preferred to palm rather than to catch.

The Irish pack compensated for their weakness by tremendous play in the loose. They laboured with great honesty in the hidden agenda of ruck and maul.

Nick Popplewell, Terry Kingston, Peter Clohessy and Michael Galwey were seldom seen – that was a tribute to their mole-like endeavours. The loose trio, Dennis McBride and Paddy Johns and Brian Robinson, excelled.

Johns had a big task in curbing Steve Ojomoh; he succeeded – nevertheless, the newcomer was England's outstanding forward.

The English pack seemed leaderless in the loose. Their aficionados will no doubt bemoan the absence of Dean Richards – he is in dry dock.

It shouldn't be forgotten, however, that the best all-round forward to wear the red rose in this generation was dropped for the final of the World Cup when he was three years younger and a few yards quicker than he is now.

Of course it will be argued that the woodwork frustrated Callard – there is another case for a post-mortem. The answer to all the excuses is that Ireland scored the only try. And it was such a beautiful score that you felt it would bring victory.

Ireland won two loose scrums in quick succession; the intervention of Wallace and O'Shea fertilised the movement.

And yet when the ball reached Geoghegan, he wasn't a man over – his little step inside and then outside wrong-footed Callard. And we all lived happily ever after – after four o'clock, that is.

The news from Cardiff was more than welcome; we were assailed before the start of the Championship with prophecies about a two-tier Championship.

Now France and England have tasted the dust. And Wales, supposedly in a crisis, are now three up – and poised for the Triple Crown and the Championship.

I find it hard to suppress my laughter at the famous prop-forward who bewailed the state of his country's rugby a few weeks ago in the *Irish Times*.

Perhaps it is true that Wales are in a crisis; if so, it is a crisis that is well disguised.

Evening Press

There was a time when Manchester United had no more devoted follower than I; it began with Jackie Carey and was strengthened when Noel Cantwell came to Old Trafford. I still follow Manchester United when they play in European competitions but my affection has waned in the domestic scene.

The reason is simple: they are no longer a football club; they are a corporation like General Motors. They try to buy success; of course most clubs do but some are better equipped than others.

It would be hard to overestimate the contribution made by Dwight Yorke this season; it is unlikely that United would have won the League without him but he started the campaign with a different club.

I think it is ludicrous that someone can play for two clubs in the one competition. I believe that buying and selling should be confined to the close season and that players should be not only cup-tied but league-tied.

I was in Rotterdam when United won the European Cup Winners' Cup and I rejoiced as much as any Mancunian or perhaps as any Manchurian; there is a little story implicit in the alternative name.

It goes back to a Friday evening long ago when I was in Mulligan's in Dublin's Poolbeg Street with my dear departed friend, Jimmy O'Connor, the blacksmith in Burgh Quay.

It was the eve of the Cup Final between United and Everton and we were getting up a head of steam for the journey. Not all of our friends were for United and we were getting a share of flak. At last Jimmy said: 'Con, us Manchurians must stick together.'

I was glad when United won the League a few weeks ago – and for two reasons: they played attractive football

all through the season and then of course there was the presence of Denis Irwin and Roy Keane.

United are now the yuppies' team; they are followed by young men who would have great difficulty in kicking a ball from the centre spot out of the circle; when United begin to wane, they will disappear like the snows of yesteryear.

Clubs are at their most vulnerable when they are strongest. A hundred years ago it seemed that the British Empire would go on forever – it crumbled like a sandcastle in the tide.

I travelled to watch United long before I came to the *Evening Press;* I was well acquainted with the joys of the Liverpool ferry and the comforts of the Victorian slum that Old Trafford was then.

I followed United when they were in the old Second Division. Tommy Docherty was then on the bridge – he talked great football and he produced great football.

Old Trafford was crowded for every game and they packed the stadiums wherever they played away. They flew back up into the First Division. I came to know Tommy and I liked him.

I came to know another United manager: Ron Atkinson and myself were billeted together during the World Cup Finals in 1986 – I liked him too. Tommy and he have an abiding sense of humour; purgatory knows, they need it in their profession.

I have never met Alex Ferguson and know very little about him, except that he is a great manager – you cannot argue with his record. I would prefer however if he didn't blame referees when things go against him – he is too old for whingeing.

Sometimes he reminds me of what Ted Walsh said one day about one of our best trainers: 'Do you see that man down there in the ring with the brown hat . . . that's so-and-so and there is no fear he is going to burst into song.'

And you can be sure that Alex Ferguson will never be found asleep in a field several miles from home with a carrier bag and two empty vodka bottles by his side – that was one of the saddest episodes in the decline of Brian Clough.

Brian, in my not-so-humble opinion, was the greatest British manager since the war; he won the highest honours with unlikely clubs – and he had the wit to produce brilliant meals from modest ingredients.

I was in his company on a few occasions and I wasn't very impressed. He was a loudmouth and I couldn't help suspecting that he was a bully. He was also embittered because he hadn't been given the job that every English manager covets most – to be at the helm of the national team.

England haven't been in the winner's enclosure since 1966; in the meantime they have made some tame exits from the Euro Cup and the World Cup. Brian was never really a contender for the manager's post – he is a strong man but not a particularly silent one.

Brian was not politically correct: you wouldn't consult him if the greenfly was devastating your roses; I doubt if he would ever write to the *Times* to complain about the decline in English marmalade – and though he endorsed Shredded Wheat, I doubt if he ever tasted it.

England's national team are woefully lacking in imagination; if they are to become champions of Europe or the world, they must learn to make the right mistakes.

*

Manchester United remind me of Éamon de Valera: to some people he represented the Second Coming – to others he was the Devil Incarnate.

I do not belong to either camp: I was a dedicated United man; now I support them in the Champions'

League – in the domestic context I have no favourite club. I suspect that my change of heart and mind owes something to the arrival of Alex Ferguson at Old Trafford. I never warmed to him.

He is now Sir Alex – but at least to me he is not the Loveliest Knight of the Year. His comments on Brian Kidd after that decent man had gone to Blackburn Rovers were unforgiveable.

Brian, after all, had to go on making a living in the game and could have done without such an unsolicited testimonial. Alex was similarly critical of Gordon Strachan; the good word seems not a part of Ferguson's vocabulary.

You will hear and read that he is the Football League's most successful manager of all time – and maybe he is. Supporters of Liverpool will contest that claim fiercely. I wouldn't look beyond Brian Clough: with homespun teams he won the highest honours.

Ferguson's fellows in management do not deem him a good tactician: they concede that he is a good buyer; that talent would of course be of little value without a deep purse. He may not be a brilliant tactician but even his severest critics agree that United on their good days are a joy to behold.

This season, they won a great many battles but didn't win a war.

Speculation about the reason for this failure is becoming a light industry. Some experts blame Juan Veron, the costliest player in United's array. He made his name as a central midfielder; unless United feared that Roy Keane might suffer a long-term injury, it was a needless buy.

The wise tell us that two circuses shouldn't be in town on the same day. Those lucky people who know all of the hidden agenda say that Veron is unhappy in Manchester. He is homesick for the wide open spaces of his native land.

Other experts – there is at least one in every pub in these islands – blame Fabien Barthez. It is difficult to find serious fault with a goalie who has won honour and honours in the World Cup and the Euro Cup and the Premiership – but there you are.

He can be a breathtaking shot-stopper; he can be equally breathtaking at giving the ball away with hand and foot.

If Rip Van Winkle woke up from his little nap last Sunday morning, he would rub his eyes as he perused the team-sheets from the previous day. What were all those keepers with funny names doing in English football? It isn't long since keepers from the European mainland were highly suspect in these islands.

They were inclined to panic under the high ball and had to punch when they should catch – so we believed. Now we do not look askance, whatever that means, at people who drink wine, even if most of it comes from the bottom half of the globe.

And we have come to respect goalies with such names as Dudek and Cudicini. Nevertheless, it is a relief to see at times that all isn't lost: good old David Seaman is as reliable as the roast beef of English tradition.

Manchester United's disappointing season may chasten their management. Their attitude towards the League Cup is unworthy of a great club. That competition was ridiculed by some leading journalists when it was mooted but it went ahead and grew and grew.

I have been at many Wembley finals but could never detect a difference in the atmosphere of a League Cup and an FA Cup final. Both are always marvellous occasions. The followers do not make any distinction. 'He that condemneth small things shall fall by little and little.'

I do not see United crumbling – but unless they win at least one trophy next season, the natives may become restless. Liverpool too had a disappointing season; they played much delightful football but ended up empty-handed. Last season they enjoyed an *annus mirabilis,* a magic year. They won the League Cup, the FA Cup and the UEFA Cup.

Newcastle United won nothing tangible but had a good season – they finished in the top four. I was pleased for Bobby Robson. He is about as nice as a football manager can be. He is the image of your reliable family grocer; you can see him waxing eloquent over the different brands of marmalade. And he is the kindly neighbour to whom you would turn if the greenfly happened to be devastating your roses.

Rip Van Winkle would be surprised too when he heard the name of England's manager – Sven Goran Eriksson. I can hear him saying to himself 'What manner of man is this?' He is the first from the outside world to manage England's football fortunes.

The arrival of a stranger to a languishing society is as old as mythology. Without it the novels and films about the American Old West would be sadly diminished. You know the story: the stranger rides into a town where the sheriff is bent and too powerful to oppose.

Someone recognises the newcomer as a legendary gunfighter who has long put aside his hardware and is devoting his retirement to creative birdwatching. A group of concerned citizens get to work on the veteran but he is loath to make a comeback. The concerned citizens stick to their guns or, if you like, to the veteran's guns. Of course he consents and the story ends with the sheriff paying for his sins in a dusty street.

The quiet Swede has no such daunting task. He comes at a juncture when English hopes are not high. An array of expeditions from the nation that founded soccer, according to themselves, have succeeded only once in a major tournament. It is a long time since the rainy Summer of 1966.

In the meantime many a collective sigh has disturbed the air, and many a journalist has scraped his barrel of words to castigate the managers and the players. Great names have come and gone. Ron Greenwood, Terry Venables, Glenn Hoddle and Kevin Keegan are among them, not to mention Bobby Robson himself.

Sven Goran Eriksson has several soft acts to follow. The new manager's squad for the Far East may appear conservative but contains two bold selections.

Martin Keown, who incidentally has four Irish grandparents, is thirty-five; obviously Eriksson believes that there was never a good horse of a bad colour.

Teddy Sheringham belongs to the same vintage. His inclusion recalls the oft-repeared story about Hector McAlpine's last words to his sons: 'Whatever you do, keep Paddy at the big mixer.' Sheringham can turn a game with one inspired dart.

Manchester United weren't very clever when they allowed him to go. No doubt it seemed a good idea at the time.

Prominent among those unlucky to lose out are Phil Babb and Steve McManaman. Babb has recovered his old self in Portugal. MacManaman doesn't start many games with Real Madrid but is very much part of their team. Perhaps Mick McCarthy has lost patience with Babb.

Philip Neville too must be disappointed: he was in all Eriksson's squads except on a few occasions when he was injured. It was the second grievous blow to his pride: four years ago most experts deemed him a certainty – Glenn Hoddle did not.

Nobody should have been astonished: Hoddle never made a major decision until he had consulted a mystic called Eileen.

David O'Leary has had a traumatic season; he can hardly be expected to keep watch over his players off the pitch. It all reminded me of what a friend of mine said about one of his sons: 'He'd be a great footballer if only you could keep him in at night.'

David has the consolation that four of his players are in the English squad. Robbie Fowler and Rio Ferdinand and Nigel Martyn were naps. Danny Mills was not.

As Arsenal bask in the glory of their double, they must rue the one that got away. They made a tame exit from the European Championships.

Rip Van Winkle may wonder at the multicultural nature of their team – but that's the way it is and that's the way it will be.

Sunday World

'A Great Three Days for Irish Tennis'

John McEnroe in Dublin

About two o'clock in Ballsbridge yesterday little steams of young girls eddied around like medieval monks who had got news of a second coming.

It would be unfair to apportion all the excitement to the young girls: the general atmosphere approached the hysteria that touched Dublin at the comings of John F. Kennedy and the Pope.

The afternoon was grey and windy and the mountains seemed to have already donned their Winter garb; a sad little moving circle of men in their working clothes protested outside the Simmonscourt Pavilion at the closure of Dunlop's – but neither the weather nor this symbol of economic distress could diminish the air of expectation.

Inside the great shed that housed the meeting of Ireland and the United States in the Davis Cup there was a heavy smell of commercialism – and it didn't involve the selling of second-hand books or used bicycles.

It was an occasion designed for the affluent – and the people you saw there were rather different from those who populate the Canal Terrace in Croke Park, not to mention the Hill.

The music, however, was familiar: the Artane Boys' Band looked like flowers that had been brought indoors as they uttered tunes that seemed more fitting for homelier places.

Among them was 'The Emigrant's Lament' – but the occasion was a reminder that not all those who sailed across the weary and stormy Atlantic failed to make their mark.

The main cause of this tumult in Dublin 4 was a young

man from New York, grandson of a Cavan peasant who went to the good.

There are those – but not many – who would question John McEnroe's claim to be the best tennis player in the world today; there is hardly anybody who would disagree if you said that he causes the most controversy.

Much of the fuel for this has been provided at Wimbledon, that quasi-sacred arena in south-west London whither the English upper classes flock every Summer to ingest strawberries and cream and give the impression that they are interested in tennis.

Until the coming of young John, protests at official decisions there were not unknown – but they were generally rare and couched in language no more violent than that used by colonels' wives when they became embroiled on the letters page of *The Times* about the best way to make crab-apple jelly.

John's protests were frequent – and sometimes he employed words that reminded us of a sometimes-forgotten truth: the working class haven't a monopoly of what is called 'earthy language'.

It was hard to blame him for these outbursts at Wimbledon: officialdom there is made up of plum-voiced and toffee-nosed people who represent all that is worst in English snobbery. Try to imagine a posse of male Margaret Thatchers plus a few female ones – and you have some idea of the scene.

And it was obvious from his first days in the big time that there was little affection going astray between him and them. Not only was he American; he had Irish blood in him – and worse still, his hair was dangerously close to red.

And so the war went on – and a phony war it was: officialdom wouldn't throw him out even if he bashed the Duchess of Kent over the head and knocked down several old ladies in the process.

They needed him: modern tennis demands huge injections of money – and when young John is on the bill, the crowds follow him as emotionally drugged as were the children who followed behind the Pied Piper.

His protesting is wearing a little thin now and is no longer much of an attraction – but the beauty of his tennis is likely to be his alchemist's stone for as long as his spirit and his body remains willing.

His opponent yesterday was a young man who is better known in this country than in his own. Matt Doyle's name meant little here a year ago – only those who follow tennis closely could tell you much about him.

Like McEnroe he is American-born of Irish ancestry – at least in part. The comparative remoteness of his Irish roots hasn't prevented him from becoming over the last few days an instant hero.

This was due in part to his unexpected victory over Eliot Teltscher on Friday evening – Doyle beat the world's number fifteen in straight sets.

On Saturday he and Sean Sorensen lost to McEnroe and Peter Fleming. It was hardly a surprise – the latter pair are current Wimbledon and United States champions.

This reverse did not depress Doyle: when I met him in the Berkeley Court Hotel on Saturday night, he was obviously still aglow after his great performance in the singles.

And well he might: he had proved that our meeting with the US wasn't altogether a case of the Christians versus the lions.

And no doubt he was pleased with his newfound status as a folk hero; his tennis was part of the reason – the other part was his personality. He is the kind of man whom you like at first meeting; he has the friendly frankness that is one of the best American traits.

On Saturday night in the Berkeley Court he was on the

eve of the most harrowing examination of his career – he seemed unbothered.

He stood in the foyer and drank a few mugs of ale. Few recognised him – most were too alert for some sign that McEnroe was about to appear.

He did – fleetingly. It is easy to understand his hatred of curiosity – but his Dalai Lama attitude draws in on himself.

The protagonists in yesterday's big game are as unlike in appearance as demeanour. Doyle has the physique associated with the denizens of the American mountain country; he is long-limbed and lean; Shylock would hardly get a pound of flesh off his seventy-six inches. And he has the kind of bony long-jawed face that would be at home in a rural Irish pub.

McEnroe is of average height and build – if there is such a thing: in rugby terms he could fit in anywhere in the backs or at wing-forward.

His expression doesn't match the boyishness of his general appearance; the eyes and the mouth suggest an unremitting wariness – he looks as if he is preparing for the role of Jesse James or, more likely, Billy the Kid.

And in play that impression is borne out. In over two hours yesterday on or near the court he only once threatened to smile – when two pigeons up near the roof interrupted his service.

And those who expected that he might play a little casually against his comparatively obscure opponent soon found out – you might as well expect sentiment from a tiger.

And if someone says that the first set was as good as ever has been played in this country, I won't disagree with him.

It was a mighty duel – and at times the excitement became feverish as Doyle played such brilliant shots that a sensational result wasn't impossible.

Some of the young people in the packed house may have come to cheer for McEnroe just as young Irish people cheer for Liverpool or Manchester United when they play in Dublin – but the great majority were behind Doyle.

They were, however, a most sporting gallery who applauded all McEnroe's winners – and only once threatened to turn against him: that was in the fourteenth game when he carelessly hit a loose ball into the crowd.

The first game was uneventful – if you exclude the spatter of applause that greeted a double fault by McEnroe. It was Doyle's only point.

The second game posed a question. Could Doyle reproduce the serving that had undone Teltscher? His first serve suggested that he could – it was a thunderbolt ace. He took the game to love – and the crowd were abuzz.

Better was to come: he led 0–30 in the next game – with a great return of service and a beautiful passing shot down McEnroe's left. McEnroe, however, increased the pace and angle of his service and won the game with a great volley – the heat was on.

If two pigeons or some moles had brought the day's play to an end after the fourth game, the crowd would still have got value: it sparkled with the wine of tennis.

Doyle started it with a great winning serve and followed with a high winning volley. Great returns of service made it 30-all. Doyle's serve put him in front again – McEnroe levelled with a good return.

A whipped cross-court stroke gave McEnroe advantage – Doyle tied the score after a great rally in which he produced three successive underhand volleys close to the net; the third was an outright winner.

He then went ahead with a good serve – and again McEnroe's all-round brilliance brought it to deuce. Another great serve brought Doyle advantage – and he won the game when McEnroe's return of serve ended at the net.

The storm abated a little after that – and it was cut and thrust until the sixteenth game when McEnroe at last broke service and won the set 9–7.

Doyle had led 40–30 – but McEnroe was now taking his serve earlier and getting in returns that gave him the upper hand in the rallies.

There was a sense of inevitability about the second and third sets. Doyle was as determined as ever – but McEnroe's wide-angled shots often left him helpless. He returned some of them – but left McEnroe with ample time and space for the kill.

McEnroe broke service in the fourth game of the second set – after Doyle had led at 40–30 again at advantage (won by a thundering ace). And the New Yorker wrapped it up at 6–3 – he took the ninth game for the loss of one point.

The pattern of the third set was much the same. McEnroe was not a model of consistency but was making fewer mistakes. Doyle played some brilliant shots – including an unforgettable winning one from almost behind the umpire's throne – but McEnroe's slight superiority in almost every department came to a big total difference.

And so the duel that had started at a quarter to three was over a few minutes before five – 9–7, 6–3, 6–3. John McEnroe had put his tennis where his mouth is – and Matt Doyle had experienced the best few days in his career.

And how did the young tiger behave? He emitted a few growls – they were of little consequence. Perhaps there were some in the crowd who had come to see his antics – if so, they were the only ones who were disappointed.

I believe that the great majority came to see good tennis – they got it. And by all accounts the game between Sean Sorensen and Eliot Teltscher was a bonus – a four-hour marathon that the American won 14–16, 10–8, 8–6.

All in all, it was a great three days for Irish tennis.

Evening Press

'WE ARE IN A GOLDEN AGE AND WE SHOULD ENJOY IT'

IRELAND BEAT WALES, 2002

Those wonderful people, the Aborigines of Australia, have only one word to express 'the past' and 'the future' – it is 'the Dreaming'. We could take a lesson from them: we are prone to indulge in reminiscing and speculation – we tend to look on the present as lacking the stuff of drama and romance.

T. S. Eliot was right: 'The task of the artist is to take the here and the now and make it rich and strange.' The same outlook should apply to our lives, including the triviality called rugby. We are in a Golden Age and we should enjoy it.

I am not going overboard or underboard because of Sunday's game at Lansdowne Road. Ireland were splendid; Wales may have looked no more than sparring partners but only because they were demoralised by the home team's blazing start.

The Welsh revealed their true selves for a little while in the third quarter but by then their task was almost impossible. Paradoxically in that stint they looked superior to Ireland but it was no more than a desperate flash of pride and couldn't be sustained.

Ireland by then were performing over a safety net; they could afford to take risks that weren't risks at all – they paid handsomely. And so Ireland's followers were left to celebrate and their counterparts to grieve – and both were left to speculate.

A shadow hangs over them both: our back-up army fear the might of England – the Welsh are fearful that the season will go from bad to abysmal. I believe that both sets of misgivings are exaggerated.

England may beat us but will not devastate us; Wales will emerge from the season with honour. England at present are perhaps the best team in the world; the home advantage may help them to beat Ireland – but we will not lose caste.

Wales will never lose their self-esteem; pride may not be enough – but we saw enough on Saturday to hint that the ability is there too.

About Ireland's ability there can be no question. Never have we had so deep a pool; there is a queue for almost every post; we could field a very good second team.

The position of hooker is an example. Keith Wood is an icon; Frankie Sheahan is a good deputy; if both disappeared from the face of the earth, Shane Byrne would be more than an adequate replacement.

Girvan Dempsey hasn't put as much as a small toe wrong – but Paddy Wallace is knocking at the door with ever-increasing vigour. David Humphreys is established at out-half. Is he clearly superior to Ronan O'Gara and Paul Burke? I could go on and on . . .

Ireland's victory was achieved without three Lions, Keith Wood and Malcolm O'Kelly and Eric Miller, and a cub, Shane Horgan; this proves something.

If there is a smidgeon of unease in Eddie O'Sullivan's mind, it is due to the danger of great expectations. We are all aware of England's power behind the scrum; they may pose bigger problems in the set pieces. England's props have long been a part of their culture, as traditional as roast beef and Yorkshire Relish and Worcestershire sauce.

We should have no worry here: Peter Clohessy and John Hayes were pillars of solidity on Sunday. Hayes, for good measure, did some great work in the loose. Clohessy of course is threatening to abdicate but he is playing better than ever. Frankie Sheahan makes up a staunch front three. Paul O'Connell's debut was a mixture of satisfaction and frustration; it was good to get that try and heartbreaking to go off injured. Gary Longwell deputised very well.

Mick Galwey made a bit of history: he is the first graduate from Castle Island RFC to captain Ireland; he did so with an absence of fuss – he is a difficult man to overawe.

Peter Stringer continues to make friends and confound foes. David Humphreys and he fit like the proverbial hand and glove.

The loose trio, Simon Easterby and Anthony Foley and David Wallace, were as sharp as hawks in Spring. Geordan Murphy and Denis Hickie were always alert for the slightest chance.

Brian O'Driscoll is a Golden Boy who will not turn to dust. Kevin Maggs is from central casting, the proverbial honest son of Ulster. He created Murphy's second try.

A few of the Welsh emerged with credit. Wing-forward Nathan Budgett had his good moments. Scott Quinnell tried to be on the bridge and at the pumps.

Full-back Kevin Morgan did little wrong and a great deal right. Scrum-half Rob Howley did all he could behind a struggling pack.

Out-half Stephen Jones posted a mighty penalty on the brink of half-time and scored a try and a conversion in the short-lived rally – it was all a wry consolation.

The Welsh followers were sadly silent; it was hardly an occasion for 'Bread of Heaven' when they were living on crumbs.

In the last quarter we heard 'The Fields of Athenry' from the South Terrace but not for long – by then the game was gone dead.

In Cork on Saturday the Welsh A team lost 55–22 to their counterparts. In Donnybrook on Friday evening the Welsh under-twenty-ones provided a splink of light at the end of a very long and very dark tunnel – they beat ours by thirty-eight points to thirty-six.

And of course those famous valleys are now alive with

the sound of theories to explain the famine. J. P. R. Williams, legendary full-back of a generation ago, was in Dublin over the weekend and was not lacking in explanations.

He was not complimentary to Graham Henry, the New Zealander who coached Wales – for a quarter of a million sterling a year. It isn't too long since Henry was canonised; now he is being demonised.

If he hadn't an outstanding record, the Welsh Union wouldn't have employed him. And it is less than a year since the Three Wise Men who picked the Lions chose him to coach them.

And in Australia he didn't do too badly. We are living in an era when there is an obsession with coaching. You can be sure that Henry had his charges well prepared for Sunday's battle; they didn't perform.

Paudi O'Shea left no people unturned before last year's semi-final with Meath; his warriors didn't get airborne.

Often a good start is half the battle; sometimes it is all the battle. The Welsh failure on Sunday may have had much in common with Kerry's pathetic showing against Meath.

Gareth Davies, brilliant winger and team-mate of JPR, was in town for the weekend too – and of course he had his own theories.

He believes that the demise of heavy industry in Wales is among the causes of the decline in its rugby. It is a familiar theory but it doesn't stand up to examination. The country has had some good seasons since coal and steel were kings.

The Scots too are searching their souls; they now have their own Parliament but haven't lost their talent for own goals. When they picked their team for Saturday, they gave England a head start. They shoved the best out-half in rugby union to the centre. Gregor Townsend has been too long on the bridge to be happy as first mate. England didn't need to play very well to win: Scotland never recovered from a nervous start.

Even though they won comfortably, England's long-running problem was palpable: they haven't had a creative out-half since Richard Sharpe. The arrival of Jonny Wilkinson a few years ago seemed to end the drought: alas for the white rose, he has all the virtues except imagination. Mike Catt is a better out-half; so is Austin Healy – he is the best all-round back in these islands.

France were disappointing against Italy, a side composed mainly of part-timers. The new ruling which obliges the loose forwards to remain in the scrum until the ball is out militates against the French. Traditionally their loose forwards have been the most skilled players in the team, combining the virtues of backs and forwards.

I will give you an example; it goes back to a day a generation ago when Ireland were playing France at Lansdowne Road. There were no substitutes in those days; when the French out-half was injured, Jean Prat the lock (number eight now) took his place – and excelled.

Sunday was a quiet triumph for men whose names weren't in the programme: down the road in Ringsend the boats were in the streets – the pitch in the old stadium was in great shape.

Let us return to Eddie O'Sullivan. He made many friends on Sunday, not only because Ireland won but because of his bold approach; he could have played safe and make a kick start – he made a hand start.

Sunday World

224

THE PUTT THAT WON THE RYDER CUP

PHILIP WALTON

Philip Walton experienced the kind of finish yesterday evening that caused him to eat a hearty supper. On the eighteenth green at sun-blessed Portmarnock he faced up to a 21-yard free – with the difference that the target was rather smaller than that in hurling or Gaelic football.

With the absence of fuss that is the coursemark of his game he stroked the ball boldly; it was clear that he had the length – the accuracy was in question. About three feet from the hole the little white sphere veered slightly to the right but quickly changed its mind. Then a foot from the hole it wobbled left and then right – and then as if drawn by a magnet, it trickled into the cup. And I suspect that the applause carried as far as Balgriffin.

Philip is a local lad – from Malahide or thereabouts – and he certainly didn't lack for support yesterday. Irish golf crowds are famous for their sportsmanship; they applaud good deeds no matter what their source – but they are human and therefore inclined towards tribalism.

There was a palpable example yesterday afternoon; it occurred on the eleventh green. Mark McNulty, one of Walton's two partners, sank a twenty-footer and was warmly applauded; Walton got down from ten feet and ecstasy erupted.

Some optimist shouted 'Here we go!' and at the next hole it seemed that he could be right. The twelfth at Ireland's most celebrated links is only 149 yards – but that statistic masks its wicked nature. Two evil humps guard the green; they are aided and abetted by a pair of steep bunkers. If your tee shot doesn't land on the green, your round could be devastated.

Walton drove first – with a weapon that resembled a

nine iron; the ball came to rest about eight feet to the left of the pin; great was the applause.

McNulty drove next; the ball ended up about twelve feet to the right of the flag; he was warmly applauded. The third partner, José María Olazabal, put his ball halfway between McNulty's and the pin. The crowd gave him his due – this was sweet golf. Walton got his birdie – and the aforementioned optimist shouted 'On your way.' I might as well tell you that the young Spaniard was also down in two; McNulty got a par.

The friendly Zimbabwean is no stranger to Ireland; three years ago he tied for second place in this tournament. Olazabal too has good memories of this country; he was joint runner-up in the Open last year.

Philip finished yesterday in 68; José María returned a 69; Mark is still a contender with 71. I followed this trio for an obvious reason; I am as much a chauvinist as the Australian prime minister, whatever his name is.

Philip Walton, fair-haired and white-visored, stood out yesterday; it is easy to understand his popularity – he is at once simple and stylish. I am not forgetting Ronan Rafferty; he went around in sixty-seven – but he was in the clubhouse or thereabouts before I reached the course, hard by the village which the locals call the Marnick.

He was only three shots behind Sandy Lyle – but most of the talk on the course and in the bars centred on the Scot. And an aficionado who had followed his every stroke said to me: 'Sam Torrance was inside him at every hole – and yet Lyle finished seven strokes in front of him.'

And he went on: 'And after his lunch he practised for two hours.' How he found out this, I don't know – and it would have been impolite to ask.

Sandy Lyle occupies a strange niche in the mythology of golf – strange even for a Scot. For long years he was the Golden Boy who was threatening to make 'potential' an extremely dirty word.

He reached his nadir one rain-drenched evening when he tore up his card a few holes from the finish in the Irish Open – at Royal Dublin, I think. And then over a few glorious days it all came right: the English-reared Scot won the British Open.

Financially that victory set him up for life – but seemingly despite all the Scotsman jokes, he is not materially minded. His life's ambition is to play good golf – something he hasn't been doing for a long time.

Until yesterday he most certainly wasn't having a season in the sun. He had invoked several coaches, including his father – all in vain.

Obviously he hadn't heard of Sean Boylan; instead of consulting Ireland's most famous witch doctor, he called in a psychiatrist – worse still, a fellow Scot. Nevertheless, it all changed yesterday – and Sandy tore up not his card but the course record.

Before setting out for the daunting North County, I watched the play on television – and saw as much as I could. Lyle's driving was steady rather than spectacular; he created the marvellous sixty-four by some super play on the green. He sank big putts at the third, tenth, thirteenth and seventeenth – and a huge putt on the twelfth, as long as Walton's at the eighteenth.

Sandy is immensely popular with Irish crowds, probably because his human frailty makes us feel kinship with him. I am not forgetting my neighbours' child, Eoghan O'Connell, the amateur (for the time being) who came home in sixty-eight.

Some people think that a Kerry golfer is a kind of freak – far from it. Eoghan is following in a line that contains Billy O'Sullivan, John Guerin, Pat Mulcaire, John C. Cooper – and Bridget Gleeson. John C., an old friend of mine, had tremendous talent at Gaelic football, rugby and golf. He was, however, always too busy making a living; running a hotel consumes enormous skelps of time.

About him there is a story which could be deemed a Kerryman joke but is absolutely true. It concerns a day long ago when he had to come up to Dublin to buy a few knives from Broderick's down the quay.

It happened to be the first day of the Irish Open – and John C. had put his name down just for the heaven of it.

He cruised around Woodbrook (I think) in sixty-six – and found himself at the top of the leader board. He was due home that night – and home he went.

His neighbour, John Guerin, turned professional and served for a while with Henry Cotton himself. Somehow I always felt that John's heart wasn't fully in the game; I lost track of him – as far as I know, he is back in Killarney. I have lost track of Bridget Gleeson too; about ten years ago she was the girl wonder.

Pat Mulcaire, whom I am privileged to number among my friends, never in his life had a lesson in golf – but this did not prevent him from winning glory in the Walker Cup.

A friend of mine who isn't short of a few pounds offered to sponsor him as a professional – but golf for Pat was always only a game. I understood; yesterday not for the first time I realised that it's a hard way to make a living.

As I watched some famous professionals struggle, I said to myself: 'It's Summer time but the living isn't easy.'

And while I am at it, I must also congratulate the good people of the Portmarnock Golf Club for the friendliness and competence of their organisation.

I felt in such form about tea-time that I decided to walk back to Dublin – I didn't get past Campion's.

Sunday World

'There's Nowt So Queer as Folk'

Ronnie Delaney, Eamonn Coghlan – and Ben Johnson

The good people of Yorkshire are right: 'There's nowt so queer as folk.' The bow-wave of the Ben Johnson–Carl Lewis duel provided an example. And it was provided not by one person, but by several, including men who wouldn't venture out of doors without consulting the weather-glass – and women unlikely to allow a cake burn because they were engrossed with a chat show. The gist of their nonsense was that Johnson had held back in the preliminaries to give Lewis a false sense of security.

You will remember that not-so-big Ben qualified only as the fastest loser – nobody dices thus with life. He is great – but nobody is as great as that preposterous theory implies. You may question the word 'great' – we'll come back to it tomorrow.

You may remember too that in the last stages of the race – if there are any last stages in the hundred metres – Lewis glanced to his right. It was an astonishing act on the part of so brilliant and experienced a sprinter – he had nothing whatever to gain by it.

It told him that Johnson was in front – something he already knew – and it certainly cost him some loss of momentum, however tiny; at this level you are dealing in hundredths of seconds.

In a middle-distance race it is common to see runners look sideways or even behind them – that is part of the tactical battle. There are no tactics in the hundred metres, no more than there is a tactical element in running from a bull.

The contenders blast away from the blocks and go like the hammers of heaven, at least the winners do – for the rest it is more like the hammers of purgatory.

Incidentally, Ben Johnson's run in the hundred-metres final wasn't the fastest ever recorded. The honour belongs to Bob Hayes of the USA – he scorched over the distance in 8.9 seconds in the Tokyo Olympics.

He achieved this time, however, in the last heat of the 4 x 100-metre relay – and, of course, from a running start. Watch out for this – it is all too likely to become a pub question.

The world of athletics is a rather strange place, not least in the way the financial rewards are apportioned. The marathon is unquestionably the most demanding both in the preparation and on the day – but you don't hear of marathon winners becoming millionaires.

The reason is probably simple: the general public cannot see a marathon in the way that they can see a sprint – it is too scattered and long drawn out. And the top marathon runners do not make much in appearance money because so severe is the race that they confine themselves to about six a year.

It is generally agreed that the four hundred metres is the race that comes closest to making the Olympics a kind of killing fields – and yet it is comparatively lacking in prestige. It is physically tortuous because it is a sprint that entails a bridge too far.

Physiologists – not to mention the athletes themselves – agree that three hundred metres is about the limit that the top athletes can sprint. From then on the body suffers from a lack of oxygen; the finish is indicative – you can see the extreme suffering in the athletes' faces.

And yet the four hundred metres exists in a kind of limbo; the two hundred is closely associated with the hundred because so many compete in both – similarly the eight hundred is associated with the most glamorous race of all.

The fifteen hundred metres is far from being the metric mile – but we think of it thus. And the mile is very much part of the collective consciousness, especially in the English-speaking world. And it goes far deeper than athletics: we speak of winning a debate by a mile – and missing a target by a mile – and we have Irish miles and English miles.

Most casual followers could at the drop of a pun sing out a list of Olympic fifteen-hundred-metre winners – they might not do so well in any other race except possibly the marathon.

And of course we in this country have especial reasons to be interested in the metric mile. Ron Delaney's victory in Melbourne is an event that often provokes a 'where-were-you-when . . . ' question. It was startling because few expected that Delaney even at his best would be a contender – and in the run-up to the Olympics he had performed poorly.

Eamonn Coghlan, in contrast, went to Montreal overburdened with public confidence. I can all too clearly remember the reaction in Dublin to Eamonn's failure – anger predominated.

Logic was suspended: Eamonn had come up against a superb runner, the tough, mentally resilient New Zealander John Walker. Eamonn, by going for broke, threw away the chance of a lesser medal – I admired him for that.

I remember it as what is called 'a tactical race'; in simple language, the pace was less than frenetic – the time was the slowest in twenty years.

I remember too a commentator saying that the rest of the field played 'into Walker's hands' – I thought they had played into his legs.

The New Zealander made his break about two hundred metres out – he took a clear lead and, though he weakened in the last fifty metres, he wasn't caught.

Jim Ryun held the world record for the mile – but in the Munich Olympics he failed to qualify for the final of the fifteen hundred metres.

I took great interest in him because he came across as pleasant and unassuming.

I watched that first round live on television; the manner of Ryun's exit seemed unreal. He ran easily at the back of the field for about three-quarters of the race – and then made his move.

He collided with the Ghanaian, Billy Fordjour – and suddenly he lay stretched with his head on the kerb. He was quickly up – within about ten seconds – and set off again; the pursuit was gallant but hopeless.

Sheer misfortune seems to have caused Ryun's failure: it can hardly be invoked to explain the failure of our athletes this week. Few expected much from Eamonn Coghlan; his presence was really a reward for services rendered; Frank O'Mara's failure was the big disappointment.

On the only occasion on which I met Frank it was a case of friendship at first sight – and so I took a special interest in his fortunes. For some reason – possibly worst known to himself – he finished far behind runners not generally deemed in his class.

Being human I am tempted to seek a general cause for our failures; the popular explanation is that lack of confidence is at the root. The achievements of The Republic's team in the Euro Cup doesn't seem to have rubbed off on the athletes.

Sunday World

We tend to think of the hare as a beautiful and timid creature – beautiful he is, but timid he is not. He will fight fiercely with his own at the mating season, sometimes even to death; he will swim miles across rough seas.

The hare is daring and intelligent and hardy. Above all, he is wary. He needs to be. Unlike the fox and the badger and the otter and the rabbit he has no bolt-hole. His bedroom is the open, utterly unguarded.

And he sleeps in the strangest places. You will not be surprised to find his 'form' in a dry ditch amidst bracken and fern or in high rushes or couch grass – and such places he favours in Autumn and early Winter. But the turn of the year affects him as it does us all.

When the days begin to grow after Christmas he tends to camp out. Sometimes you will find him in a little hollow in a bare field; more often you will find him snuggled down in ploughland.

The weather may be cold and wet but it hardly seems to matter; he draws warmth from the earth; his eider-like fur keeps him dry. And in ploughland, especially when it has been harrowed, he is amazingly difficult to discern.

His colour merges in with that of the earth; the untutored eye could mistake him for a stone. And there he lies from about an hour after dawn when he returns from feeding until an hour before dark when he sets out again.

He sleeps very lightly, even when the day is calm and warm; when the day is windy he hardly sleeps at all. His scent is being wafted abroad; his ancient enemy, the fox, is likely to be creeping up on him – it is no time for slumber.

And on Monday morning at Donabate the wind was the main worry. It was coming from the west, the kind of weather men describe as fresh. Behind it the sky was a slaty-grey; there was every indication of a small storm.

And the crowd, gathered in little knots in front of Smyth's pub, were apprehensive; in the great fields of lea and ploughland beyond the village were plenty of hares, but they would be awake and watchful and difficult to drive into the field chosen for the coursing.

And so it proved. A little after ten the crowd were in a ragged line along the southern fence of the first chosen field; the slipper in his red jacket was midway at the eastern hedge; the judge, red-jacketed too on a piebald pony, was a little to his right and infield; the beaters were busy behind the slipper's back – time passed, but no hare came.

The day was darkening now and was stormy rather than windy. Greyhounds on leashes amidst the crowd yawned and whimpered; the slipper and the pair under his command seemed as if they had been there forever – and then at last came sounds of excitement.

A hare was up in the strawberry beds; the beaters were urging him on the required route with a frenzy of cries; a whistle blew – the official signal that a course was expected.

The knowing ones keep their eyes on the gap to the slipper's left. And suddenly there he is, the first hare of the day – pale brown above, ears back, scut up, eyes huge, the great hind legs driving him on in a fluid chain of movement.

He veers outfield from the crowd, veers again a little from the judge and his pony – and when he is about seventy yards away the slipper runs a few strides and looses the hounds.

They have perfect sight of the hare against the green lea and come from the slips close together, a brindled and a white-and-brindled, snouts low, fierce of intent. The crowd is silent.

The field is a few hundred yards long and the hare has

almost reached the safety of the western fence when he is forced to change course to avoid capture – the hounds are within feet of him, the white-and-brindled slightly in front.

The hare turns with incredible adroitness, so sharply that he is almost going back the line on which he came; the dogs brake violently and little tufts of grass fly in the air.

Quickly they are again in pursuit and in fifty yards the hare is again forced to change course – death seems imminent. But his sleight of foot is marvellous – and there in the south-western quarter of the field he time and again evades the eager jaws.

Almost a score of times he changes direction, sometimes going away at right angles, sometimes swinging around. At last the distance between turns begins to grow – the hounds are tiring.

And finally the hare makes a little half-circle and straightens out to run back in the direction whence he came; the hounds labour behind – they are not coursing now, but hunting.

The hare goes through a gap in the hedge to the slipper's right; the beaters are silent as he runs past them – he has come through the dance of death to freedom. The judge signals the winner – and the Donabate January meeting is under way.

Soon the whistle blows again; a hare comes through the hedge a little to the slipper's left and goes towards the right – when the dogs are near he swings towards the northern hedge and before they can recover he is into it and gone. Then comes another blank; it is decided to move north to the next field – its hinterland produces only two hares, both magnificent creatures who seem to toy with the hounds. By now it is twelve and a major change of territory is decided upon.

First there is a break for lunch. There is no bar or

restaurant – but boots of cars are opened and seem stocked for Arctic expeditions. People you never met until a few hours before offer you an abundance and variety of food and drink. There is great camaraderie: for the day at least, age and sex and status seem irrelevant in the freemasonry of hound and hare.

The new field is a magnificent green plain; east of it is a great area of ploughed upland – here the beaters are busy, the whistle soon blows, and you can see the hare long before he runs down into the coursing space.

The whistle blows frequently now; not all the hares that get up run obligingly into the slipper's territory, yet there is a course about every seven minutes. The meeting is now certain of success; even the wind has died down and the sky has brightened.

The mood is now of relaxation. There is comment on how dry the land is and how soft the Winter – here and there are daisies, months before their time.

The aficionados of open coursing, a rare and special breed, are in their element. There is talk of Waterloo, of the great difference between park coursing and of coursing in country where the hare knows every blade of grass.

We spend the last hour with Tom Lonergan. Tom is now nearly thirty years in Walkinstown, but he reminds you of Cavafy's famous lines – that in the fields in which you grow up, there you will give your life, no matter where you may roam.

Tom is from Doon in east Limerick and his talk is all of the country – the dogs and hares and cattle and land and of how great it is to spend a day out here where the city for all its nearness might be a thousand miles away.

And perhaps it is the very nearness of the city that makes Donabate so rural – you find that same quality in Essex and Kent. Back in Smyth's pleasant pub you might be in a different century.

The aficionados talk with the marvellous innocence of

their kind. The meeting has been a great success. There is only one regret – that one hare failed to get away. At the November meeting all went scot-free.

We were near the unlucky hare when he was caught. A steward was on hand to end his suffering quickly. The hare died with less mental and physical pain than did your Christmas turkey. Coursing would have few opponents if it was always as in Donabate on Monday.

Evening Press

THE SHIFTING FORTUNES OF THE ANCIENT GAME

The creation of the Aswan Dam was a boon to the economy of Egypt but it did no good for the fishermen in the Nile Delta. The invention of plastic was hailed as a step forward but it did no good for the jute workers in Pakistan.

In 1800 the Act of Union abolished the Irish Parliament – it too had unforeseen consequences. Dublin was no longer a capital; it became a provincial city. Most of the landlords took up residence in London.

No doubt many people said 'good riddance' – but it didn't work out that way. The most surprising consequence was that the ancient game of hurling went into an almost permanent decline. The landlords were its greatest patrons; many of them kept stables of hurlers, just as their counterparts in Britain kept stables of cricketers.

In both cultures the landlords competed with their fellows, sometimes for big wagers. When Michael Cusack embarked on his epic endeavours, hurling was almost extinct. The Famine of course had been a factor: there was little inclination to play games in the grim years after 1848.

Cusack's ambition to see Ireland have its own distinctive games succeeded – up to a point. By taking what he deemed the best elements of soccer and rugby, he created a new game – shrewdly he christened it Gaelic football.

One historian tells us that the new association, the GAA, 'swept the country like wildfire'. That was true but in a limited way: the new game took root in every nook and in several crannies – the remains of hurling languished.

Hurling today is little more widespread that in the days of the landlords. Indeed, despite many efforts to promote it, the ancient game is sadly narrow-spread. There are many reasons for this lack of growth.

Not least is the mysticism that surrounds the game: it has the albatross of 'tradition' hanging from its neck. In the old husbands' tales you are told that hurlers must be born.

We all must be born – but I doubt if small boys in Cork and Kilkenny and Tipperary come into this world with 'hurler' stamped on their wee backsides. Of course this concept of 'born hurler' is a total myth but sometimes myths can be more powerful than truths.

The big three – Cork and Kilkenny and Tipperary – won seventy of the first hundred All-Irelands. It wasn't until 1981 that the All-Ireland was won by a county where hurling isn't the dominant game.

Offaly, wherein it is confined to a few parishes, made the breakthrough and shocked most of Gaeldom and almost all of Hurlingdom. The old husbands, otherwise the traditionalists, were unruffled: it was an aberration – it wouldn't be repeated. It was – and more emphatically – in 1985.

And yet on the night of that final in 1985 I discovered that old attitudes die very hard – some do not die at all. I was in Paddy Morrissey's, that great Kilkenny pub in Dublin's Leeson Street. I met a normally very intelligent girl who said to me: 'Offaly are only scoopers.'

Her words came back to me on a Sunday in 1995 in Croke Park when Offaly met Kilkenny in the championship. A deluge postponed the start for twenty minutes; the teams re-emerged onto a sodden pitch.

Offaly put on as fine an exhibition of hurling as ever we have seen in Croke Park or in any park. Kilkenny were bewildered; the contest was over long before the interval. That game, or if you like, that exhibition, was seen by a big crowd and by many more on live television.

It should have slain the 'born hurlers' myth and buried it at a crossroads with a stake driven through its silly heart. Alas, it is as alive and as unwell as ever.

The other bar to the advance of hurling is the provincial system on which the All-Ireland is based. The year of Our Lord 1955 will suffice as an example. Cork and Tipperary were joint favourites to win the All-Ireland – Clare sent them both tumbling out of the Munster Championship. Limerick put out Clare in the Munster final. Wexford beat Limerick in the semi-final and went on to beat Galway in the All-Ireland final.

Now here is the summary: if Clare had been fated to win that year's All-Ireland, they would have needed to win five games; Galway got a bye to the final and needed only one game to win the All-Ireland. It was ridiculous but few people shouted 'Stop!'

The provincial system mocks logic and fair play but it is still with us. The few who dare suggest reform are shouted down by the traditionalists. What would hurling be like without the Munster final . . .

The Munster final is sacrosanct. And it isn't really a Munster final unless it is played in Thurles between Cork and Tipperary.

The best Munster final I ever saw was played in Killarney between Limerick and Tipperary. Of course it wasn't the real thing: you need to see the dust rising around the goalmouths in Thurles.

Television has helped to clean up hurling: that famous dust didn't always come from strokes aimed at the ball. That's another story: more relevant is the bizarre tale of Galway's attempts to get into contention for the All-Ireland.

They won the All-Ireland in 1923 – and then an interim during which it seemed that the gods would never smile on them again. And some time in the sixties they asked to be allowed play in the Munster Championship.

Their argument sounded simple: because they had no competition in Connacht, they had to start out every year in the championship without the benefit of a game. They got their wish. It didn't seem to dawn on Galway's Brains Trust that every other county started out in the same way.

Galway got their wish – and suffered years of humiliation. They almost disappeared from the map of Hurling. Eventually they had to be asked to be allowed to get out. It all resembled a story about W. B. Yeats.

The great man had never consumed a pint of stout – or even held a pint. And so he asked his friend and fellow poet, F. R. Higgins, to help repair this flaw. Higgins took him into Mulligan's in Dublin's Poolbeg Street about six o'clock on a Friday evening.

It was pay day and the dockers were building up a head of steam. 'Higgins,' said Yeats, 'please take me out.'

Television has been a boon to hurling; so has the coming of the helmet. This was inspired by the revolution in cricket. A new breed of fast bowlers had sprung up in the West Indies; they stood about two metres – thus came the helmet. It was a matter of life and death.

Hurling faces a few problems: one resides in the decline of the Christian Brothers. Some of them were not particularly Christian or brotherly but the order played a mighty part in the propagation of the game. They were like Johnny Appleseed, the legendary American pioneer, who travelled the length and breadth of the New World spreading the precious fruit.

Another problem resides in the greater carry of the new ball. Many puck-outs land within thirty yards of goal. If all puck-outs and frees were taken off the ground, as with sideline cuts, it would revolutionise the game. As things are now, the middle third of the pitch is like land set aside by decree of the EU.

Recently Kerry gave Antrim a good game in the final

of League Division Two. That, I fear, was another false Spring; almost always such promising displays are followed by heavy defeats in the championship. It all recalls the story of Sisyphus who was condemned to roll a stone up a hill until it rolled back down.

There was no tradition of hurling in my part of Kerry but we had a game of our own. We played in the road with improvised camáns; the ball was the lower half of a small polish tin.

Many years later I was delighted to learn that we had been playing Winter hurling, just as the two men in a play by Moliere were thrilled to discover that they had been speaking prose all their lives.

Magill

I know a few people who believe that they understand the New Zealand mentality. Now read on . . .

The Kiwis have never fought a war on their own – and look on rugby as a substitute for battle. Some people will tell you that war is a substitute for rugby – we will skip that.

There is a book about New Zealand called *The Passionless People*. It was written by a native son – I fear that he wasn't 'into sport'. I know that when New Zealand are playing a Test in the Northern Hemisphere, even the dogs and the cats stay up late.

I have a piquant memory of an afternoon in Dunedin during the World Cup in 1987. I went to cash a traveller's cheque and found myself a hero for a few minutes. All the staff gathered around to see the man who had come all the way from Ireland for the World Cup.

And all the staff, men and women and boys and girls, were wearing shorts and numbered All Black jerseys. It was a charming little scene. I didn't spoil it by revealing that I had been paid to come.

On the following day, we experienced a fine game between Canada and Ireland. It came perilously near producing a sensational result. The men who sported the Maple Leaf went into the lead in the seventieth minute. Tony Ward mounted a rescue operation.

A barman told me about a little snatch of dialogue he had overheard. A veteran said: 'That man Ward could walk on water.' His friend said: 'He couldn't. He's a Protestant.'

I cannot forget the courtesy and generosity that I encountered in Dunedin. I was ferried back in time. Those virtues are not a prominent part of our culture in this country today.

Brent Pope, incidentally, is a native of Dunedin. He is a decent man who believed that he knew everything about rugby until he came to manage Clontarf.

On the way back to town after that game in Dunedin, I remarked to the taxi driver that the attendance had been rather small. And he said: 'We don't get many fine Saturdays at this time of the year. People are out sailing or walking up in the mountains.'

That underlined something I had known – the New Zealanders love the out of doors. In Wellington, I saw men of four score and more out running in the dawn. It was a heartening sight.

Their status in the world of sport reflects this love of the open. They have never been far from the top of the tree in rugby. They are formidable in cricket and athletics and sailing and are an emergent force in soccer.

I fear, however, that they love rugby not wisely but too well. We remember the outrage in New Zealand when Colin Meads was sent off in a game in this part of the world.

There could be no doubt about the great man's guilt. The television camera couldn't have made it clearer. The 'logic' of the reaction down below was that Meads was above the law.

And, in the course of the World Cup in 1987, I discovered that criticising New Zealand rugby wasn't the best way to make friends and influence people.

The general expectation was that the final of the inaugural World Cup would be between Australia and New Zealand. It didn't work out that way. On a fine Sunday afternoon in Sydney the scenario became unstuck.

The home team were warm favourites to beat the French and seemed on the way to victory until David Campese made a cardinal error. At the time, he was just about the best attacker in rugby union and certainly the worst defender.

Alas for the gold-and-green, he hesitated to catch a lofted ball; it bounced wickedly – France got a try that turned the game.

The run-up to the final was of the kind that I had never known before. The hostility against France bordered on hysteria.

The French are the most civilised people in the world; they tell us so themselves – but at the time their government was behaving outrageously. They were testing nuclear bombs in the south Pacific. The people of New Zealand were not amused.

Their argument was simple: 'We depend on agriculture and fishing – pollute our land and our water and there is no more New Zealand.' On the night before the final, I met sensible people who forecast that a French win could provoke riots.

The win, if not the riots, seemed likely in the first half – the Tricolours were waxing. Then on the brink of half-time came what may have been a turning point: France were denied a penalty try.

It was blatant injustice. Then the gods took a hand – during the interval came wind and rain that would favour New Zealand.

The last quarter was only a playing out of time. The riot police went home. The people of New Zealand, as we have seen, never fought a war on their own.

They have another reason for looking on rugby as more than a game. Most of them look to Scotland as their spiritual home – it is a long way from the south Pacific. They have a sense of isolation, of being exiled in hostile surroundings.

Australia is only a thousand miles away across the Tasman Sea – it is little more than two hours' journey. There is, however, little love lost between these two peoples.

Small countries tend to resent being in the shadow of

245

big countries. We here in Ireland know the feeling. So do the Scots and the Welsh.

The Kiwis have another pan of fried potatoes on their shoulders. They are aware that the outside world looks on them as culturally backward.

They are not – but this belief persists. It is engulfed in a story that is long part of folklore.

The time was the early twentieth century and the location was a hotel in Auckland. Most evenings when the bar was at its busiest, a little old man (do we ever hear of big old men?) used to run in and shout: 'John Keats was the greatest poet that ever lived.' Then he used to flee for his life.

In the meantime, this supposedly cultural backwater has produced two of the world's greatest writers of short stories – Katharine Mansfield and Frank Sargeson. For good measure they have produced some good films – and their wine is now making a name with the best.

Nevertheless, rugby occupies a huge place in the national mindscape. And the Kiwis, even in bad times, look on themselves as the game's chosen people. The good people of Kerry used to have a kindred belief about Gaelic football – but that was a long time ago.

We tend to take people at their own valuation – most rugby nations look up to the All-Blacks. Why should the hookers put the ball into the line-out? The answer is simple – because the All-Blacks started the practice.

In more civilised times, we saw the winger put the ball in – it made sense. The ball should be put in by the best man in the wingers and the three loose forwards.

Our management slavishly follow the general example although Keith Wood and Frankie Sheahan seem not to be related to William Tell. Indeed, if I ever go fowling with them, I will keep well back.

Sunday World

'This Dog Won't Fight'

The Proposal to Split the Dublin GAA in Two

The Brains Trust that planned to divide Dublin into two Gaelic football teams didn't know their social history. If there is to be a breaking-up, it will be on the lines of Fingal and Tallaght and Dublin City.

I believe that the proposal is a non-runner – or as my Kerry neighbours would say: 'This dog won't fight.' My friend Mick O'Dwyer wasted no words: 'It's daft, plain daft.'

When did the Liffey become a line dividing two tribes? The people of Dublin are hardly aware of it. When Dublin were represented by fourteen Vincentians and one outsider, their support was no less in the Deep South.

And if Thomas Davis or Ballyboden St Enda's or Kilmacud Crokes reversed the act, their support would be no less in the Far North.

I find it hard to understand why this kite was set aloft. Dublin are not dominating Gaelic football to an embarrassing degree. Indeed their record in the senior and under-age championships is rather thin.

We are told that the size of Dublin's Gaelic-football population makes administration very difficult. There must have been some substance to this in the days of pen and ink and school copybooks. Now when small boys can be seen with a computer game in one hand and a camcorder in the other, administration should be no problem.

Of course it seems ridiculous to have Dublin and, for example, Leitrim in the same competition – but the 'daft, plain daft' proposal will not correct that imbalance.

The club All-Ireland gives the so-called lesser counties a good chance of a place in the sun. That was the format for the championship in the good backward old days.

Our forefathers were not out-and-out daws.

If the lesser counties are to be given a fair chance of progress, it should be in the context of a league, as in soccer here and elsewhere. I have been advocating this since the days of Robin Sarch and Reckitt's Blue and Custer's Last Stand.

The ongoing trauma of Kerry's hurlers is in itself sufficient example of the need for change. They are landlocked in Munster; with a bad draw they would need to beat three major powers to break out; with a good draw they would need to beat 'only' two.

When the founding fathers of the GAA adopted the county as a unit, they backed a winner. It was a rather strange choice for so Gaelic a body: the counties were imposed by Britain – and especially England. The counties had no traditional unity – and even less geographical unity. The lines were drawn for convenience in administration.

Some counties, at least in the realms of hurling and Gaelic football, manage to cook up grievances against each other. Kerry and Dublin are an example.

We were told that this hostility originated in the primary schools in the capital. The early governments in the young state attempted to revive the Gaelic language with a reign of terror.

There was a preponderance of Kerry teachers in Dublin; they suffered from guilt by association. Perhaps this was a factor in the bitterness between the counties in the seventies.

A bigger factor was the city-versus-country mentality that is known the world over. It is – or was – expressed as jackeen versus culchie.

I experienced a rather extreme example of this attitude in the aftermath of the All-Ireland Final. This was the occasion when the names of Mikey Sheehy and Paddy Cullen became as inextricably linked as those of Caesar

248

and Brutus, not to mention those of Jack Dempsey and Gene Tunney.

Next day in the *Evening Press* I dared to make a mild joke about the goal – little did I know. I suffered a stream of communications by post and phone – they weren't all complimentary. One from a fourteen-year-old boy was memorable: it ended – 'From now on it's death to the Culchies.' He was from Ballyboden.

The bitterness between Dublin and Kerry turned into an unlikely friendship. Jimmy Keaveney and his merry men began to look on going to Listowel races as an essential pilgrimage.

I experienced a piquant symbol of this in the Black Forest in Germany. It came in the wake of that game against England when an ethnic Donegal man, Ray Houghton, scored a magic goal – and a fully fledged Donegal man, Packie Bonner, made many magic saves.

That evening we were up in a hotel in the mountains; the craic was well above the international average. Late in the night or perhaps early in the morning, I found myself in a quiet corner, kind of, with Kevin Moran.

In a lull in the storm he turned to me and said: 'Do you know something . . . I'd give anything to be in Ballybunion tonight.' If I had happened to be in Ballybunion, I would have wished to be in Stuttgart – such is human nature.

Anyhow, it is good that the bitterness between Dublin and Kerry has diminished to insignificance. There was hardly a trace of it, either on the pitch or in the ground, during those two tumultuous days in Semple Stadium last Summer.

Now the generality of Dubs look on Kerry as a Promised Land. The Dingle Peninsula is the main beneficiary; South Kerry was always tourist country.

The Dingle Peninsula owes some of its popularity to that wretched movie *Ryan's Daughter*. And of course

Paudie's Pub in Ventry has become a place of pilgrimage.

Let us suppose that Dublin is divided into two regions in Gaelic football: can you see the faithful followers being divided into warring tribes . . . I can't – once a Dub, a Dub forever.

The Dublin question is only a makey-up problem; there are real problems facing the GAA. Hurling is already a minority game; Gaelic football could go the same way.

Football enjoyed a season in the sun last year, due in the main to the 'back door'.

But such changes are only expedients: the All-Ireland as we know it must be scrapped – and the game itself must be radically reformed.

The young people of today, both genders, are fortunate. They have a choice of several games. That is real freedom; a generation ago in rural Ireland there was hardly any choice at all. This is freedom in a real sense.

Magill

'GALWAY HAVE TAKEN TRADITION AND WRUNG ITS SCRAWNY OLD NECK'

GALWAY PLAY KILKENNY IN THE ALL-IRELAND HURLING FINAL, 1987

No doubt they had weather forecasters in Spain in 1588 but they seem to have been on the blink in July of that year – otherwise the Armada's sailing would have been postponed. Francis Drake could afford to be laid-back as the great fleet came across the Bay of Biscay; he knew that the tempest was his ally.

About ten o'clock in Dublin yesterday morning the rain, which had been no more than a faint moistness, made up its mind and started to come down straight from a leaden sky.

And with it one's mental images of the impending battle began to change shape. And a question sprang up: whom would the rain favour?

The obvious answer was that both teams would prefer that it had held off; a wet surface adds to hurling's inherent uncertainty. In such conditions the ball can change pace and direction in a way that makes you suspect that its Gaelic name was something to do with the word 'slithery'.

And some Galway folk no doubt had memories of the 1979 final, when a ball skidding on a wet surface found its way into the net at the Canal End and visibly wounded the maroon-and-white.

There was, however, the consoling memory of two years ago when Galway beat Cork in an amphibious semi-final. That was the occasion when most of this year's Galway team faced their first big test; the new wave came through so well that someone referred to them as 'the Raindance Kids'.

And yet the wet sod and the slippery ball would hardly favour the short passing that their front six have developed so well. And the changed going would diminish the big advantage of this sextet; it was generally agreed that at least five had more pace than their markers.

And yet it is probable that Kilkenny saw it differently. Their tradition puts great store in the long-range score: their unspoken motto is 'Take the points and let the goals look after themselves.' And the better the conditions, the more likely there would be a point-storm.

The rain ceased about half past two and held off except for the first five minutes of the second half. It turned out that the conditions weren't too bad at all.

The pitch held up well. No doubt it was slippery but that shouldn't have mattered; if we are to believe the advertisements about the modern boots, they would enable you to walk on water. The conditions should not be used as an excuse for this undistinguished game.

Two years ago in the semi-final Cork and Galway served up a classic on a day when heaven's cocks were open and you could expect to encounter a seal in Croke Park.

The reasons for yesterday's less-than-graceful encounter was not on the pitch or in the sky but in the minds of the players and possibly their mentors. Both sides were so bent on winning that some players weren't over-concerned about the means.

Mr Terence Murray booked seven players – all were lucky to escape the shameful walk. And a few more were lucky to escape his censure.

Let there be no disguising the fact that this was a dirty game, heavily marred by off-the-ball 'incidents' and much vicious 'tackling'. The inexplicable fact is that nobody was sent off. It is remarkable that in Gaelic football you can be dismissed for a blow with the fist but on yesterday's evidence you can only be booked for a blow with a hurley. It was hardly surprising that the quality of the hurling was poor; too many players were bent on spoiling rather than creating.

Kilkenny folk may have been loath to admit it but they were still suffering from the deep wounds inflicted in last year's semi-final. And Galway were facing the appalling prospect of three lost harvests in a row.

The mental climate of this match didn't excuse the skulduggery of which some players were guilty – but it explained the ragged texture.

When a man is on trial for his life, you do not expect him to offer epigrams – so it was yesterday.

This hundredth playing of the All-Ireland hurling final produced some astonishing statistics. For example, Kilkenny's original sextet of forwards produced only one score, a great point by Harry Ryan in the thirty-seventh minute.

And Kilkenny got only one score in the last twenty-five minutes, a point by substitute Tom Lennon in the sixtieth minute.

Kilkenny have a marvellous tradition of long-range points – yesterday they uttered fifteen wides, nine in the first half. Their woeful waste recalled Kerry's eighteen wides in the replay of this year's Munster final.

Galway were more thrifty: six wides, three in each half, is an acceptable level of inaccuracy. And now for the good news: we saw some great hurling, all the more pleasing because it sprang up like flowers in a desert.

And at least one man kept his head while many around were losing theirs. Galway's left half-back, Ger McInerney, was more than the man of the match – he was the man of the season.

He exemplified Ernest Hemingway's most quoted phrase: 'grace under pressure'. He also recalled a fragment from the national anthem: 'Some have called from a land beyond the sea.'

In the second half especially he showed a radar-like instinct for being where the ball came within reach – and almost always he used it well. He seemed to have remarkable freedom but he made it for himself by amazing anticipation.

And, strange though it may seem, this was not a tight marking game; it seemed to be but it wasn't. The impression of tight marking came from the sight of players jostling one another far off the ball.

It was common to see the man in possession being harassed by two or three – therefore one or two of his colleagues must have been unmarked.

The ball rarely was sent to an unmarked man; the number of passes that went astray was probably a record for a final. It was common to see a man work wonders in winning the ball – only to give it away.

Galway's short passing produced little. Brendan Lynskey exuded ideas but he failed to unite the attack. It was only in the last ten minutes that the maroon-and-white flowed. The Kilkenny attack never flowed at all.

McInerney, Tony Keady and Peter Finnerty were the best line of the day. Behind their brilliance was the solidity of Sylvie Linnane and Conor Hayes and Ollie Kilkenny.

And behind them was John Commins; yesterday he entered folklore; his two marvellous saves from Liam Fennelly were the game's highlights.

Neither side could claim a clear advantage in midfield: Ger Fennelly played soundly – apart from inaccurate shooting; Pat Malone flowered late; Steve Mahon was as usual cool and resourceful – and scored two precious points. Lester Ryan began well but faded.

Kilkenny's suspect defence did well. Joe Hennessy struggled in the first half; he was brilliant in the second.

Paddy Prendergast did his part shrewdly. And John Henderson was always in command of his corner. Ger

Henderson took unwarranted punishment but managed to show his greatness. Liam Walsh and Sean Fennelly gave little away.

The Kilkenny unit failed as a unit. And yet the black-and-amber favours were dancing in the early passages of the second half.

Galway had led by five points to four at half-time; Kilkenny resumed as if determined to put the pretenders in their place. In the first minute of the new half came a glorious seventy-five-yards point from Ger Fennelly.

Anthony Cunningham quickly replied. Then Harry Ryan wriggled free in the right-hand corner and from an unlikely angle posted the ball over the bar.

Mahon regained the lead; Ger Hennelly levelled from a free. Now it was head to head; one sensed that a goal would win the day.

Liam Fennelly was almost through but Hayes brought him down; Ger Fennelly pointed the free. Twenty-seven minutes remained.

Now Kilkenny were in front for the first time. Away below on the Hill the black-and-amber danced. The huge Galway following on the Canal Terrace were silent in foreboding.

Joe Cooney eased their worries with a point from a free. In the fifty-third minute he put Galway ahead from another free. Mahon added a mighty point.

Then a minute later came what many will see as a turning point – it was almost a turning goal. For once Liam Fennelly got behind the backs and with the ball in hand looked certain to beat Commins. An underhand flick would surely have left the keeper helpless – but the most celebrated golador in the game held up the ball and palmed it; somehow Commins kept it out.

That was in the fifty-third minute. Two minutes later Liam fired in a great shoulder-high shot from the right – again Commins parried. The ball wasn't cleared – and

Lennon pointed but now you felt it was Galway's day.

The denizens of the Canal Terrace had seen two near-miracles under their noses – now they were in great voice.

Just on the hour Cooney from a free made the score eleven points to nine. By now Galway's equivalent of the US Seventh Cavalry, Noel Lane and P. J. Molloy, were on the pitch.

And in the sixty-second minute Lane's great instinct for putting the ball in the net blossomed again. Cooney had made a great run down the middle and passed to the right; Lane shot from a narrow angle – the ball went in off Kevin Fennelly's near foot. Now all but the Hill was an ecstasy of maroon and white.

Kilkenny fought back valiantly but against a raging tide. Keady signed off with a point from away out in the country.

Spare a thought for Kevin Fennelly: Kilkenny's keeper was woefully unlucky for the goal; his puck-outs and frees devoured space; he had a fine game.

And spare a thought too for Martin Naughton, Eanna Ryan, Anthony Cunningham and Michael McGrath. The ball didn't run too kindly for them yesterday, but they have played a great part this season. I suppose you could say the same for Kilkenny's forwards – Christy Heffernan especially will understand.

The final score – 1–12 to 0–9 – wasn't a fair reflection: the margin might have been the other way if Liam Fennelly hadn't missed that great opportunity. Anyhow, Galway have now made a clean sweep: this year they have won the Railway Cup, the League and the Golden Fleece.

And like Down and Offaly, they have taken tradition and wrung its scrawny old neck.

Evening Press

ITALIA 90

Some day somebody will get a doctorate in philosophy or perhaps in psychology for a thesis on the failure of soccer to take deep root in the USA – perhaps somebody already has.

We all know the standard explanations. The vastness of the subcontinent is blamed; so are the burning Summers and the sometimes savage Winters.

These factors are found elsewhere; Brazil is an obvious example; we must look elsewhere for the primary causes.

The people of the US are still immature. They are only feeling their way towards nationhood; a concept that may prove elusive on account of deeply rooted racial divisions.

It has been said that the US has a civilisation that went rotten without ever having been ripe. This is outrageously unjust. It is perhaps better to say that the people of the US still have their frontier mentality. The Indian with his bow and arrow or perhaps his rifle is still lurking in the wood waiting for the chance to slay the white devil as he goes about his work.

Immature people like their sports to be simple and full of action – hence the enormous popularity of basketball all over the US. They also like sports in which achievement can be measured mathematically, as in baseball and in gridiron football.

The North American Soccer League never prospered in the US; neither did the experiment of assembling such all-star teams as the New York Cosmos.

The Cosmos experiment was woefully ill-conceived; it was synthetic; there was no real competition. And few people will go back again and again to watch the same circus.

Over the last few years we have experienced some ludicrous suggestions designed to make soccer attractive in the US. One scientist with more imagination than common sense proposes that some godlike figure high up in the control room in the stadium will expand or contract the goals as he sees fit.

Another would-be expert proposes that not all of the players would be given a free role; some should be defenders; others should be attackers – and so on.

And yet all is not lost – the National League is being revived. This is part of a promise given when the US applied for the right to stage the Finals of the World Cup.

It is rather a strange kind of a deal – it was to have been fulfilled before the tournament. Now it is scheduled to start on April 2 next year, not on April 1 – and I need hardly say why.

One obvious question arises. Where will this new League get its players? Most of the experienced players from the US are plying their trade in Britain and in Continental Europe.

The *New York Times* was less than enthusiastic this week. It said in a headline: 'MAJOR LEAGUE SOCCER HAS MORE SCEPTICS THAN FRIENDS.' This is the only piece on soccer in its ten pages of sport – there isn't a mention of the World Cup.

The more popular paper, *USA Today*, did rather better. It carried details of the new league and devoted a good page to the World Cup.

The page includes a summary of the rules but there is no mention of offside. This is hardly surprising when you consider that the forward pass is so big a factor in American football.

In that same paper you will read a description of the long ball in relation to this evening's game between Italy and The Republic of Ireland. Obviously this was included in case some people might think that the Irish will be playing with an oval ball and the Italians with a round ball.

The experts in this same paper are not too optimistic about our chances. They say that we have only two players of world class – Paul McGrath and Roy Keane. This is less than encouraging: Paul is possibly over the hill; Roy is certainly under it.

The home team expect to reach Round Two. John Harkes, whom we know from English football, says: 'In Italy in 1990 we were only a bunch of kids out of college – we have learned from our mistakes.' His colleague, Alexi Lalas, says: 'This is a great team, the best ever to represent the US. All we have to do is play our natural game.'

The Irish over here from the homeland had only one topic of conversation over the last few days. What team would Jack play? I would have preferred if Jack hadn't been making such arrogant noises over the last few weeks. He has been quoted as saying that he is the best coach in the world and that when something is going wrong with his team on the field, he can sense it without thinking.

Napoleon used to say that the best general he ever knew was a man called Luck. Our Jack has had a share of good fortune – we can only hope that it won't desert him here on the East Coast of America.

If we fail to reach Round Two, his boasting may haunt him. Where does an ostrich hide his head when there is no sand?

In this evening's game you will see a palpable contrast between the two leaders – Andy Townsend and Roberto Baggio. Townsend relishes the hard aspect of the game; he excels at the kind of shoulder tackle that has almost disappeared from Gaelic football. Baggio avoids physical contact as much as possible – he is a one-touch player.

You could say that the approach of each epitomises the approach of his team.

I expect a draw – possibly scoreless. Incidentally in *USA Today* we were told that a goal is worth a point. It could be worth three points this evening.

That little item of misinformation makes you wonder about the future of soccer in the US.

*

On Saturday morning I was reminded of a film which was a classic and is a classic and belongs to a generation ago. It was called *The Wages of Fear*. The principal characters were Yves Montand and Charles Vanel.

The story is set in a godforsaken town in Latin America where a small number of Europeans are desperate to get away to a better world. The chance comes when fire breaks out in an oilfield a few hundred miles away. Two truckloads of dynamite are needed to cut off the fire. The two drivers chosen are Montand and an actor whose name I have forgotten but whom I remember as being quintessentially Scandinavian.

They set off. Montand is a good distance in front. When the Scandinavian comes near journey's end, he shaves off his beard with enormous concentration as if he felt some momentous event was about to occur. A few miles down the road his lorry explodes and he dies clean.

On Saturday morning another memory came back to me. It concerned the occasion of my First Holy Communion. I wasn't worried about the experience itself but about my clothes.

My mother had ordered a new suit; we had the jacket but the trousers weren't ready. And that morning as I went towards the town, I experienced for the first time in my life what I now know as nervous tension.

I was terrified of going up to the altar rails with my

splendid new coat and pants that had known a long and hectic life worn by a small boy devoted to hunting hares and rabbits and winkling fish out of their watery homes. The pants was ready and all was well.

That is all a very long time ago but on Saturday morning I felt a tension of a kind I hadn't known for years.

I was fearful that our football team would be devastated by Italy. And then all the great deeds of the past would be turned to dust and the great celebrations at Dublin Airport at the homecomings would look like fool's gold.

Italy's team-sheet bristled with great names; at least six would be candidates for a world team and at least two, Paolo Maldini and Roberto Baggio, would be almost certainties.

Some of our best team were perhaps a little beyond their best and others were very short of experience. I was thinking especially of Phil Babb; he had excelled in manoeuvres but I wondered how he would fare in war.

I was out at the stadium two hours before starting time. And the heat and humidity and the huge presence of Italians increased my fears.

At last the magnificent opening ceremony was over and the warfare began. After the first minute I knew that we wouldn't be devastated. Packie Bonner radiated confidence and Stephen Staunton fired in a shot that indicated that Republic weren't overawed.

Ten minutes later we saw Ray Houghton score a marvellous goal: from twenty-five yards he sent in a dipping shot that deceived Gianluca Pagliuca and went under his bar. The great keeper looked like a king who, though hedged by minders, found his pocket picked. This marvellous opening gave the Irish tremendous confidence and, backed by the great following, they took on the Italians in every department.

Our full-backs, Denis Irwin and Terry Phelan, were keeping house tidily and occasionally foraging into the big world outside. Phil Babb was playing with the coolness of a veteran and the zeal of a newcomer.

And what can we say about Paul McGrath? In his long career he has never been more brilliant. He took the ball with every part of his foot: instep, side, heel and at times even sole.

He looked as casual as if playing with his two small boys in his back garden. He was doing things that surely had Jack Charlton demented because our Jack likes things plain and simple.

Our Paul is a law unto himself. You cannot regulate genius. We were seeing the gospel according to Paul.

And in midfield we saw Andy Townsend and John Sheridan and Ray Houghton and Steve Staunton take on their illustrious counterparts and lose no caste.

And while all this was going on, a young man from Cork called Roy Keane was hinting that soon he would be deemed a great master.

It was a marvellous game and we were thrilled to see our players hold their own in such illustrious company as Paolo Maldini and Franco Beresi and Roberto Baggio and Roberto Donadoni and Giuseppe Signori.

The Republic dominated the first half. Then the Italians came out and put men forward and for about twenty minutes besieged Packie Bonner's goal.

Our keeper excelled himself; he was in the heroic form which we saw in Stuttgart on that famous day when we beat England.

And up in front Tommy Coyne was waging a great battle though outnumbered two to one. It all ended happily and for a long time I will remember my great friend Paul soaring to rule the sky and crouching to rule the earth.

By the way, the first truck of dynamite got to the oilfield and helped to quell the blaze – as Jack Charlton would say, they closed it down.

*

Back at home long ago there was a saying: 'It's six o'clock and there isn't a cow milked or a pig fed or a child washed.' I have a strong suspicion that this morning you could change the word 'six' to 'nine' and the same thing would be true.

I remember an evening long ago when I was on the train from Fishguard to London; it was crowded with people from the valleys who were going to London to see Dai Dower fight for the flyweight championship of Britain.

A friend who was on the same train told me that down at the bar Aneurin Bevan, then a minister in the Socialist government, was waxing indignant about the number of hours that would be lost as a consequence of this fight.

What he didn't realise is that it is such occasions that many people live for – and what they lose in hours of work on a given day they make up for by working better if the result on the occasion goes their way.

I know that at home in Kerry my neighbours are at present drawing out the turf and making the silage; I wouldn't be surprised if some of them started late today and knocked off early – but, believe me, they will make up for it when life returns to what we call normal.

A young man who is well known to me rang his parents in Dublin last night; they couldn't talk – all they could do was sob uncontrollably and put in the occasional word which meant that it was great.

By now you will have guessed that the man at the end of the phone was David O'Leary. Never before in his seventeen years as a professional footballer has he walked such a knife-edge between being a hero or a scapegoat.

As he stepped up to take that fateful penalty, I was reminded of a story that was in our school books long ago, a story which we could never forget. It concerned

William Tell, a famous Swiss hunter whose marksmanship with bow and arrow was the talk of the country far and wide. William was a rebel; he fought against a cruel overlord; he was captured and sentenced to shoot an apple off his son's head.

It may seem ludicrous to compare his trauma with that of Dave O'Leary last night – but, believe me, if David had missed, it would have left a mark on him for the rest of his life.

David missed the Euro finals two years ago because he was not in Jack Charlton's good books. And it seemed last night that he would go through these finals as no more than a substitute. Then, late in the game, Stephen Staunton became so leg-weary that he was called off and David was sent in. And so at thirty-four he got his very first taste of action in a cup final, whether World or European.

In his short stint in the actual game he did very well but if either team had scored before the end of the hundred and twenty minutes, his part would have been forgotten except by himself and his friends and family.

Then came the dreaded penalty shoot-out. And while the players decided among themselves who would take the penalties and in what order, I was back in Seville in 1982 on that burning night when the best-ever French team fell out because they missed a penalty.

And I couldn't help remembering that less than two months ago in the final of the Scottish Cup our keeper Packie Bonner went right every time the ball went left and went left whenever the ball went right and ended up being beaten nine times.

In years to come you can be certain that the following question will be asked in many a pub: 'Who took the five penalties that put The Republic of Ireland into the quarter-finals of the World Cup in 1990?'

As we all know, Romania had the first kick. And after

eight penalties the score was 4–4. Then Romania's substitute Daniel Timofte reminded us of Jimmy Keaveney in his heyday as he decided to let fly without taking a run-up. His kick seemed a model; the ball flew about chest-height away to Bonner's right but Paddy got a touch with both hands; the ball spun away to his left – and all heaven broke loose.

Near me in the press box there were many seasoned campaigners; some were incoherent – other sobbed unashamedly. And I hardly exaggerate when I say that it was the most dramatic moment in the history of our football.

There is a famous quotation from W. B. Yeats: 'Romantic Ireland is dead and gone – it's with O'Leary in the grave.' When I have time, I will amend this extract: 'Romantic Ireland is far from dead and gone – it is very much alive and well in a stadium in the heart of Genoa.'

If a writer of schoolboy fiction had brought this scenario to his editor, he would have been told to go back to his desk and write something that readers might believe.

From being an almost forgotten hero, my friend David O'Leary sprang last night to the top of the tree in popular acclaim. He and Paddy Bonner were our especial heroes and it couldn't happen to two nicer or more modest people. The American cynic who said that nice guys always finish last may have known all the answers, but he hadn't heard all the questions.

I have never quite known the Irish followers to be so quiet in the immediate aftermath of yesterday evening's game; they seemed like men and women and boys and girls who had seen something that was almost unbelievable and they were still trying to come to grips with it.

What made our victory – such as it was – all the sweeter was that for the first twenty-five minutes of this game we seemed doomed not alone to be beaten, but to be humiliated.

The man we had feared most of all, Gheorghe Hagi, lived not only up to his reputation but far beyond it: he seemed like a combination of Ruud Gullit and Marco Van Basten at their very best.

In that period the Irish midfield quartet went through a terrible trial. Andy Townsend, who had been deputed to mark Hagi, seemed like a collie being teased by a grey-hound.

Kevin Sheedy was hardly in the game at all. Paul McGrath was retreating more and more into defence. The hour, however, found the man: Ray Houghton has had a traumatic year with Liverpool; injuries and loss of form had diminished him until he was scarcely more than a name player – yesterday evening when it was most need-ed he recovered his old form. Nevertheless in those twen-ty-five minutes or so The Republic was living on the brink.

The young full-backs, Chris Morris and Stephen Staunton, were being tormented not only by the roving Hagi but by Ioan Sabau and by Iosif Ratariu. And it seemed that scores must come.

This, however, was to be Mick McCarthy's finest hour – or, to be precise, his finest two hours. He began badly and was lucky to avoid a yellow card for a succes-sion of crude fouls but when he settled, he played with an artistry and a wisdom which must forever silence his crit-ics. Yesterday evening he didn't rely on the long ball; he uttered some beautiful chips and some very neat ground passes.

Kevin Moran may not be as mobile as when he tor-mented Kerry in 1976, but he has great vision, and time and again last night he was the little Dutch boy with foot and head in the breach in the dam wall.

The game began to change in the second quarter. Houghton's influence was spreading to his midfield col-leagues; Sheedy was showing flashes of brilliance; Paul

McGrath was playing more in midfield – and Townsend was beginning to cope to some degree with the magnificent Hagi.

Up front Niall Quinn was getting the occasional touch in the air but once again John Aldridge had no luck in the green shirt. He got the yellow card for what was no more than an accidental late tackle and in that same moment he damaged an Achilles tendon; for him it seems that the war is over.

Tony Cascarino came on and proved that he is more than just a header of the ball; he did very well on the ground. And as half-time neared, the Romanians began to look a little ragged; passes went astray; clearances were hurried. And in between the fortieth minute and half-time their goals had two very narrow escapes.

Their keeper, Silviu Kung, made a marvellous one-handed stop from Kevin Sheedy. And a few minutes later a flying header from Niall Quinn went just wide of the keeper's left-hand post.

Both teams were glad to hear the half-time whistle; it was a burning evening; the temperature was in the high seventies and the humidity was 65 percent.

There wasn't the slightest breath of wind. And it was obvious that the second half would be played at a slow pace. The conditions favoured Romania; when England played them in Bucharest this time last Summer, the temperature was ninety degrees. It was hardly surprising that some of the Irish players were palpably weary long before the end; indeed, in the last twenty minutes Niall Quinn, who had played gallantly, was hardly able to run.

It was in this time that Ray Houghton showed his marvellous energy; he chased everything and whenever he won the ball, he made good use of it. It was almost impossible to get in behind the back four; Gheorghe Popescu, their brilliant sweeper, mopped up whatever little crept through. And their keeper Kung looked very happy under the high ball, whether chipped or crossed.

Cascarino came close with a header from a cross by Morris – that was the nearest we came to scoring in the second half. Paul McGrath might have had a penalty but referees are very loath to point to the spot in games of this nature. And it was with a feeling of inevitability that we watched the late stages of normal time.

And in extra time neither team seemed to have the energy or the inspiration to put the game beyond the lottery of the penalty shoot-out.

Yesterday morning at about eleven o'clock I sat with Jack Charlton and Paul McGrath as we watched the full video of the game between Argentina and Romania. Jack took copious notes. About one thing he was very worried. Hagi is dangerous from anywhere within thirty yards. He has an explosive left foot. And I know that Jack instructed his warriors to keep him out of the penalty box at all costs even if it meant committing a 'professional foul'.

The plan worked but Bonner's goal had some very close escapes. Packie made three great saves, but of course they will be all forgotten in the light of his stop from Romania's fifth penalty. It was an evening which has left behind so much talk about it that I doubt if we will think about our meeting with the Italians until the day comes.

I have never known so many happy people in Genoa and Rapallo as last night. And I can only imagine the atmosphere in Dublin and all over the country.

Nevertheless life goes on and I have no doubt that down at home today the cows were milked and the pigs were fed and the children washed. We are now in the last eight of the World Cup – such mighty powers as the Soviets and Holland and Brazil are out. Football is surely a strange old game.

Evening Press

'MICK DOYLE HAD FREED HIS PUPILS FROM THE FEAR OF MAKING MISTAKES'

IRELAND BEAT WALES, 1985

Two sacred beliefs were severely shaken in Cardiff on Saturday. The more important is a pillar of rugby logic – or perhaps I should say 'It was.' Just as the gurus tell us that Gaelic football battles hinge on midfield, so too are we told that in rugby if you are dominated in the set pieces, your house is built on a quagmire. The second belief – widely held in Ireland – is that our neighbours across the sea from south Leinster are bad losers!

A Welshman could be excused if he asked: 'How do the Irish know?' Well, on Saturday we got another opportunity to test this belief. And though a Welsh defeat was likely long before the final whistle, this was a wonderfully sporting occasion.

I spent most of the night in Welsh company: there were no excuses and the singing was grand.

Well, I suppose there could be no excuses: Wales had nobody to blame except that back seven. The Welsh pack played splendidly: perhaps the wing-forwards, David Pickering and Martyn Morris, may occasionally have been marked absent in defence – but the eight won an enormous amount of possession. And never has possession been more crazily squandered.

You couldn't blame the forwards if they felt like diligent peasants whose industry went for naught owing to a profligate aristocracy. Indeed Saturday's game gave me an insight into the excesses of the French Revolution.

And the aristocrat who must take most of the blame is Terry Holmes. The scrum-half missed much of the season through injury: his return a month ago was hailed by the Welsh papers and sport magazines as a second coming.

His skills have been little impaired by his lay-off but his tactics made one suspect that adulation has gone to his head. A Latin proverb came to mind: 'Whom the gods wish to destroy, they first make mad.'

Perhaps Holmes was not to blame: Wales, after all, have a coach, John Bevan. However, it isn't easy to foresee the course of a rugby game – at any level.

The coach or manager – or whatever he is called – sits in the stand: once the ball is kicked off, he is cut off from the battlefield. And it was hard not to believe that he had fallen in love with the Australian concept of rugby – and fallen rather blindly.

Holmes seemed obsessed with elaboration. He and his fellow backs were attempting moves that the Australians through long practice carry out instinctively.

Richard Greenwood is right: you cannot give a rugby team a brain transplant overnight. And as the Welsh backs overlapped and underlapped and dummied and scissored, they usually went more across the field than forward. And the Irish were given the time to seal off the threatened break.

When the ball reached the would-be scorer, he found himself like someone lost in Hampton Court Maze, with the added hazard that men were waiting in the bushes to clobber him.

What made this all the more puzzling was that one of Wales's straightforward movements brought a lovely try. This came a few minutes before half-time, and the Welsh following had a right to expect that the interval talk would produce an outbreak of common sense.

It produced even greater absurdity, so much so that you felt that if a Welsh back found himself clean through, he would look around for a colleague with whom to bring off a scissors or an overlap.

And while all this was going on, what were Ireland doing? They reminded me of what someone said about

Guy de Maupassant: 'He elevated common sense to the point of genius.'

Mick Doyle's greatest asset as a player was his tackling: it is hardly a coincidence that it is also the greatest asset of the current Irish team.

Doyle has a precious mental asset too: from bitter experience he knows that the parable involving the buried talents has a wide relevance.

Ireland got hardly half a dozen try-scoring chances on Saturday: they took two. While Wales wasted manna, Ireland prospered on crumbs of heaven.

It was a remarkable game: if you had seen only the figures – which no doubt some bright young people compiled – and then looked at the scoreline, you would have to assume that the computer had gone on the blink.

It hadn't: it was Holmes and his fellow backs that had gone on the blink. There was also the case of Mark Wyatt: he missed six penalties – four of them looked easy for such an accomplished kicker as he. And his general play seemed to suffer from his misses.

Such was the Welsh dominance that he got little to catch – but his intrusions into the attack were unhappy. He seemed to have forgotten Carwyn James's advice – that a full-back must come into the line at a subtle angle. Wyatt merely came in straight and cluttered up the moves: on several occasions the out-half seemed surprised by his presence.

Gareth Davies did many neat things but needs to be sent back to that famous factory to have his confidence repaired. Mark Ring was the best of a three-quarter line that had a genius for running into cul-de-sacs.

I heard bitter criticism of Richard Moriarty from a few Welsh journalists – I thought he was Wales's best. He amazed me. I thought of him as a not-so-gentle giant whose main value was in the line-out: he looked the complete forward on Saturday.

Some of his line-out work was messy – but he won much clean possession too. And time and time again he was first up to the break-down.

Robert Norster controlled the middle of the line-out. And Syd Perkins and Morris got the odd ball there too. Bill James was outstanding in the loose – and, all in all, there was little wrong with the home pack.

The *Western Mail* told the world on Saturday morning that if Wales didn't give away reckless penalties, they couldn't lose. Their control was far better than in Murrayfield: they gave Michael Kiernan only three penalty shots – but he put them all over as if he was a direct descendant of William Tell. How long must he go on finding the target before he is a recognised kicker?

Kiernan and his fellow three-quarters provided further evidence for something I have long been saying: this is the best line in the five countries. And with Paul Dean and Brendan Mullin he formed a great barbican in midfield.

Trevor Ringland was his usual serendipitous self – but even he was excelled by Keith Crossan, the little man with the built-in radar. This honest Ulsterman is so unobtrusive that you are hardly aware of his presence until he pops up to seal a leak – he is the invisible mender.

Hugo MacNeill had one terrible moment when he knocked on a long harmless ball under the post. But typically he put it behind him. And typically too he left his mark with a glorious deed. In Murrayfield it was a great catch when only he stood between Scotland and six points – on Saturday it was his part in Ireland's second try.

And his ability to transcend mistakes is typical of this team. On Saturday, for example, Michael Bradley threw out a few woeful passes – but seemed utterly unaffected.

I believe that this attitude owes much to Mick Doyle: he had freed his pupils from the fear of making mistakes.

He is achieving a kind of men's liberation.

And it is probably a product of the new attitude that the Irish pack, though beaten in the set pieces, did so well in the loose. Usually when forwards are in trouble in the line-outs and scrums, their spiritual barometer sinks.

Brian Spillane didn't let Moriarty's line-out dominance demoralise him: he excelled in the loose. His kick-ahead that lifted the siege and led to our second try was like a proclamation of freedom for forwards.

Not since Ken Goodall have we seen an Irish forward with such a sensitive foot. Most forwards – apart from the French – in such a situation would have kicked for length or contemplated setting up 'second-phase possession'.

Nigel Carr's mobility and aggression upset many a Welsh move. The other wing-forward, Philip Matthews, did well too but he gambles too much on the offside.

It may seem in bad taste to utter criticism of a team that achieved such a famous victory – but once again Ireland failed to establish a solid set-scrum. Why, I do not know: I am not one of those lucky people who can see through solid flesh. And the giving away of penalties may yet prove a costly pastime.

Ireland made much of their own luck on Saturday – but can take no credit for Wyatt's misses. This is the area that needs most correction. And next time out they may not start so well. After fifteen minutes they were nine points ahead.

Kiernan kicked a middle-distance penalty in the ninth minute. And then came a beautifully simple try.

An Irish passing movement went left but was frustrated. Ireland retained possession – and from about thirty-five yards out and in the middle Bradley angled a high ball to the right.

Ringland, jostling with Phil Lewis, won the race to the touchdown. Kiernan converted from about twelve yards from touch.

For the rest of the half we saw Welsh dominance. And they got their first score in the thirty-third minute – a sweet drop goal by Davies from broken play.

Five minutes later came the high point of Wales's day. From a set-scrum a little to their left and close in, Wales heeled smoothly. Holmes sent Davies away on the narrow side; a long pass put Lewis in near the flag. Wyatt struck the conversion beautifully – ironically he scored only from the most difficult of his seven kicks.

From the restart Wales were penalised for obstructing Donal Lenihan – Kiernan scored. And so it was 9–12 at half-time.

Wyatt missed a simple penalty just after the resumption. Wales then put in a fierce series of attacks – but it was Ireland that scored.

A breakaway led to a charge by Ringland. Ireland won the ball in the right-hand corner and it was spun across the line.

MacNeill came outside the centres – and his long, accurate, well-timed pass sent Crossan curving away from Mark Titley – he scored close in. Kiernan converted. In the seventy-fifth minute he scored his third penalty. Wales were now in bits and pieces – and glad to hear the last whistle.

Nine–twenty-one was a strange score for a game in which the territorial graph would show that Wales spent almost two-thirds of the time in Ireland's half. If there is a moral, it may be that a great player such as the Welsh scrum-half can be too much of a father to his side.

The Welsh might have been better off if they had no Holmes to go to – sorry about that.

Evening Press

'The Most Glorious Road That Ireland Have Travelled for Many a Day'

The Republic Beat the Soviet Union, 1974

It was a bad day for the experts. Before dawn, the news had come from the heart of Africa that Muhammad Ali had torn up their script and written a wild poem of his own.

As we hastened into town in the early morning, we could see the evidence of this fermentation: friends greeted one another with pugilistic gestures; there was an inchoate excitement that made the grey air seem like the light of Spring. It was as if the heretic from Kentucky had given us all a new charter.

And again in the afternoon there was a glorious divergence between prediction and fact. We had listened to the experts and been swayed by their solidly delivered opinions that there would be a small crowd at Dalymount – but when we set out for Phibsboro in what should have been good time, it was soon obvious that whatever the state of the economy and the need for humble toil, there were a great many wheels with no shoulders to them for the time being.

Streams were hurrying northwards as if to storm the Bastille. We were glad of this unforeseen congress even though it meant that the game would be in progress for several minutes before we could glimpse the white-lined rectangle and its living drama.

The chaos at the entrance was so complete that one suspected it was the work of some malevolent prankster, and by the time we had scrambled to the top of the Tramway Terrace, the clock on St Peter's Church showed twenty minutes past the hour and Don Givens had just erected the first milestone in the most glorious road that

The Republic have travelled for many a day.

We had come in the hope of being able to analyse the game with near-scientific precision – but it would have been as relevant to attempt to transmute the voice of the wind into words.

A storm had sprung up and when again Givens propelled the ball into Pilgui's net, the powerfully efficient Russian team looked like a ship that had lost its masts.

Their captain, the admirable Serge Olshansky, looking like a Bobby Charlton from the Steppes, laboured frenziedly to integrate his crew – but one felt that this Irish team would not be easily thwarted from writing an astonishing chapter.

And so it proved – although in the third quarter the Soviets played with a power and precision that threatened to chasten and subdue. Paddy Roche brought to mind what Dick Fitzgerald, the great Kerry footballer, wrote about goalkeeping: 'The custodian may get little to do but he must do that little well.'

Twice in that uneasy period he made saves that looked easy because they were unspectacular. Had he failed, brightness might have fallen from the air. But the world has no time for what might have been; it is what happened that counts – and for once we can look back on a game without summoning up that sad pretender: 'if only'.

This was The Republic's greatest sporting occasion since the grey day at Cheltenham with nibs of snow in the wind when Arkle stormed past the 'invincible' Mill House and won his first Gold Cup.

And the news of Ireland's victory was as stunning to the sporting world as was Ron Delaney's miraculous run in Melbourne on that December day eighteen years ago.

Twenty minutes from the end a decent wee man from Ballyfermot asked us to put his little boy on our shoulder that he might savour this famous victory. With a heart and a half we suffered the child to come unto us – and when in unborn years he tells his own children how he got his grandstand seat, we hope they will believe him. Johnny Giles and his heroes, like Muhammad Ali a few hours earlier, restored our belief in the romantic.

Hemingway used to say about aspiring fishermen that enthusiasm was not enough. He was right – it is equally true that good works without faith are of no avail. Ireland's albatross around the neck is the national sense of inferiority; at Dalymount yesterday the men in green shattered that grey image as explosively as Ali demolished Foreman.

It was great to be in that crowd on the Tramway Terrace. Seldom has joy been so unconfined. At last the hungry sheep had looked up and been fed. And the most heartening aspect of a gloriously memorable afternoon was the spirit of the Irish team.

Here were men reminiscent of Matt the Thrasher when he strove until it seemed his heart would crack for the honour and glory of the little village. And that new climate was symbolised especially by Steve Heighway.

A few days ago the familiar story of players withdrawing because they preferred club to country seemed about to be repeated; Heighway's casting-off of injury was a harbinger of Spring.

This Irish team is not invincible – no more than were 'the Dubs'. But like the Dubs, they have tremedous heart. And that, allied to skill, makes a formidable coalition.

Evening Press

Under the Eye of the Volcano

Mexico 86

The message-bag is now forgotten. A generation ago it was as much a part of rural Ireland as *Old Moore's Almanac* and the alarm clock and the bellows and the tongs. The coming of the motor car and electricity and sophistication did away with all four.

The message-bag was made of straw and was very deep and had two handles, in case of accident. The second handle was the insurance.

And when you set out for town you could be sure that on the way you met many a housewife who would make you into a postman in reverse. So now you can see the need for two handles. Those of my generation were familiar with words long since forgotten.

Who now understands the meaning of 'Killowen'? And who now understands the meaning of 'Blarney'? Both were kinds of thread.

And in those days you could hardly enter a house without hearing the womenfolk talking about two-ply and three-ply and Fair Isle and a great many other things associated with making your own clothes.

Many is the morning I set out for town with my message written down and my timescale worked out so that I could be home within an hour. But, invariably, funny things happen on the way to the marketplace.

Mary stopped me at her gate. She wanted two ounces of Killowen. Hannah wanted three-ply and it should be Blarney. Peggy wanted knitting needles and she insisted that they should be made of bone. And so an ordinary male in rural Ireland became acquainted with the deeper intimacies of the feminine world.

A few mornings ago all this came back to me in downtown Mexico City. I went into an airline office to buy a ticket for a flight to Las Vegas and never was I more aware of how much the world has changed since I was a boy.

Long ago with my faithful message-bag I could buy fifteen things and pay for them in half an hour. To get this simple air ticket took more than that. You may wonder why. The answer is simple – the computer struck again.

It was early morning. I was the only customer. The decent woman behind the counter knew her job. But before she could tell me that I could get a flight she had to press about ten thousand buttons, make several phone calls and eventually tell me that no flight was available.

Mexico is in many ways a marvellous country but it has an element known locally as *la mordura*. This means 'the bite' – in other words the bribe you must give on such occasions.

I suspected that I was about to pay my first bite in Mexico and so I called in David, my taxi driver, who has been to me a godsend in the last three weeks.

And he spoke to the good lady and I discovered I was hopelessly wrong. There was no flight. But what amazed me was that it took so long to find out. Anyhow, she went to great pains to make alternative arrangements and we were about to part in a haze of goodwill when a terrible thing happened.

She said: 'You have come for the World Cup?' I said: 'I have been here three weeks.' And she said: 'Have you seen many games?' I said: 'As many as was physically possible. And I have seen all the others on television or on video.' And she said: 'Who will win?' And I said: 'I fancy Brazil.'

Oh dear, I have never seen such transformation in anybody's face. From being a very polite and almost cold person she turned into a raging partisan. I could not believe that an educated, middle-aged woman could harbour such emotions; to me it was a symbol of something I had almost forgotten – the spiritual investment of the Mexicans in this tournament is beyond our understanding in Ireland.

Over a cup of coffee and a glass of beer in a local cantina my friend David explained this hunger to me. David himself is a symbol of Mexico's trauma. He is thirty and has a first-class degree in Communications but to make a living has to drive a taxi about fourteen hours a day, seven days a week.

He is a man of extraordinary intelligence and integrity of the highest kind. He would love a job in television but in Mexico it is a matter of being on the inside, and he isn't. The people in general are friendly and kind and competent and hard-working but this is a very corrupt country and the badness comes down from the top.

There is a slight improvement but the life of the ordinary Mexican is hard beyond our understanding. The tortilla is for many the staple diet, just as it was for their ancestors who scraped the soil for a living a thousand years ago.

And meat and rice are almost luxuries. Incidentally, the price of all three has increased in the last few weeks. The government has taken away the subsidy on such basic foods, hoping that it will pass unnoticed in the heat engendered by the World Cup. My friend David says: 'This is a sign of how childish the Mexican people are and how much the government scorns them.'

The government has taken a huge gamble in staging the World Cup. The devastation caused by the earthquakes last September is far greater than the world outside knows. The official figures are obviously false. The world was told that eight thousand people had perished but the figure is far more than that. The demolition workers are still finding bodies.

There is no social security worthwhile in Mexico and

so millions of people are born without being registered. Their deaths are known only to their own.

I will now give an example of how unprepared this country was for such a huge tournament. I was in March the Third Stadium in Guadalajara for the first game there. It was to start at twelve o'clock and it did but the team were on the pitch while the post-office engineers were still putting in the phones.

But all life in Mexico is a gamble. A few days ago during the interval in that great game between England and Paraguay I looked around me. The Aztec Stadium is almost in the country, if you could imagine such a huge conurbation as the capital having any surroundings.

And above me I saw the peaks of volcanic mountains which often have poured out lava and killed thousands. Technically these volcanoes are extinct but nobody knows. It's like Sellafield – the official story cannot be trusted.

Nevertheless, poor people are putting up houses and shacks on the slopes of these mountains: they are gambling that the volcanoes will never again strike, just as those who are building tall office blocks are gambling that the earthquakes will never come back.

Twice recently I saw examples of how accustomed the Mexican people are to natural violence. On the plane between Guadalajara and Mexico City last Monday I experienced what it is to be on the back of a bucking bronco. But the passengers didn't seem to notice.

They went on eating and drinking and talking away as if the flight was the essence of smoothness. Then on the evening of the England–Paraguay match I was in a café when a ferocious thunderstorm cut loose. I and my two companions were less than happy but the locals all around us didn't seem to notice.

Nevertheless, I am worried about the reaction of the people when their team falls out of the World Cup. In

1970 Mexico were hosts to the World Cup but their own team fared badly. In the meantime they have staged the Olympic Games but no local made the headlines. And now they are tired of being spectators at the wedding feast and they hunger for a sign that the gods haven't forgotten them completely.

And so now you can understand the reaction of the decent woman in the travel agency. Why do I believe that Mexico won't win? Almost every team that wins a major tournament is strong in two positions: it has a goalkeeper who is dependable and at least one forward who can smell scoring chances.

Go back over the years and you will see for yourself. In 1966 England found an unlikely goalador in Geoff Hurst. In 1970 Brazil had at least three, especially Jairzinho. In 1974 West Germany had Gerd Muller. In 1978 Argentina had Mario Kempes. And in 1982 I need hardly say that Italy had Paolo Rossi. And in all those years the goalies were good too. Felix in 1970 was much criticised but he gave nothing away.

Mexico's keeper, Paolo Larios, is very dodgy. And the man who should be their goalador is not playing particularly well. The story here is that some of the team aren't even on speaking terms with Hugo Sanchez. They say that he is out of Mexico most of the time and then comes back home and reaps the harvest which they have sown. In other words he is the only one in the squad who is making money out of endorsements.

Before this tournament started I put my cards on the table. I believed then that Brazil would win but that their price of eleven-to-four was a bookmaker's joke. And I said that the best value was the sixteen-to-one for West Germany and the twelve-to-one for England. My opinion stands.

Evening Press

Do you remember Talgo Abbess? It was a strange name for a gelding but it didn't prevent him from being one of the best hurdlers in his day. He went within a few lengths of winning the big prize at Cheltenham in a very good year.

His owner was well known to me; I used to meet him almost every Tuesday at Castle Island pig fair. Michael Healy was a gentle son of Macroom, the town that proverbially never raised a fool; the pig business was no territory for anybody who hadn't all his wits about him; Michael was brilliant.

Our entry into the Common Market brought a change in the business; Michael had a pub in Cork for a while; with typical boldness he emigrated, not to Australia or the United States but to Brazil.

He spent a few years there and became friendly with another emigrant, the alleged great train robber, Ronnie Biggs. Biggs seemed destined to spend the rest of his life in exile. It is unlikely that he will ever see Westminster Bridge or watch Arsenal or eat jellied eel in Aldgate or in the Mile End Road itself.

No doubt some enterprising newspaper will someday do a 'Where are they now?' on the robbers; it will probably reveal that they are leading very quiet lives.

Buster Edwards used to sell flowers outside Waterloo Station; I didn't see him when last I was there – but then it was Derby Day and perhaps he was gone off to Epsom.

Gordon Goodie, the leader of the gang, is in the vegetable business; he learned a great deal about potatoes and carrots and beans and the rest during his years in prison.

A rumour persists that the real leader was never

brought to court; I have heard him named – he was, we are told, the masterind. He may have been the real leader but he was certainly no mastermind; the famous robbery was about the worst-planned coup of all time.

Its only serious rival was the Gay Future affair; some of those who were involved are well known to me; I couldn't believe that such normally sensible people could act so crazily.

I lost all touch with Michael Healy when he left the pub business; he surfaced again last Sunday. We met on the way down from Croke Park; Michael was radiant. And could you blame him after that famous victory.

And with a famous rugby player of yesteryear we adjourned to the Plough and we were back again on Tuesday mornings at the pig fair in Castle Island.

And of course we reminisced about his assistant, Dinny Counihan, a famous Gaelic footballer in his day, long since gone to his rest.

Some day someone will do a thesis on the relationship that existed between rugby and the pig business. It was remarkable; I never heard it explained.

Noel Murphy spent his working life at the trade; if you saw him in his ancient raincoat, you would hardly believe that he held the highest post in the Irish Rugby Football Union.

There were other Cork Murphys in the business too – and all were stalwarts of the Constitution club.

Paddy Reid, one of our Triple Crown heroes and an old friend of mine, followed his father into the trade but found it too precarious and eventually settled for a job with a steady income.

Pig buyers, as anyone who knew the business will tell you, were a special breed; they were civilised men and great company. Cattle buyers were a different species; I am talking about those I encountered in the days of the fairs; they weren't all bad – but enough of them were.

I would be tempted to refer to them as cowboys but I believe that the word in its present sense is being abused. There was a time when it symbolised the essence of romance; every small boy dreamed of riding the range and frying sourdough and beans and brewing coffee for his supper and bedding down under the stars.

Now 'cowboy' signifies someone who is bent on making money but not too worried about how; they are not scarce in the brave new Republic of Ireland.

Michael Healy wasn't the only Cork friend that I encountered on the way down from Croke Park last Sunday.

I had no difficulty in recognising Michael; he has changed hardly at all over the years; believe it or not, I took a few minutes to recognise Peader Ó Riada.

He was a slight youth; he is now a sturdy man; he attributes the transformation to all his work in the bog; like myself he loves that aspect of our culture.

Peadar, like his father, Seán, God rest him, is a great musician but, as far as I know, he doesn't play professionally. He made no secret of his allegiance on Sunday; the fact that he wore so much red-and-white didn't help me to recognise him.

Peadar lives near Ballyvourney; it is not hurling country but this doesn't prevent it from sending its quota of aficionados to Croke Park.

Ballyvourney is just across the boundary from my own county; Peadar knows South Kerry well and loves it; he tells me that it is being desolated by emigration – too well I understand.

I know of once-proud Gaelic-football clubs that now cannot field a team; the ailment is not confined to Gaelic football; rugby is suffering too.

We do not see some things clearly until time sheds its elucidating light: we are seeing in this generation a new kind of great hunger.

Not all the cause of emigration is economic; people are going away who have lost faith in the country; one of our more prominent politicians is never done referring to Northern Ireland as a failed entity; I am not so sure about The Republic. Peadar Ó Riada fears that great tracts of South Kerry and West Cork will end up as forest; he could be all too right.

We hope to meet again in the Shakespeare after the football final. It will be our last day there with Séamus Nolan as host.

That celebrated house has changed hands; the new proprietor is, as far as I know, a Corkman who made his fortune in London. Over the past year or so the number of pubs sold in Dublin has been far above the national average; whether that means trade is good or bad, I do not know.

And of course more and more sports stars are infiltrating the business. Paddy Cullen was perhaps the first in this generation. P. J. Buckley and Paddy McCormack also have pubs in the city.

Eugene Coghlan has a pub in Birr; Brendan Lynskey and Tony Keady have the Galway Shawl – in Galway, of all places; Larry Tompkins is across the road from the railway station in Cork.

And of course the man of the moment, Mick O'Dwyer, has been in the catering business for a long time.

Evening Press

It is easy to visualise one of our ancestors protecting himself with a stick while another man threw a round object at him. Cricket today is essentially the same.

It is of course akin to rounders, the game that developed into baseball. Rounders was very popular with the Nonconformists of Northern Ireland; they took it with them to America. Unlike those who emigrated from the South, most of them became settled on the land.

Thus baseball developed as a rural working-class game and changed very little for generations. It was a simple game for a young nation. Its rules remained more or less unchanged.

Cricket had an equally simple origin; it developed into the most sophisticated of all field-games. Just ask yourself in how many ways can a batsman be given out. You think you have all the answers – and then somebody adds one more. And then somebody else adds another one.

I doubt if the greatest expert would get 100 percent if he sat for an examination on the rules of the game. It is also the most democratic of field-games in that it caters for all shapes and sizes.

You needn't be very big to be a great batsman. Don Bradman was an example. Nor do you need an exceptional physique to be a great bowler. Think of Ramadhin and Valentine. And your career needn't end when you come to thirty. I watched the wonderful Cyril Washbrook play in a Test when he was well over forty.

If some people believe that Cricket is a game of the upper classes, they are mistaken. Long ago when I worked in Sussex, I had two friends who played professionally for the county. In the close season one of them worked as a van driver; the other became a bookmaker's clerk.

Cricket is, of course, the ruling passion in Sussex. When I first went to work there, a certain aspect puzzled me for a little while. I could see lights on in many houses in the small hours. I soon discovered the reason: it was Autumn and England were playing Australia down below in the bottom of the world. The people in England's south-east are friendly and easy-going – but very serious about Cricket. At certain times it is a big topic in the pubs – so is the size of the crops, especially the corn and the hops.

I was away from Sussex for a long time until I landed at Gatwick on the way home from the World Cup Finals in Spain in 1982. It was too late to get to Dublin and so I stayed in the Crest Hotel. The bar was in no hurry closing; the conversation was going strong. I was ferried back thirty years by the time machine. The topics of the conversation were much the same. And of course because it was Midsummer, Cricket predominated.

Cricket was once fairly widespread in Ireland. The Act of Union, passed in 1800, caused a decline. Dublin became a provincial city; many landlords moved to England. They had been big patrons of Cricket and Hurling – both games suffered in their absence.

When Michael Cusack began his revolution, Cricket lost more ground. By taking what he deemed the better elements of soccer and rugby, he created Gaelic Football. It was easy to play and easy to understand – it quickly spread all over the country.

If you read Canon Sheehan's *The Literary Life and Other Essays*, you will see that Cricket was very strong in Cork in the late nineteenth century. Sheehan was born in Mallow and knew Cricket from childhood. The local club was then a big power in the land.

They were champions of Ireland on several occasions. Sheehan took great pride in seeing the pennant flying over the clubhouse. In later life he ministered as a curate in Hampshire and no doubt enjoyed the game there too.

Cricket is still strong in Cork but mainly in the city. In rural parts of The Republic it is strongest perhaps in East Galway and Kilkenny and North County Dublin. It survived in parts of Kerry until well into the twentieth century.

Then a few years ago there was a revival. A number of doctors and medical students from the Indian subcontinent formed a club. They were augmented by local lords who had been at schools where Cricket is on the curriculum. Tralee Cricket Club, to the surprise of many, won the Munster Junior Championship.

In this generation we have seen a huge change come over the ancient game. A new breed of fast bowler has sprung up – giants about two metres in height. This is especially true of the West Indies. They hurl the ball down at a frightening speed.

The batsman in his county cap is part of the past. His counterpart now is like a medieval knight about to go into battle. Incidentally, this revolution has influenced Hurling – it led to the helmet.

Another change is the coming of the one-day limited-overs game. This is the prodict of social and economic changes. It is a long way from the time when the five-day Tests were the basis of the game.

Of course they are still there but somehow the game seems to have lost its leisurely texture. I think of Neville Cardus, who wrote about Cricket from his standpoint as a music critic. Sometimes he wrote about a Test as if it had a kinship with a symphony. And then there was the most famous of all commentators, John Arlott of the cider-apple voice. One of his phrases has passed into folklore: 'The men in their shirtsleeves and women in their Summer dresses.'

I know a host of Cricket stories – allow me to tell one. It concerns a young man on a holiday from South

America who discovered that the English people practised magic.

He was taking a walk one morning near Regent's Park in London when he got caught up in a crowd all going in the same direction. He went along with them until he came to a gate, where he had to pay a few pounds to follow them in.

Eventually a very large crowd was gathered around a big field. England was in the middle of a heatwave; the leaves on the trees were shrivelled and the grass in the field was brown.

About five to eleven, two men in white coats strode onto the field. Each man carried three white painted sticks: they stopped in the middle of the field about twenty yards apart.

They drove the sticks into the ground – and the rain came down.

Programme note for Ireland v. South Africa match, 2003

'KNOCKNAGOSHEL HAS ITS OWN PLACE IN RACING HISTORY'

It isn't as resonant as other Kerry names such as Coomasaharn and Lyrecrompane and Gleannsharoon, but Knocknagoshel has its own place in folklore. Whenever its name comes up in conversation, it is odds-on that somebody will recall a war cry associated with it. I was up in that mountain village a few days before last year's All-Ireland football final and was glad to see a plaque embodying the famous war cry.

The story goes back to 1880, when the bitterness aroused by the Parnellite split was at its most virulent. Parnell's campaign had brought great benefit to the farming community; ironically, many of his staunchest supporters were people of little property.

These, incidentally, were the same people who played a big part in the proliferation of Michael Cusack's new game, Gaelic football. This class was well represented in the parish of Knocknagoshel. When the split came, they stood up to be counted.

Parnell was due to hold a rally in Newcastle West. His supporters in the mountain parish were determined to attend. They would have to pass through Abbeyfeale – it was enemy country.

The bold peasantry marched behind a banner that said: 'ARISE KNOCKNAGOSHEL AND TAKE YOUR PLACE AMONG THE NATIONS OF THE EARTH'.

When I was up in the village in September, I met its most famous citizen. Eddie Walsh was sitting in the sun in front of his public house.

He carries his years lightly. It is hard to believe that he was an especial star in the Kerry team that won five All-Irelands between 1937 and 1946.

He played all his inter-county football at left half-back;

with Bill Dillon and Bill Casy, God rest them, he formed a line of most resistance. Gaelic football in the good old days wasn't always a thing of beauty.

The all-seeing eyes of television had yet to come. Many sports reporters were inhibited by fear of libel and by subservience to the governing bodies. It was a regressive age: Joe Sherwood was barred from the press box at Lansdowne Road; John D. Hickey fell foul of the Cork County Board.

Eddie Walsh was the ultimate knight in shining armour: he was often provoked but never lapsed from the standards he had set himself. In the real world he was modest to a fault; he took little part in the life of his native village.

He was content to run a good pub and help to bring up his young family. His friend and fellow publican John Curtin looked on himself as Mayor of Knocknagoshel. Listowel had a well-established Harvest Festival, built around its race meeting – John decided that it shouldn't have all the glory.

And so he founded the Knocknagoshel Harvest Festival, even though the harvest consisted mainly of potatoes and turf. I have fond memories of the first race meeting ever held there.

I travelled up with my great friend, the legendary Tom Deane. We were in the front of what he called his horse-box, though it was really a small turf lorry.

He had only one horse at the time; he was seventeen years old – the horse, that is – and was the veteran of countless races. And to prove it he had lumps on both front knees the size of turnips.

As we unloaded him in the village, he caught sight of the bunting and the streamers – he pricked up his ears and his nostrils flared.

The racehorse bore little resemblance to that at Ascot. It would have delighted Jack Yeats. And the atmosphere seemed a proof of the belief that life in Ireland has a kind of wild taste.

The time was late October; the track was very heavy. It suited Tom Deane's veteran – he was the first past the post. He wasn't declared the winner; there was an objection.

It came from an English girl called Patsy Hand who had brought a small farm near Kenmare and kept a few horses. She claimed that Tom's horse, not to mention his jockey, had gone outside a pole at the most distant point in the track.

And she took the stewards to show them the evidence of the hoofprints. The two good men and true went into conclave; in other words, they had a few bottles of stout in the tent.

The fact that they had backed Tom's horse may have influenced them; they decided that the hoofprints were not conclusive evidence – and announced 'Winner all right.'

*

Knocknagoshel can be quiet enough in the late Autumn and in Winter and in early Spring – many of the younger men go to England for at least part of the year. Some settle in our neighbouring island and come home on holidays, usually in August.

That is nearly always a lively month in the village: you can see the hens pecking around under a Mercedes or a BMW or a Jaguar. The four pubs are busy in those August nights; it is and always was a heartland of what is loosely called country music.

Knocknagoshel is a far-flung, well-populated parish; it breeds a hardy people – but few of its footballers have worn the county colours. They are too busy in those months when Gaelic football season is at its height.

Much of the work on the bog and in the fields is done by hand; a broken finger can discommode you. I do not know any people more dedicated to Gaelic football but the work comes first.

How did Eddie Walsh become so eminent a footballer? He never worked on the land: in his early life he helped in the family bar – eventually he got a job as a travelling ganger with the County Council.

It may sound a rather sinister title, but in fact there was little to it. Eddie merely went around on his trusty bike to see that all the men working on the roads were present and correct. His travels took him by our house three or four days in the week.

He hardly ever passed without coming in; he became almost part of our family. My mother was a dab hand at making apple cake; it was always on the menu. And of course the teapot never left the hob. They were simple times.

Another eminent footballer was a regular visitor to our house too. Frank Kinlough was an inspector on the land-drainage scheme in our area; he too travelled around on a bike. He was a member of the Roscommon team that won the county's first-ever All-Ireland when they beat Cavan in the final in 1943. Roscommon won their second All-Ireland when they beat Kerry in the final in 1944.

And therein hangs a tale. Eddie and Frank never met in our house – perhaps their bikes recognised each other. The gods of football, those expert catchers in the wry, con-trived that they would meet in Croke Park.

It wasn't only that they were on opposite teams: Frank was at right half-forward and thus was marked by Eddie.

There is a common belief that if two men are marking each other, both of them cannot play well. Indeed they can: both Frank and Eddie excelled in that final – Frank scored two points; Eddie looked on that as a reflection on his manhood.

The counties met again in the 1946 Final. Kerry won – Eddie was happy that honours were shared.

*

Last Autumn a few of us travelled the width of Knocknagoshel parish from west to east – I couldn't help feeling a little sad. I recalled a line from 'Dublin in the Rare Old Times': 'And the grey unyielding concrete is making a city of my town.'

The green unyielding conifers are making a forest of my heartland. The patchwork of neat houses and well-kept small farms is being replaced by a green anonymity.

And of course the people are going. I think of Goldsmith and 'The Deserted Village':

> A bold peasantry, their country's pride
> When once destroyed, can never be supplied.

In the pubs in the village you can see the symbols of emigration. The walls are adorned with big pictures of Manchester United and Liverpool and Arsenal – and many others.

I think too of James Connolly: 'Ireland without its people means nothing to me.' And I think of a paragraph written by my friend Ned Walsh, the local correspondent with the *Kerryman:* 'Eileen and Mary O'Connor, daughters of publican Dan C. D. O'Connor, emigrated to Leeds last week. The village will never be the same again.' Alas, two lovely ships passed in the night.

Eddie Walsh retired from serious football about 1950 but still played in casual practice matches. One evening a man from the heart of the mountains gave him a hard game, even though this man was wearing his working boots.

The local parish priest was delighted with this

prospect for his team. He bought him a pair of lovely Cotton Oxfords. He never saw the promising newcomer or the Cotton Oxfords again.

The boots were too valuable to use playing football. They were ideal for the bog.

Magill

'Con Houlihan Says that Pat's Will Never Die'

The Triumphs and Tribulations of
St Patrick's Athletic

Kerry County Council have few equals as catchers in the wry. When I was down home lately, I witnessed two examples of its mindiwork. Pound Road was a collection of mud and thatch houses in the old quarter of Castle Island. About thirty years ago its people were given houses in a new estate. Pound Road was razed until not a crumb of mud remained. The council, nevertheless, erected a handsome signpost proclaiming Pound Road.

Their second nugget is even more mind-boggling; it concerns our late lamented railway line. It is long since gone; in its place a sign says Station Road. It wasn't enough to close down our rail line – the track was uprooted. In its place there is an extense of weeds 'unprofitably gay'. We miss the rail line; we miss that lovely horizontal ladder that was our link to the big world.

We didn't see roads in the same way: to travel by road was a journey – to travel on the train was an adventure. And for us in the primary school long ago, the railway line had an especial virtue.

The midday train brought the English papers – we were intimately in touch with London. Of course we small boys didn't buy those papers; we hoarded our pennies whenever we had them – but some of the parents, all 'townies', did.

At school next day there were usually a few copies doing the rounds – we devoured them. The *Daily Sketch*, now only a memory, was a great favourite – because it gave so much space to soccer.

It may seem off that we were so fascinated by a game that we had never seen in the round – there's no boundary to the imagination. It was all the more fascinating because we saw it only in flickering snatches in the news-reels in the cinema.

And it was odder still to hear small boys arguing fiercely about the merits of teams they had never seen in action. Some were devoted to Arsenal, some to Tottenham Hotspur; Chelsea had its devotees – and so on and so on. London was then the capital of our football world. I doubt if any of us could explain the origin of our devotion; at some time a seed had fallen and germinated.

Scunthorpe is a modest town in the Yorkshire Coalfield – I know mature people, kind of, who are pas-sionately loyal to its football club, even though they have never lived there. Stenhousemuir is hardly the most famous club in Scotland – it too has its disciples here in Ireland.

My own devotion to St Patrick's Athletic is hardly a secret. And I think that I can trace its origin. It probably goes back to a Sunday in the late forties when Pat's were playing Evergreen United in the FAI Cup. The venue was the Mardyke. Inchicore is a railway village. The faithful travelled down to Cork in a special train.

The nucleus of the following was family groups, some represented by three generations. They seemed to fear that Cork was experiencing a food shortage: they came well supplied. They took out their flasks and their sand-wiches and picnicked on the green green grass during the interval. I liked it and I liked their sporting attitude to the game. Pat's lost with honour. It was all very civilised.

I didn't see such family involvement again until Derry City joined the League of Ireland. And I didn't see the Saints in action again – except on television – until I came to live in Clondalkin and then Portobello in the seventies.

In the meantime the club had led a rather nomadic existence. They had no ground of their own and had played in several locations. Eventually they settled, kind

.n a decidedly modest stadium called Richmond Park the living heart of Inchicore. The playing surface wasn't quite state of the art: indeed it vied with Sligo Rovers' pitch for the honour of being the craziest in the League of Ireland – or in any league. The Showgrounds sloped so much from midways that when the keepers stood on their lines, they could barely see each other. The pitch in Richmond Park sloped so much that if the keepers stood on their lines, the man in the upper goal could kick the ball into the hands of his counterpart down below. For bad measure, the pitch was liberally pitted with mini-craters, which the most diligent care could not make behave.

And yet for a generation this unlikely setting was the stage for vibrant football, dramatic and melodramatic, and never less than colourful. A saying evolved: 'Richer is the ground where anything can happen and often does.'

There was the occasion when Pat's were down two goals against Sligo Rovers and reduced to eight men with ten minutes to go – they won 3–2.

And it was in this modest arena that Paul McGrath first unveiled his genius in a senior game. The Black Pearl of Inchicore went on to world fame with Manchester United and Aston Villa and The Republic.

Curtis Fleming was Inchicore's second Brown Pearl: after a fine career with Middlesbrough, he went to play with Crystal Palace. Paul Osam is Brown Pearl Number Three: he is the only player to have won four League of Ireland medals with Pat's – and looks forward to a few more.

Underpinning all this endeavour and excitement are the ever-faithful who have followed the Saints through thin and thinner. I have been privileged to drink with them and exchange songs with them and lament with them and rejoice with them.

They are the salt of the asphalt and the tarmac and the

concrete, men and women who have given \ more than it ever gave to them.

A time came when the Brains Trust in Inchic ed that the crazy pitch should be tamed and ci took two years of patient toil; Pat's found a tei location in the greyhound track in Harold's Cross.

On its good surface, Pat's were able to practise the creative football that Brian Kerr preached. The ever-faithful were not too happy about the exodus. The new venue was little more than two miles from the old – but they complained about the weather there.

It was much colder – and the people in the pubs were strange – so they said. It's an ill wind that doesn't blow some good: while Pat's were in exile, they won the League for the first time in a generation.

The climax came in the last game of the season, against Drogheda United in Lourdes Stadium – we needed to win. Ironically, I couldn't be there: I was under orders to be in Fairyhouse to see Desert Orchid in the Irish Grand National. I got the news within a few minutes of the final whistle and celebrated in Benny McDonald's in Clonee. With me was another Patrician: my friend Paddy Freeman is an aficionado of many sports – he could have walked out from the pages of Damon Runyon.

I was in Oriel Park when Pat's won their next League title. They took the lead ten minutes from the end and then came almost unbearable tension as Dundalk laid siege to our goal. The celebrations that night in Inchicore and next morning in the market pubs are part of folklore. I cried off: I spent the night in the Derryhale Hotel and celebrated next day in my favourite pubs in Dundalk.

In the meantime Pat's have added to Brian Kerr's double with two more championships – the third masterminded by Pat Dolan and the fourth by Liam Buckley.

Incidentally, one of the most famous days in Pat's history had nothing to do with winning a league title. The

ular keeper was unavailable one weekend; somebody was inspired to sign Gordon Banks for the game. The World Cup hero had lost the sight of an eye in a road accident and had no regular job.

Inchicore was in carnival mood for the big occasion. The stadium was packed long before tip-off time. A multitude of small boys and small girls kept chanting: 'Gordon Banks, Gordon Banks, Gordon Banks, Gordon Banks, Gordon Banks.'

He wasn't seriously examined until about five minutes from the end, as Shamrock Rovers desperately sought an equaliser. Then a rising shot from twenty yards seemed certain to send the ball into his top right-hand corner. Gordon made a great leap and turned it outside. It was just what the crowd needed to give him a rapturous ovation at the end.

There is a rumour now that the club may relocate across the road when St Michael's Flats are pulled down. If this goes ahead, there will be blood on Emmet Road. The accountants will hang from the lamp-posts.

We love the Camac, the river that flows down by the pitch. It is like a girl behind a bar. And for good measure it provides work for a friend of mine. He stands guard at the south-west corner of the ground. His primary job is to prevent the occasional ball from being carried down to the sea. His secondary job is to pull out any small boys who may have jumped in after it. Incidentally, Hereford United for this same job keep two men in a boat on the Severn.

St Patrick's Athletic have survived many crises. At times it seemed that they might cease trading. In this context, I got the highest tribute of my life. One Sunday long ago I saw it inscribed on the back of a toilet door in Inchicore: 'Con Houlihan says that Pat's will never die.'

Magill

ACKNOWLEDGEMENTS

The publishers would like to thank Niall S
Magill and Colm McGinty of the *Sunday World* fo. _
ng permission to use material that originally appeared in
their publications. They would also like to thank the staff
of the National Library in Dublin for their assistance and
Jason Michael for proof-reading the text.